"We have much to say about this, but it is hard to make it clear to you because you no longer try to understand. In fact, though by this time you ought to be teachers, you need to someone to teach you the elementary truths of God's word all over again. You need milk, not solid food! Anyone who lives on milk, being still an infant, is not acquainted with the teaching about righteousness. But solid food is for the mature, who by constant use have trained themselves to distinguish good from evil."

Hebrews 5:11-14 NIV

Finish Your Milk

and "Don't Drink the Kool-Aid"

All emphasis within Scripture quotations is the author's own. Sean Barron wishes to thank all those who have contributed testimonies used in this book. They are not owned by any person or that any person would take credit but that each and every testimony is for God's glory and He delights in them. Psalm 119:11

This book is available at Christian bookstores and directly from the author.

For purchasing directly from the author or to discuss speaking engagements, email sean.barron@gatheringpeople.family

For more information about Freedom Ministries of the South, please visit:
www.freedom337.org and www.finishyourmilk.org

ISBN: 978-0-692-19926-8

SAN NO: 991-1235

For Worldwide Distribution. Printed in the U.S.A.

Dedications:

To all of those who have sown into me and to those whose desire is to change the world.

Rowan

My family

My friends

My Freedom family

Those gone from this earth that remain in our hearts

Those in "the struggle"

Table of Contents:

Special Thanks:

Matt Cooley:
Grammar and Refining Content Edits

Miss Coralie Chatagnier:
First Grammar Edit and Encouragement

Clark Miller:
Cover Art, Picture, and Temple Diagram

Linda Barron:
Leading by example, and being a rock for our family

Danny Barron:
In memory of Danny and his wisdom

Dear Friends:
Those who had the courage to publicly share personal testimony in this book.

I have known Sean B. for more than ten years, and with each passing year, I am amazed to see just how much he has grown and matured spiritually, even though it has not been easy or without pain and tears. He has always had a very determined attitude and spirit, which has not always been beneficial to himself or others, but he has now resolved that determination to become a man of God, a humble servant of Jesus Christ, and a close, dear friend who is willing to sacrifice anything to help a friend or save a lost soul. His life's story is colorful and graphic, but his willingness to humble himself and to seek God's will has paved the way for healing and restoration in his life and in the lives of others.

"Blessed be the God and the Father of our Lord Jesus Christ, the Father of mercies and God of all comfort, who comforts us in all our affliction so that we will be able to comfort those who are in any affliction with the comfort with which we ourselves are comforted by God."
2 Corinthians 1:3-4

Mike Richard
"Godfather" of Christian Recovery in Sulphur, Louisiana and servant of the Lord Jesus Christ.

Preface

It is the heartbeat of my existence to reach people with the truth. For much of my life and early ministry, I was led to pursue the proverbial "one sheep" and allow the rest of the flock to tend themselves. That portion of the flock always seemed so safe, pure, and "dignified." In other words, they had their church faces on, but believers and non-believers, alike, can carry a façade of external peace but remain broken within. I learned early on that most people inside the church carry on the same type of charade but just conceal it within a different language and culture. Let me tell you that God really has no interest in our games, toys, intellects, talents, conquests and achievements. They only honor Him and advance His kingdom when they are used in humility to glorify Jesus. The Lord is still interested in winning our hearts, saving lost souls, and radically setting people free. Today there is so much "pollution" in our lives, minds and hearts that many churches have lost sight of the concepts of loving and reaching a hurting people, let alone teaching the believer how to mature in the Lord.

I hope this book challenges your heart and opens the door for real change to take place. Ultimately, my prayer is that the reader may discover who he or she is in Christ and, in that identity, walk in purpose. This is a ten-year work in progress. In these pages, you will hear directly from the word of God, testimony of my own life experiences walking with the Lord, and out-of-the-box analogies, poems, essays, verse by verse breakdowns and testimonies of real life people. The world's systems and the enemy will be exposed. Things that are normally swept under the rug will openly be discussed. Many of my own heart felt experiences are laid bare in the hope of sparing or relating to those who wish to pursue more. As I began writing this work, my target audience or demographic was initially geared toward the seeker, the new believer, the blue-collar worker or the religious person who may have taken their eyes off Jesus. As the Lord brought the chapters together and these pages come to completion, my perspective has changed. My eyes are now open. The purpose of this book is to deepen our spiritual understanding, share the complete Gospel and encourage all believers to do the same and "finish their milk." This book may not be for everyone or any certain demographic at all. However, it is for all who would receive it and desire to grow up and *Finish Their Milk*.

"Therefore, rid yourselves of all malice and all deceit, hypocrisy, envy, and slander of every kind. Like newborn babies, crave pure spiritual milk, so that by it you may grow up in your salvation, now that you have tasted that the Lord is good."

1 Peter 2:1-3

This is my testimony…

My name is Sean Barron. I am forty-two years old. My parents were divorced when I was two years old. I lived with my mother. Because she worked shift work to provide for my sister and I, I spent a great deal of time with both sets of my grandparents. My Granny taught me the Lord's Prayer and prayed with me. I was not forced to attend church though at times I attended different denominational services with my older sister and few other family members. It was during one of those services when I was ten years old that I responded to an altar call and accepted Jesus as my Savior. Deep in my heart, I believed in the Lord and salvation through Jesus Christ. However, there was so much I did not understand with no one to guide me in His ways.

In the following four years after my salvation, I suffered through a mountain of tragedy. I lost two of my grade school friends from unforeseen accidents and all but one of my grandparents. Two of my cousins suffered tragic deaths. In a short amount of time, I had seen so much death. God did not seem fair or "good" and my heart grew bitter. When I entered high school, I had no desire to fit into any of the cliques. I felt uncomfortable, unhappy and confused. I was exposed to and experimented with recreational drugs and alcohol abuse at an extremely young age. By the age of fifteen, I chose to start using alcohol and drugs habitually. During the early years of my usage, I had a good time and seemed to have found the escape I was desperately seeking. However, for the subsequent twelve years, I battled a vicious cycle from which some never break free. My life was defined by broken relationships, loneliness, extreme highs and lows, dangerous situations, drama, death, overdoses, addiction, extreme anxiety, and depression. I was arrested more than twelve times and spent a part of my life living on the run from the police. I took pride in myself for being tough, strong-willed, and uncompromising. My heart was broken and troubled. I fully understood and expected that I would die if I continued to live that way, and most of the time even that knowledge did not scare me. The most troubling fact was that, through it all, I always knew *"there's got to be more to life than this."*

Toward the end of this time in my life, I had an encounter with the Holy Spirit, and despite this, I would run from God for four more years. Finally, deep in my spirit, I knew I could no longer make it without Jesus in my life. I knew that He was the only hope of me becoming a "good" man. In the latter part of 2003, I asked Jesus to be Lord of my life! After a year or more of constant struggle, the Lord led me to Life Church in Sulphur, Louisiana. I soon joined the church and its Celebrate Recovery program. I began to study the Word, take discipleship classes, serve others, and make my own quiet and study times. I truly began to seek His face and His will for my life. Ever so slowly, I was being led into complete surrender and The Lord raised me up. I learned that He has a plan for us all and everything I had been through prior to this point in my life was for a reason. In June of 2005, I went with my church to the nation of Lithuania. We had two teams, one for evangelism and one for construction. I was on the construction team. We were responsible for remodeling at a Christian-based Recovery house. There, we were able to connect with the people and leaders in a special way. For the first time, I was able to share my testimony with others. I prayed not only in front of others but for others and was comfortable doing so. I received healing and peace in my heart. This trip changed my life forever. The Lord used me for His glory!

When I returned home, I started a Men's Bible Study group. The Lord led me to begin reaching out to my friends and family. I began to serve more deeply at my church through increased discipleship, cell (or small) groups, and Celebrate Recovery. I was wide open seeking and serving. Even though I did not fully understand why the Lord led me as aggressively as He did until at the end of a Sunday service, He called me back to Lithuania. In April of 2006, my church returned to Lithuania. This trip involved evangelism and performing drama and worship to present the Gospel. Once again, He pushed me well out of my comfort zone performing a drama. Souls were saved and lives were changed. During this trip, resident Pastor Milton Magalhaes asked me if I would serve with him and his family for two years. After three days of procrastination, I surrendered to the ministry. I returned to Lithuania in September of 2006 and through the power of the Lord, I honored my commitment. I experienced more life, growth as a Christian man and learned to trust Him.

Those years were two of the best years of my life. The Lord used me in ways I never dreamed possible. I found myself preaching, working with youth, serving on all levels, evangelizing, and working with people who struggle with addiction. I immersed myself in the national culture. Playing soccer, weight training, visiting festivals, traveling, fishing, hosting Bible studies, working on farms, feeding the poor, picking seasonal mushrooms, and serving people were all common events in my life. This made it easy to meet people and make friends. Trust is not something easily given in the nation of Lithuania. However, once you truly make friends with a Lithuanian, it is often for life. I am blessed to now have family and friends across the globe.

I returned home in September of 2008. It was a warm homecoming. I returned to find that my home, which was damaged by Hurricane Rita, had been re-roofed and remodeled. It really touched my heart that my friends and family believed in what God was doing in my life enough to bless me that way. In December of 2008 and 2009, I was part of the "Big Feed" in Mexico. We worked with Way of the Cross Ministries. Four hundred missionaries from all denominations worked to serve twelve thousand people and preach the Gospel of Christ! In the summer of 2009, I also traveled to Nicaragua with Way of the Cross for a youth crusade. We were able to go into many schools and preach the Gospel of Jesus Christ. Many souls were saved and many hearts were touched. I returned to Lithuania to share my faith, maintain relationships and assist with youth camps in 2009 and 2010. The Lord has taught me the importance of sharing my faith and loving people. I clearly see now that the Great Commission is so much more than merely sharing the Gospel.

I returned home to attend college in 2010 while simultaneously serving with my church's prison ministry, men's prayer group, discipleship, and cell group programs. To the

Glory of God, I was able to graduate McNeese State University in December of 2012 with a bachelor's degree in Sociology. Throughout 2011, I did an internship with the ministry teaching *Life's Healing Choices* by John Baker. I was called to officially relaunch the Celebrate Recovery Ministry in my area in 2012 and became the Recovery Pastor while attending college and working two other jobs. I spent three years managing a car lot and would later work thirty hours a week as a painter in 2015. In 2014, I briefly returned to Nicaragua and was able to experience the Lord on an even greater level, which you will hear more about later in this book. During this season, I was a bi-vocational pastor pouring my all into the ministry.

Through this process of growth and change, the Lord began to do a new thing in me. We officially changed the name of the ministry from Celebrate Recovery to "Freedom Friday." Currently, several life-changing ministries fall under the Freedom Ministry umbrella. In late 2015, a door opened for me to handle more duties and further the ministry. By faith, I walked into full-time ministry with a part-time salary, and the Lord always provided. In 2016, I became a full-time pastor on staff at our church. It was a difficult year of transition, change, relational, and personal development. With these changes came a new Senior Pastor and a new name to embrace this exciting new season. We are now called "The Gathering" and focus on faith, community, and purpose. Now, I currently serve as a Volunteer Pastor, have a vested interest in our community and seeing churches work together.

My cousin April and her family moved to Pachuca Mex-ico to teach English as Christian missionaries. However, the Lord had bigger plans. They would end up successfully planting a Freedom Ministry there in Pachuca. I was invited to join them and in May of 2017, they would host a "Freedom Conference." More information about the conference weekend can be found in the testimony section of this book. The move of God there prompted the official launch of "Freedom Ministry of the South." April is now stateside and planting a Freedom Ministry in another local church. We now have four local Freedom Ministries operating in our area and one in Mexico. We focus on helping people with their "next steps" in life, whatever those steps may be. It is also my heart to connect people and ministries together for the Kingdom. More information, including mission and vision statements, bylaws, action plans, and current functions, can be found at www.freedom337.org. *(author's blog - www.finishyourmilk.com).*

I do find myself busy at times, but there is no denying the fruit of God's hand at work. I attempt to always make my-self open to my family, friends and anyone ready to change. Starting my day in the Word of God always helps the process. Jesus has recently pressed into my heart the importance of honoring the sabbath. Throughout this time, Jesus has taught me to be a friend to myself by establishing boundaries. Still, I am a work in progress and do not claim perfection. The Lord is not a respecter of persons (Romans 2:11). Apart from the blood of Jesus, there is nothing special about me. Be encour-aged, if God can use me, He can most certainly use you. The Lord has a plan. Let us submit unto it.

CHAPTER 1

Where do you stand?

In my youth, I was a loyal fan of the band Kiss. I was amazed when I first bought the Kiss *Alive 2* album at a garage sale. To me, it was like each member of the band was a super hero. The band blew stuff up, breathed fire, spit blood, smashed guitars, and set off fire horns in their concerts in the 70's. Each band member was given a "spot" in the show to showcase his talent. I stumbled across the record at maybe six years old, and I was mesmerized. Later, one of my older cousins told me that he saw Kiss in '76, and he gave me the concert ticket stub. He verified that there was no greater concert that he had ever seen. If a wild, good time was what you were looking for, you could find it there. He told me that all the stuff I saw and read about was true, and the energy and excitement could not be matched. This verified what I already believed (by faith) to be true. Unfortunately, the band had disbanded and had taken their makeup off by this time, meaning I would never get to see their show. I would always tell my friends that I was a Kiss fan and why, but most of the time, they would just give me a hard time. Eventually, I got my hands on a video with Ace Frehley's guitar solo from '77. I finally had evidence to show when my friends would say, "Kiss? They are no good." Each time I heard it, I would say, "Do you have eight to ten minutes to change your mind?" I would show them that guitar solo, trying to plant a seed. In many cases, it opened their eyes or changed their perspective.

Things changed with Kiss in the mid 1990's. The band eventually put the past aside and began touring again, playing the old songs, sporting the same old makeup, and giving the same wild show. There was no way that I was going to miss this reunion. I saw four shows with the original band in three different states. I can say this from experience- there is a strange unity amongst the real Kiss Army. You could see a complete stranger singing the lyrics or witness something cool happen, and you just have to give them a high-five. Most of the people were there for the right reasons on the first reunion tour, and I noticed that there were a few different types of fans at the concerts.

First, you had the **die-hard,** loyal fans. Like me, they either believed by faith in the greatness of the band from what they heard from others or from what they had already experienced. Nothing was going to ruin their good time. They would sport old, faded concert shirts that can only be bought on tour. Some of the shirts were from the original tours and some were from the band member's solo tours in the 80's. Most of the shirts were tattered and worn, but the people were proud to wear them. These are the types of fans that I loved to stand by. They were just as excited as I was. There was no trouble, violence, messing with your girlfriend, or crossing any lines. These were the types that were more likely to buy you a drink, treat you like family, and exchange pleasantries.

Next, you had **the seeker**. These were the people who were fans, but they did not quite believe that Kiss was the "Hottest Band in the Land." They had to see and experience it for themselves. They were different than I was because I would have believed that they were the best even if I never would have got to actually see their show or not. These fans needed confirmation. The seeker was a cool fan and easy to get along with because you knew deep down within you that, in most cases, they would leave from that place and evolve into a diehard fan. Generally, the music and the show would speak to them personally. Seekers could come from different generations, and you wanted them to have the good time experience that would open their eyes. For some, this could be their first show or live concert, and they were expecting to have a good time and experience all that they had heard about.

Third, you had a fan that was **going through the motions**. They were possibly once die-hard fans but had a bad experience. Maybe Ace (lead guitar) was too drunk, or the band gave a shout out to the wrong city because they were on tour so long. Maybe they had their feelings hurt, or a drunken group of guys disrespected their women. It could have been any random number of things because not everyone was at the show for the right reasons. This disrupted the unity of the good time. It is possible that this fan may not have been in a good place mentally. Life could be hard at the time. They were at the show because they knew it could be awesome, but their level of expectation had been reduced. Past circumstances had eroded their hope and level of excitement. Despite it all, they knew they were part of something bigger than their own circumstances and that there was always the potential for them to snap out of it.

Lastly, you had my least favorite group of fans- **the posers.** These people pretended like they were die-hard fans.

They wanted to enjoy the culture of the concert but had no real loyalty to the band. It was safe to say that they had no core and were overly concerned about what other people thought. They loved Kiss around the fans at this concert, but they loved another band the most around the next group. They behaved differently and claimed loyalty to others. They projected one thing and lived another. These people had new Kiss shirts but couldn't name their favorite albums or five of their favorite songs. They had no remembrance of the first time they heard or saw Kiss. This usually meant that they did not have the experience that real fans share. These people had no testimony of how a song related to their life or how it impacted them. I'll admit that we sometimes laughed to ourselves at these people, but I always greeted them and tried to be nice, hoping that this would be the show that helped them cross that line into loyalty. My hope was that they might actually let their guard down long enough to experience more than just the explosions, girls, and nostalgia. I knew that if they could stop worrying about what people thought and let go, they could leave differently than how they came. I also hoped that they would come to the revelation that they could be part of something bigger than themselves.

I see the same types of people in The Church. Either you are a follower of Jesus or you are not. Hopefully, you are a **die-hard** and nothing that life or the devil can throw at you will stop you from believing and living what you know to be true. A genuine follower of Jesus can hold his or her joy close and remain focused no matter the crowd. In fact, these types of people will set the tone at a gathering and understand the importance of ushering in the anointing (God's presence).

You can spot a true die-hard a mile away and enjoy their testimony and company. A true believer, full of love, will respect and love others whether they "see it" exactly the same or not. When you are truly about God's kingdom, you can rejoice with another believer's victories and pray for their struggles. Why is this? We are all in this together until that day or until we go on home.

If you are a **seeker**, keep seeking the truth. Open your heart to Jesus and the Word of God. Coming from a die-hard like me, let me tell you, He will change your life. Do not put God on a clock. Please allow Him some time to show Himself to you. Jesus is real, and His plan is good. Keep seeking and believing; visit a few churches until you find a place that is genuine. Find a place that preaches the Word of God and challenges you to grow and get involved in ministry. Good "music" and warm teaching will not get you through the deeper trials of life. The Bible warns about such "fluff" environments that teach and express what "itching ears" (2 Timothy 4:3-4) want to hear.

Even the best of us are guilty of **"going through the motions."** I commend you for still pressing through and seeking Him anyway. The truth is that if you are looking for a reason not to follow Jesus, the enemy will gladly give you one. No church is perfect. The only perfect Church was put on a cross. People are messed up, and not everyone is what they seem. Keep in mind that Jesus said, "*It is not the healthy who need a doctor but the sick*" (Mark 2:17). The church is supposed to be the hospital for the broken, a safe place to heal, grow, and confess. If you have had a bad experience, seek

God before you seek another church. Sometimes, when we get challenged or held accountable, naturally, we want to leave. Reject the instinct to run and receive the pruning. Other times, we are destined to serve for a season and get called elsewhere. The truth is that we should be following Jesus, not man. Many believers are struggling with the "felt led" syndrome. Meaning, when things are wonderful, "peaches and cream," and spirit-filled, they "feel led" to be part of it. However, when the enemy attacks and challenges the work (what God is trying to accomplish), the same people, often, "feel led" to chase that "good time feeling" elsewhere. Herein lies the problem-once you achieve a certain level of maturity, you, yourself, should give back to the work instead of crying that you aren't getting fed or, worse, slandering the very work you once shared in or help build.

The truth will, in fact, stir in your belly, promote change, and convict you toward righteousness. Do your best not to let your frustration develop into a cancer (Hebrews 12:15 - *a root of bitterness*) that can destroy relationships and fellowships. If it is time to move on, do so gracefully and without gossip or slander. If you are truly being led by God, there is no need for justifying why you are making changes to others or on social media. Always check your heart's motive to evaluate if you are acting out of pain. This applies to all relationships and transitions in life. It shows no physical or spiritual maturity whatsoever when someone feels the need to publicly (such as social media posts) "throw people under the bus." Attacking others and rationalizing or justifying your actions will only keep you locked in chains. It also further gives a lost world the conformation that Christian people or full of as much garbage as everyone else. We should have and display the fruits of the Spirit. Throwing fits on social media like a two-year-old child in Wal-Mart will not do the Kingdom of God any good. Truthful and genuine confession, healing, and repentance are the only things that will set you free. I pray the Lord lights your fire, heals you, and sets you back on His path.

The **poser** is the completely "double-minded" (James 1:8) person. They possibly know Jesus and what is right; however, they remain yoked with darkness. They are afraid to let go because they fear that they will lose themselves. Jesus said, *"Whoever finds his life will lose it, but whoever loses their life for my sake will find it"* (Matthew 10:39). You will never know who you really are until you "let go" of yourself. We have to allow the Lord to shift us into our new identity. The Bible says, *"If you are in Christ you are a new creation"* (2 Corinthians 5:17). Pride is the main difficulty of accepting wise council. It is easy in today's world to believe that we need to listen to no one but ourselves. Our modern culture teaches us to please ourselves first and to be selfish. The good news is that Jesus paid the price so that we can be set free. The Lord is still calling to the lost, luke-warm, broken, hurting, confused, and poser, alike. The power of Jesus Christ can set you free.

I never completely understood this next point until recently. The Lord has taught me, through very tough life experience, what these verses in James really mean. I always tended to bypass the "grieve mourn and wail part" or, at least, read over it quickly.

"Submit yourselves, then, to God. Resist the devil, and he will flee from you. Come near to God and he will come near to you. Wash your hands, you sinners, and purify your hearts, you double-minded. Grieve, mourn and wail. Change your laughter to mourning and your joy to gloom. Humble yourselves before the Lord, and he will lift you up."
James 4:7-10

We must learn to stand and fight. However, it must be done in humility and in love. In verse 9, the "grieve, mourn, and wail" is our flesh or "self" dying. This is highly symbolic of true repentance. When the Holy Spirit confronts your pride and your own way of doing things, you have a choice. The process is laid out in these verses. First, we are told to actively resist the devil. If you are not in a "warring mode," you will never get free. This positions you to be able to initially draw close to God. We are then told to wash our hands of our old life and ways, thus allowing the Holy Spirit to purify our hearts. The actual repentance and change, or the "pruning process," (John 15:1-5) will usually require tears and pain. The old man and the old ways do not depart easily. Without true repentance and daily pruning, we will not be able to shift into "die-hard" status. Sometimes, it requires us hitting our knees and forgetting all of the things that we think we know. Let go of religious pride and of who we deem to be right or wrong. Cut the formalities, and get real with God. This is true humility. When we admit that we are truly clueless without Jesus, the Holy Spirit can teach us. Once we allow ourselves to become moldable, teachable, and useable, the Lord will lift us up in His time and in His way. Not by man. Not even by our hard work, but by the hand of God! Psalm 1 clearly shows the Lord's desire for us all.

"**1** *Blessed is the one who does not walk in step with the wicked or stand in the way that sinners take or sit in the company of mockers,* **2** *but whose delight is in the law of the Lord, and who meditates on his law, day and night.* **3** *That person is like a tree planted by streams of water, which yields its fruit in season and whose leaf does not wither—whatever they do prospers.*"
Psalm 1:1-3

Keep it Simple

Religion can produce an element of control and complexity that Jesus came to correct. I was not what many in the South refer to as "raised in church." That simply means that I was not exposed to the Gospel of Jesus regularly or to any denominational belief system. At the onset of my walk, I thought this to be unfair. Many of my friends grew up with some type of faith or religious based foundation. I tended to be a little jealous of these people and their "perfect" families. I reasoned that if had I known Jesus earlier, I could not have possibly gone down the wrong road and lost everything. The truth is that it happens every day to believers and non-believers alike. Often, we lose focus or get blinded to the things that matter most. I remember one day in particular, while walking home from work, I begrudgingly asked God "Why didn't you call to me earlier?" I was a twenty-eight-year-old man who lost everything three or four times and recently quit a decent paying job and sold my Chevy Suburban all to seek Christ. Simply put-I was having a rough day. Amazingly, just a few minutes later, the Lord showed me several of the times he did send people and tug on my heart throughout the years. Unfortunately, I wasn't able to recognize or to respond because of the condition my life was in at the time. My eyes were veiled, and my heart was in bondage.

Initially in my spiritual walk, I was angry because I believed that I was behind in life and didn't truly understand or know by verse the Holy Bible. I declined invitations to attend Bible Study groups. After all, how could I possibly attend a Bible study if I did not even know the Bible? Being the prideful man I was, I secretly started reading the Bible. I was determined to learn its contents and its mysteries. I read and studied *Purpose Driven Life* by Rick Warren and many other books about overcoming addiction and depression. When I finally met some "Christian" people, I was determined to fit right in. Though there is no doubt that this year of my life was beneficial to my spiritual growth, I can honestly admit that I missed out on many blessings as well. For some reason, I was blind to the fact I needed fellowship and encouragement from other believers. The Bible reminds us in Proverbs 27:17 that "*iron sharpens iron, and one man sharpens another.*" It is a lie from the enemy that we must first get our life together before we go to church or seek God. Point blank, Jesus says, "Come to me all who are weary and need rest" (Matthew 11:28-30). We are supposed to come as we are addicted, ashamed, broken, or self-conscious. The Body of Christ, which is The Church, should strive to create a welcoming, loving, non-judgmental, and genuine environment.

The fact that I was not force-fed doctrine or born into a God-fearing family was, in fact, a blessing. When I heard about this man named Jesus, what He did for me, how He lived and what He taught, it changed my life forever. I was not hindered by any preconceived notions or opinions; therefore, I could simply just receive and believe according to my own newfound understanding. Let me be clear. I don't have a superior opinion of myself nor do I claim to understand everything. I love and respect all believers and have friends from several different denominations and walks of life. The Lord wants His people to love and respect one another. This is how others will come to know Jesus. The love of God leads man to Jesus. When I thought I was far behind everyone else, God knew that I was right on track. If we can remain or become humble like Jesus, we can love like He does and, perhaps, truly open our hearts to Him. Only within the bounds of humility can we learn from the words and life of Jesus.

To anyone reading this book that has been burned by a church, has been hurt by a Christian in a relationship, has been violently force fed religion in your youth or has been shunned by your religious family, on behalf of the true body of Christ, I would like to apologize. The enemy is real and will hit low and hard to keep you from finding the true Jesus or the purpose and peace He offers. There is no tear cried (Psalm 56) or situation in your life the Lord does not know. Maybe this is the time to let go of the past and seek Jesus? Religion and man's interpretation of it has not done the world or most of us any good. I encourage you open your heart as you read this chapter and the remainder of this book. You could be a struggling pastor or someone simply seeking answers to what we call "life." Take a deep breath and simplify. Let's shift our focus to Jesus and let Him speak to our hearts.

Thinking Point: Jesus did not die so we could become locked into a certain denomination, He died so we could live and love like Him.

Jesus wants to be "your everything." He is the Alpha and Omega. He is the way, the truth, and the life, and no one comes to the Father except through Him (John 14:6). You can know about Jesus and attend church and still miss heaven. Good works and Bible study are expected, but they will not get you into heaven. They will not get you into a relationship with Christ. Getting an honorific title in front or behind your name, leading a board committee, teaching children, or working with youth will not open the gates of heaven for you. The Holy Bible says in Ephesians 2:8-9 *"for it is by grace you have been saved, through faith, and this is not from yourselves, it is the gift from God not by works so that no one can boast."* Many people, even good Christian people, do not teach the truth of heaven. Simply put- you can know beyond a shadow of a doubt that you are going to heaven when you die. 1 John 5:13 reads, *"I write these things to you who believe in the name of the Son of God so that you may know that you have eternal life."* Blessed assurance is there for those in Christ. It is a choice to invite Jesus into your heart and make Him Lord of your life. The faith of your parents, pastor, priest, or spiritual friend may help you grow spiritually, but it is still your choice to receive salvation. It is a heart, mind, and spirit decision. The choice to follow Jesus is the most important decision anyone can make in his or her life.

In John Chapter 3, Nicodemus, one of the most influential religious scholars of Jesus' time, approaches Jesus at night. He wanted to ask Him a question. It is commonly preached incorrectly that he asked, "How can I become a Christian?" or "How can I be born again?" In reality, he was indirectly seeking eternal life and its mysteries. John 3:2 reads *"He came to Jesus at night and said, "Rabbi, we know you are a teacher who has come from God. For no one could perform the miraculous signs you are doing if God were not with him."* Nicodemus knew the law and books of the prophets for he was a highly educated religious man. He met Jesus at night because he did not want to be seen seeking Jesus. Following what the Holy Spirit was doing in his heart, Nicodemus did what he had to do. Jesus already knew why he was there and what he was seeking. Jesus directly declared, *"I tell you the truth no one can see the kingdom of God unless he is born again."* In one of the most beautiful scriptures of the Bible, Jesus further explains in verses 15-16 "that everyone who believes in him may have eternal life. For God so loved the world that he gave his one and only Son, that whoever believes in him shall not perish but have eternal life." The Lord wants you to know His son Jesus. How do we know this? Romans 5:8 says: *"But God demonstrates His own love for us in this: While we were sinners, Christ died for us."*

The choice is yours. This isn't a choice to become a member of a church or denomination, but to become a member of the Body of Christ. It is only through Jesus one can be saved. It is not Jesus plus something else that makes you right with Him. It is Jesus alone. No person, no denomination, no spiritual gift, or baptism can assure your salvation. Salvation can only be given through the name above all names-the name of Jesus. Acts 4:12 reads, *"Salvation is found in no one else, for there is no other name under heaven given to men by which we must be saved."* There is no greater thing than knowing Jesus Christ and the power of His resurrection! When you give your heart to Christ, the angels rejoice! The beautiful thing is that there is no one certain prayer that is said to make this happen. There is no "sinner's prayer" in the Holy Bible. However, Paul writes in Romans 10:9-10,13: *"That if you confess with your mouth," Jesus Christ is Lord," and believe in your heart that God raised him from the dead, you will be saved. For it is with your heart that you believe and are justified, and it is with your mouth that you confess and are saved for everyone who calls on the name of the Lord will be saved.* You may have a grounded Christian pray with you or lead you in a prayer, you may pray with a pastor on television or the radio or you may get on your knees and pray with all your heart alone. What matters is that you mean it, that you understand that Christ lived, died, and has risen for you, and that you want to know and surrender to Him. This is the first and most important step for true repentance. It is the key to finding purpose, having peace, maintaining healthy relationships, and becoming and discovering who you really are in Christ Jesus. It is about surrender. It is coming to the end of yourself and your own ways. If you have never received Jesus Christ as your Lord and Savior and don't know how to specifically pray for salvation, I urge you to use this example to receive Christ. "Father God, today I realize what You have done for me. I want you to come into my heart and life. I thank you for the forgiveness of my sins, and for living, dying and rising for me. I now turn from myself toward you. Fill me with your Holy Spirit. Help me to seek your ways, Word, and will for my life. Light the path of my feet and use me for your Glory! In JESUS name Amen."

Truly accepting and embracing Christ is where the Christian walk begins. I encourage you to seek fellowship and growth in a local church. You may have to visit a few churches to find the place where you belong. The Holy Spirit will let you know if you are where He wants you to be. You will receive confirmation in your heart. If you just prayed a prayer for salvation for the first time or have never told anyone that you have accepted Christ into your life, you need to do this. God did not intend there to be closet Christians. We need each other to stand. Hebrews 10:24-25 says, *"and let us consider how we may spur one another on toward love and good deeds. Let us not give up meeting together, as some are in the habit of doing, but let us encourage one another-and all the more as you see that Day approaching."* Now is the time to stand up and move forward with Christ. No more half stepping! Now is the time to do whatever it takes.

CHAPTER TWO

Whatever It Takes

So for all you young people who are out there who have hopes, dreams, desires, it doesn't matter where you are as long as you hold tightly to those, because it can come to pass if you don't give up and practice perseverance
Walter Payton (Hall of Fame running back), *Never Die Easy*

I can remember watching the Bears play football when I was growing up. To this day, there has not been a more complete football player than Walter Payton. Tears still come to my eyes when I think of how he lived and died. Payton came from a humble, but family-oriented background. Family values and a never say die attitude were instilled in Walter. In his first NFL game, he rushed for zero yards. He would later become the NFL's all-time leading rusher. Throughout his entire pro football career, he missed only one game-a game in which he wanted to play in but his coach would not allow. He ran hard every play. He ran hard with poor blocking on subpar teams and always kept coming at the defense. Unlike today's players, he never cried to be traded or begged for more money. He did not make a spectacle of himself when he scored a touchdown. In the latter part of his career, he would eventually hold the Super Bowl trophy, an honor some Hall-of-Fame players were denied. More importantly, he never let his fame go to his head. He always made time for family, friends, and fans alike. Even as he battled terminal cancer, he never quit. He never cried out "Why me?" He continued to encourage other people until the day he died.

Despite some personal struggles, his faith, life, and legacy will live on forever. Yes, Walter Payton was a "whatever it takes" man.

What ever happened to perseverance? We must be willing to fight until the end. We must choose daily to pick up our cross and follow Him. This may sound extreme to some, but the enemy plays for keeps. If you honestly gave your heart and life to Jesus Christ and prayed, "Here I am, use me" then prepare yourself. Trouble is coming. I bring this to your attention not to scare or discourage anyone. I only want to make you aware of the very real struggle that happens daily. The fight for your soul, your family and friends, your ministry and witness are on the line each and every day, but there is good news. He gives us strength, blessings, rewards, power of His name, and the grace, forgiveness and love that we need to persevere. We, as Christian people, must be willing to get over ourselves. It takes brutal honesty and humility to admit that we struggle daily and that we are nowhere close to per-fect. When we judge others we are, in turn, judging ourselves and crush our witness. How we relate to people is a reflection of our relationship with God. Everyone struggles in different areas, but everyone is gifted in different areas as well. We are the Body of Christ and no one part of the body can function alone. *"Iron sharpens iron, so one man sharpens another,"* says Proverbs 27:17.

Pride can keep us from growing spiritually, or even worse, send us down the wrong road. Every human being needs someone in which to confide. In the Christian walk, we need one another to provide true accountability. An accountability partner will stand in the gap, pray for you, listen to your victories and your fears, and, at times, offer a swift kick in the bottom. These are the characteristics of a real friend. I am not referring to your wife or husband. I am referring to a true brother or sister in Christ to confide in. Choose your accountability partner wisely. You don't want someone to sit on the pity pot with you. Anyone can do that. You don't need someone in worse shape than you so that you can feel better about yourself or situation. You need a solid person who will do his or her level best to follow Christ. You need a person who can pray for you and with you. It says in James 5:16, *"Therefore confess your sin to each other and pray for each other so you may be healed. The prayer of a righteous man is powerful and effective."*

The sin, struggle, problem, or hindrance in your life may be different than mine. However, we all have sinned and fallen short of the glory of God. The battle may differ, but the war is the same. Paul discusses in Romans chapter 7 and the book of 2 Corinthians 12 the struggle of the flesh. He also points out that His, Jesus', power is made perfect in our weakness. We must first acknowledge that there is a weakness within us. We must be willing to look beyond the surface and into the very depths of our own heart and soul. Psalm 139: 22 says *"search me O God, and know my heart; test me and know my anxious thoughts."* For some, it may be easy or blatantly obvious what their hindrance or shortcoming is. However, for others, there may be walls built up to guard their scars, hurts, or addictions. The only way to know is to start praying and asking the Lord to show you the vines that need to be pruned (John 15:2). Being honest with yourself (not beating or bragging on yourself) is the key to the road to victory over your struggle. As a Christian believer, it is your duty and privilege to read the Word of God regularly. This book or any other book from your favorite spiritual author may help you gain understanding in your walk, but it is paramount that you read the Word of God for yourself. Hebrews 4:12 states, *"for the word of God is living and active. Sharper than any double-edged sword, it penetrates even to dividing soul and spirit, joints and marrow; it judges the attitude of the heart."* The Word of God is God. If you claim to be serious about following Christ and bettering your life but you do not spend time reading and meditating on the Holy Bible, you are lying to yourself. Though the Holy Spirit can speak however He chooses, He often speaks through the Word. It is amazing how much confirmation and guidance can come by reading the Word of God with an open mind and open heart. If you struggle hearing from the Holy Spirit, I advise praying beforehand. Ask for help in understanding what you are reading or reflecting on that day. If you doubt the sovereignty of the Holy Bible and Jesus as Lord then try Him at His Word. When you seek with your whole heart, you shall find (Jeremiah 29:13). The only wrong way to read your Bible is to not read it.

Today's world has been desensitized to sin and morality. Family values are laughed at, divorce is normal, and having affairs is acceptable. The American father is made to look like a slothful loser, milking the system is normal, porn is rampant and glamorized, and sexually transmitted diseases are on the rise world-wide. Women think they don't need men, and men don't respect their women, and neither gender respects their parents. Several ministers are beginning to preach, and write books that promote "itching ears" doctrines. Even worse, people are willingly drinking the Kool-Aid even though it is laced with poison. What has caused this rapid decline in our moral compass? Quite frankly, a lack of Jesus Christ has. Without Him in our hearts and minds, our own values will decline until we are just like everyone else in this broken and hurting world. Whatever "good" an individual possesses was bestowed on them by their creator. The beauty of it all is that once we receive the healing, we are supposed to go into the world and preach the Gospel (Matthew 28 and Mark 16). You and I are supposed to let our light shine. We are called to make a difference. It is never too late if you are willing to do whatever it takes!

Everyone is different. The Lord created us that way. Different colors, backgrounds, personalities, and traits compose the human race, and we all need each other. Hebrews 3:12-13 says, "*See to it, brothers that none of you has a sinful, unbelieving heart that turns away from the living God. But encourage one another daily, as long as it is called Today, so that none of you may be hardened by sin's deceitfulness.*" We all have different strengths and weaknesses; therefore, it is important to discuss a few common areas of life's weaknesses, struggles, and topics and questions which are common to the Christian walk. I have learned in my personal experience dealing with my own addiction and through helping others that it is a personal choice, and to be set free, it always involves a soul-searching and Christ-seeking process. I am not putting God in a box. The Lord can set anyone free however He sees fit. For some of us, this is a constant process. It can be similar to pulling weeds from the garden or peeling an onion. You must learn to be honest with yourself, God, and your accountability partner in order for the healing to begin. The walls of pride must come down, sometimes one brick at a time. Learning to trust God and step into the unknown is a scary thing, but you can't walk on water unless you get out of the boat. What I have learned is this: everyone has a past, everyone has pain, and everyone needs Jesus. For me, it is a daily choice. Will I cast my cares on Him or will I take it back? Will I live in my own strength or the strength He provides?

Real-talk on some serious Life Issues

*ADDICTION

My various issues with addictions, anger and pride came very close to destroying me. My heart was dirty and hardened, and I was no good or help to anyone, including myself. Unfortunately, I have seen firsthand that many people must hit bottom before they look up toward God. I have seen many people I love destroy themselves along with their families. No one will change until they are ready. My prayer is that these next paragraphs may open eyes, soften hearts, and help others from crashing to the bottom and losing everything, in particular, their life. Depending on how serious the situation is, in-patient or out-patient rehabilitation may be needed. When fighting against drug, alcohol addiction, and porn you will, in fact, have to do whatever it takes to have peace.

If you are serious about change, I would recommend the *Celebrate Recovery* program for any and all addictions and issues. Moreover, I think it would be wise for ANYONE who wants to participate in ministry to complete a "step study" program. God designed us with a desire to love, encourage and help people. *Celebrate Recovery* teaches us to deal with our past and character flaws and prevents them from hindering our current growth and the growth of others. This program puts the Lord on His throne. The twelve steps are all Biblical in nature and origin. I recommend seeking wise council and prayerfully considering the available options.

Denial and pride are powerful suppressants. Admitting "I need help" or "I can't do this on my own" is not easy. Pride is so powerful that most of us have a hard time just confessing we are hurting in the first place. I recently spoke with a friend who struggles with methamphetamine and other drugs. This person said, "Don't worry. I do not pay for it. People just give it to me." Rest assured, a price will be paid, along with all those who actually care for this person. Every person who chooses to go down this road, in fact, will pay for it. When all the trust people once placed in you is gone, when your relationships crumble, when you lose employment, when you think you cannot function normally without it, when everything seems so overwhelming, when you consistently lower yourself and standard of life to maintain addiction based relationships, and when you can no longer face yourself in the mirror, you will pay for it. It happens to everyone. For some, it takes longer than others, but it will eventually happen. I promise that you are not the only exception to the rule. I know from experience that life is exhausting when you have to pick yourself up off the ground over and over again, but by the grace, love, and power of Jesus, the cycle can be broken. Most people have no idea of the level of spiritual warfare that was required to gain their freedom. The next battle will be to maintain that freedom and to stand your ground against the enemy.

The enemy is a great deceiver that plays for keeps. He will try to convince people that they don't need rehabilitation, to attend meetings, or church. If a person is not willing to change their phone number, shut down or safeguard all of their social media for a season and avoid tempting places or triggering situations, I am inclined to believe that they are not serious about lasting change. I went to every extreme when I was involved in the drug culture. In order to get and remain free, a person must be as radically extreme in their freedom as they were in their addiction. It may be necessary to attend *Celebrate Recovery*, faith based groups, Narcotics Anonymous (NA), and Alcoholics Anonymous (AA) meetings in the same week. During my path to sobriety, I attended each of those programs (and worked the step study), attended discipleship classes, and got involved in my local church. I found areas to serve and give back. I eventually made new friends and found a sponsor and mentor. Romans 12:2 says, *"Do not conform any longer to the patterns of this world, but be transformed by the renewing of your mind. Then you will be able to test and approve what God's will is-his good, pleasing and perfect will."* We all mess up, but never give up. Never accept the negative things you have been told. In Jesus name, you can deal with anything and move forward! I ask only that you are honest with God and yourself and obey what the Holy Spirit is putting on your heart. If you keep doing the same things, you will get the same results. The greatest tragedy would be to continue to live in a life of bondage and miss the freedom Jesus offers us all.

It is important to do whatever it takes. However, at some point after the initial admitting there is a problem, one should shift focus to the solution. That solution is Jesus and your personal relationship with Him. You can respect a group's culture to get the support you need until you have more viable options. In my life, Jesus used every situation, court ordered program, and less than desirable job held during my climb up as a testimony and relationship building tool. Remember, God wastes nothing if we give it all to Him. Let us never stop praying for those who are bound by addiction.

*RELATIONSHIPS

"Life is relationships; the rest is just details."
Gary Smalley, *The DNA of Relationships*

You may ask yourself, "What does a single man know about relationships?" My response would be, "Can I tell you what I do know?" I know I have destroyed my share of relationships. I also know that there is almost no relational sin I have not committed. When I was younger, though not obeying Christ, I had a good heart. I only desired to be with one woman at a time. Unlike many of my friends who were with as many women as possible, I thought I was the nice guy. Before my life with Jesus, my dating life consisted of four long-term, serious relationships over the course of ten years.

Without a doubt, I cared deeply for these women. Unfortunately, I carried my past into these relationships. Feelings and emotions began to overlap and confuse my heart. My substance abuse, trust and anger issues, and past hurts from others would eventually bleed into and destroy my good intentions. I grew bitter, and try as I might, my castle was still built on the sand (Matthew 7:24-27). It would be easy to label me an extreme case and say that I don't or can't understand what you are going through. I challenge you to listen with your heart, and you may learn from what the Lord has allowed me to experience.

If you are married then this paragraph cannot truly express the level of scriptural commitment you have made. No matter what the world says, marriage is sacred bond. Matthew 19:4-6 says, "*and He [Jesus] answered and said unto them, Have ye not read, that he which made them at the beginning made them male and female, And said For this cause shall a man leave father and mother, and shall cleave to his wife: and they twain one flesh? Wherefore they are no more twain, but one flesh. What therefore God has joined together let man not put asunder.*" I purposely used the King James translation. It uses the word "cleave." Cleave means to hang on like your life depends on it. When difficulties arise, learning to cleave to your spouse is wise. Two people must become one flesh. This is not only talking about being sexually joined but about being joined on every level. The next scripture says, "*what God has put together let no man come between.*" This means forsaking all others and going all in. The clear implication is that there should be no "back-up plan."

If you are married, engaged, or claim to be in a serious relationship, and you are communicating with past lovers or flings, "catching lunch" with them, or social networking for attention, then my friend, you are setting yourself up for ruin. This is called emotional cheating. If the other party in the relationship is not aware of the communication taking place, it is cheating. If they are being told "we're just friends" when it is clearly more than that, it is cheating. When you are deleting messages and pictures off your phone so your significant other will not see, it is cheating. If this paragraph makes your skin crawl and you are not yet married then remain single. Stop "playing the game" and take time off. Seek God and make peace with yourself and your past. Do this before entering into the next relationship. Maybe a season of singleness and healing is what is needed.

There is no wisdom in confiding in the opposite sex while in a serious relationship. We should all be careful who we confide in. It is not possible to communicate honestly or on a deep emotional level with your significant other when your mind is in the past. Having an affair or contemplating a liaison later down the road hinders any possible healing or growth. The Holy Bible says, "*Let no one come between*" (Mark 10). We do not need to become stumbling blocks in the kingdom for others. We need to be solid stones to help people climb closer to Christ. We should love, honor, and respect the people in our lives to the best of our ability. Prayerfully evaluate what is important to you and your life's relationships.

The above scripture and 1 Corinthians chapter 13 is often read like poetry at a wedding ceremony and has become just as much a ritual as throwing the bouquet to the bridesmaids. In reality, it is the Word of God. His words and instructions on how to live and love are right before us. They are not to be taken lightly. If you have messed up, have fallen into the rut of day-to-day life, or have had tragedy or other adverse situations hinder your relationship with God, do not give the enemy the final word. Repent, get your heart right with Christ, make amends, and move forward. Simply ask the Lord for wisdom and strength to not only make it better but to make it permanently "good." The Lord is still in the miracle business. Don't walk away from your spouse and family. These are the most important things in life besides Christ Himself. The greatest tragedy would be to never attempt to do your level best in Christ before walking away. This means allowing Him to cleanse and teach you. Receive God's wisdom and grace then choose to do whatever it takes. Remember, change starts with you and Christ. You can only clean your own back yard. Hopes of controlling someone else are mere fantasy.

If you have this book in your hand, I hope that you are willing to admit there are areas of your life that need to change and allow Christ to work in. You may ask, "How can I change?" These are just a few helpful pointers. Put Jesus Christ first in your life. Seek His face and read his Word. Pray and develop faith through focusing on your relationship with Him. Absorb all the things of God in like a sponge. Let Him begin to change you from the inside out with the power of the Holy Spirit. I strongly recommend reading books about the five love languages and becoming the man or the woman that you're truly called to be. For some men this may seem like a stretch, but I wish I had read those books twenty years ago. Christian counseling may be needed to work through some past issues. Real love is a choice; it is not a season or a passionate summer. Learning to communicate with your spouse and all people you love will make everything run smoother. The ideal situation would be for the marriage to function as a team in all facets of life.

"Dying to self" daily is not fun, but it is what Christ commands us to do. Luke 9:23 says, *"Then he said to them all: If anyone would come after me, he must deny himself and take up his cross daily and follow me."* We must learn to forgive each other and let those things of our past go. Progress will be made when we learn from our past mistakes, not when we hold onto them. Compromise may, at first, seem like a painful word, but we must learn, grow and change. Some behaviors may have to be eliminated by both parties. It is ridiculous, immature, and childish to do things to purposely hurt the people we love. We must be open to listening to each other and moving in the right direction, thus seeking God's perfect will. Forgiveness through God's power and love freely given are what builds lasting relationships; however, once trust is violated it must be earned. Through Christ all things are possible. Wise men and women seek Jesus first rather than half-heartedly asking Him to bless their endeavors.

Thinking Point: If you are not yet in a covenant relationship, it would be wise to discuss the material mentioned above with your future spouse. Communication is the key in all relationships; therefore, laying all your cards on the table together would be wise. Each spouse is supposed to offer a covering of protection and prayer over the other. The Bible calls our spouses "help mates," and its literal translation from Hebrew means "a strong rescuer standing in front of." Learning to cover each other's blind spots and weakness will ultimately strengthen your relationship. This should always be done in wisdom and love.

Keep this fact in mind: no single person on this earth can give you real joy. Our true joy and peace only come from Jesus and our relationship with Him. Only within this relationship will we find the wisdom and strength to love and its divine source. Never put your happiness eggs all in another person's basket. You will not only set yourself up for disappointment, but you will place an enormous amount of pressure on the person you love. Focus on Jesus. You cannot bring anyone a glass of water when you are dying of thirst! You have to drink a big glass of Jesus before you can lovingly share a sip. Sometimes just a taste of God's love can become a foundation of change. Throughout this book we will take a closer look at wisdom and relationships.

*GRIEF

This is where it gets deep. This is where the difficult questions arise such as, "Why do bad things happen to good people?" I wish I could give you a sound answer. Life happens. In brief, we live in a fallen world, and the Lord gives us free will. The enemy prowls like a lion seeking someone to devour (1 Peter 5:8). The book of Romans proclaims that God makes all things work together for the good of the believer in Christ (Romans 8:28). That is a profound promise. Neck deep in pain, it can be hard to receive or believe that God is in control or that His plan is good. In these moments, keep in mind that grace is enough (2 Corinthians 12:9). It is a good thing that He is holding us regardless of our emotions.

I had a very weak faith-based foundation when I was growing up. I heard "God is good" and believed Jesus did live, die and rise for me. However, I experienced much pain and loss in my early years. Shortly after I called on Jesus as my Savior, I watched my granny die a slow painful death from emphysema. She, of all people, spoke life into me. She taught me the Lord's Prayer and gave me hope that there was something good in this world. The attention, time and affection she gave me, and those who loved her, was an example of genuine love. Why did she have to suffer? Soon after her passing, two of my cousins died tragic deaths, both of my grandfathers passed away, and two of my classmates were killed. The pain I felt and witnessed, brought a sense of hopelessness. It was a raw feeling that I could do nothing to comfort my hurting loved ones. I did not understand why my family seemingly had so many problems. My family was broken, buzzed, and angry. During this time, my heart slowly grew hard. I honestly did not think the Lord was so good anymore. These combined events slowly eroded my shallow faith.

This confusion, coupled with daily teenage peer pressure, pushed me into alcohol, drugs, and women as an escape.

Eventually, I would be totally immersed in the drug culture. I thought I dealt with all my past. Things seemed to be going well, and I had everything I ever wanted at nineteen years old. My world came crashing down when I received a life changing message at work one day. One of my best friends was killed making a drug transaction. In the coming years, nothing worked to ease my pain. The culmination of everything I had ever lost was more than I could endure, and the hollowness and shallowness of my faith left me sinking fast. There were so many questions and no legitimate answers. His death led me into my first real season of addiction and depression. The aftermath cost me a very special relationship, seriously damaged several others, and momentarily stopped my future. I became a loose cannon and honestly did not care whether I lived or died. There are many days I cannot even remember-more than I care to speculate. From this point on, pain and depression consumed me until the day I met Jesus. Then the real fight was on. It is only by God's grace and mercy that I am alive.

Grief is a process. We all need support and time. With that being said, I do not agree that "time heals all wounds." Time may lessen the blow or allow for a comforting perspective to form, but Jesus Christ is the healer. In my case, the wild life was not the problem. The problem was my pride. I had no real knowledge of God's Word or who Jesus really was. I allowed pain to consume me, and it slowly blinded me to all the good things left in my life. The fact was that my house was built on sand. It became easier for me be numb than to feel any more pain or disappointment. A vicious cycle had formed without me even realizing it. No one gets a pass. It is human nature to look for escapes in such things as prescription medication, toxic relationships, solitude, socializing, computer games, anger and control, fighting, exercising, drinking, working, gambling and other compulsive behaviors. Any of these behaviors can be used to mask grief or any other "issue." The enemy's fog first blinds and then robs you of every blessing in your life. The good news is that this can occur only IF you allow him to.

I had to learn to humble myself and allow the same God that I was furious with to bring peace unto me. The comfort that I eventually received changed me forever. I learned to *"call on me in the day of trouble; I will deliver you, and you will honor me"* as written in Psalms 50:15. My pride was and still can be a hindrance in my walk with Jesus. The Holy Spirit once gave me a word. He said, "It is alright to be mad at God. It's alright to not understand. It's not alright for us to **stay** mad at God." We are supposed to give those emotions and pain to Jesus. Put them at the foot of the cross. The only way it worked for me was to be totally honest and real. As King David bled his heart throughout several of the Psalms, so should we. We should then allow ourselves time to cry and vent and let the Holy Spirit minister healing. Some refer to this encounter as a moment or "touch of grace." In our Christian walk, it is important to recognize such moments. Let go and let God. Say out loud, "Lord, I receive the healing power of the Holy Spirit. Help me now, today, and each day forward to cast my cares on You. Teach me to do Your will. In Jesus' name, Amen". Let the roots of bitterness toward God be removed and be replaced by the comfort of Jesus.

Later in life, when I was in the mission field and two months before my scheduled return from Lithuania, I lost two of my very close friends. There was an ocean separating me from my family and friends. I knew in my heart that one of these friends was in a battle for his life because the Holy Spirit told me. On a seemingly normal day, I was checking my email and social media. I received the life changing message telling me that my friend had taken his own life. I immediately went to my knees in tearful prayer. The only peace I found in the situation was the thought of being present when he prayed to receive Jesus as his Savior. He was a baby in the faith. It was hard for him to read his Bible and take things on faith. The Christian walk is extremely hard with little or no support system, and there should be no lone rangers in our walks with Christ. About one month later, I lost the other friend to a drug overdose. Once again, I was far from my family and friends. This blow hit me much harder. He once visited my home church to hear me preach. He mentioned to another friend that he felt the Lord pulling on his heart and that he should have responded to the alter call by going to the front for prayer. Only God knew his heart. If you feel the Holy Spirit tugging on your heart then respond immediately. No one is promised tomorrow. We often overlook just how special it is when Jesus Christ is speaking to you. I still pray to this day for hurting families that have suffered unfair or unexplainable losses. Because dealing with a loss was a weak point in my armor, the enemy attempted to bombard me with negative thoughts and emotions. I was able to recognize the enemy's attack. It was a blessing to have real friends to pray with me and support me while I was so far away.

That fall, I found myself seeking the solace of the Baltic Sea. It was an attempt to get away from it all. The cold wind blows in strong gusts as the waves crash onto the shore-line. The cloudy, hazy grey sky in the afternoon was my refuge. I realized that the Lord had been speaking to me about friendship and loss for quite some time. I allowed the Holy Spirit to minister to me along those shores. This turned into a moment of grace and receiving. The Lord showed me a different perspective about thankfulness and love. I began to thank God for the time I did have with each of my lost family members and friends. He taught me to not only be thankful for but to cherish who remained and honor those who have passed. The reality was there were areas where I had buried shame and unwarranted guilt. He showed me all my regrets. I had to let them go. There are many different customs in which cultures honor their dead, and each individual person has their own method, time frame, and support needed to overcome grief. Clearly, I developed several methods that were selfish and toxic. That day, the Lord told me the way to honor my fallen loved ones-**live!** He didn't mean just "go on with life" but for me to live it to the fullest.

Do not miss any opportunities with those you hold dear. Tell people you love them. Hug them often. Serve and love people like Jesus did. The Bible says in 2 Corinthians 7:10 that *"Godly sorrow leads to repentance which leads to a life of no regrets...."* Where I once felt that I fell short in sharing my faith with these two friends, the Lord showed me that I had done my part in sharing my life, my home, and my time with them. It was not a burden but a blessing. The real blessing is to have ever known love at all. I had to seriously thank God that He entrusted me to share His love with them. The blessing of the time I had with all those I lost was no longer a trigger for pain, but a warm spot that will forever hold a special place in my heart.

Do not allow the enemy to steal seasons of your life with guilt, regret and confusion. I pray this helps everyone gain some hope. The Bible makes it clear that we need support and accountability. Please do not fight or attempt to carry your burden alone. Sometimes being humble and making a call or text asking for prayer can be a difference maker. People may already be praying for you and wondering how to reach out. Dealing with grief, like most other struggles, is a process. Jesus says we should approach them "one day at a time" (Matthew 6:34).

*STRESS

Stress is a normal physiological response to an event that makes you feel threatened. Stress can steal your joy. The human body has a natural "fight or flight" mechanism, and every living organism on this earth will respond to stress in some way, shape, or fashion. Therefore, it is a natural response. How we deal with stress defines our level of peace and joy. As taught in *Celebrate Recovery*, denial is a symptom of stress or other life changing or life-threatening events. Stress can be linked to forgiveness in the form of extreme hatred. It can, if allowed, destroy and mold the very nature of someone's life. Worry and stress are toxic and must be replaced with faith, hope and love! Let's look at some of the detrimental impacts stress can cause.

Common effects of Chronic Stress: Pain, heart disease, digestive problems, insomnia, depression, obesity, weight loss, nausea, immune system breakdown, autoimmune disease, and skin conditions such as rashes or eczema.

Common external causes of stress: Major life changes, work frustration, relationship difficulties with family and friends, financial problems, overall sense of being too busy.

Common internal causes of stress: Inability to accept uncertainty (worry), pessimism, negative self-talk, unrealistic expectations, perfectionism, lack of assertiveness, FEAR.

Other Various Symptoms: Poor judgment, difficulty remembering details, focus on negativity, anxious racing thoughts, body aches, chest pain, rapid heartbeat, loss of sex drive, frequent colds, moodiness, irritability (short temper), loss or gain in appetite, change in sleeping patterns, isolating behavior patterns, procrastinating and neglecting responsibility, the use of alcohol, drugs, or sex in an attempt to relax, and various nervous behaviors such as nail biting, pacing, or picking at an imperfection.

These can be signs, symptoms, or doorways for the enemy to attack. What can be done? What is the answer? In John 14:1, Jesus says, *"do not let your hearts be troubled. You believe in God; believe also in me."* Matthew 6:33-34 says, *"but seek first his kingdom and his righteousness, and all these things will be given to you as well. Therefore, do not worry about tomorrow, for tomorrow will worry about itself. Each day has enough trouble of its own."*

Here are some helpful pointers. Take the necessary steps to let God position you to seek Him diligently and with your whole heart so that you can ultimately experience the total freedom that Jesus has for us all. Learn to identify your stressors or triggers, and learn to be honest with God and yourself. Be real about the causes of stress in your life. This will help in the preparation to an improved reaction. Remember, you are trying to achieve progress not perfection. Learn how to manage stress until your complete victory happens. Formulate a plan. Pray and then establish realistic healthy boundaries.

I have found that I manage stress much better if I choose to persistently meditate on a verse from the Bible or a POSITIVE lesson Jesus is teaching me. By focusing on the solution, Christ and His promises, overcoming stress is possible. It takes constant effort and honesty to resist our emotions and situations (pouting, anger, spending money etc.). Call your accountability partner or someone spiritually mature enough to hear your heart and pray! Exercise regularly, eat healthier, rest, and honor your time with God with study, prayer, worship and listening to His voice. When it comes to accountability always remember, Ecclesiastes 4:9-12 *"Two are better than one, because they have a good return for their labor: If either of them falls down, one can help the other up. But pity anyone who falls and has no one to help them up. Also, if two lie down together, they will keep warm. But how can one keep warm alone? Though one may be overpowered, two can defend themselves. A cord of three strands is not quickly broken."*

*WORSHIP

One of my friends in Lithuania shared his favorite Psalm with me in 2006. It has stayed close to my heart ever since.

Psalm 100

1 Shout for joy to the LORD, all the earth.

2 Worship the LORD with gladness;

come before him with joyful songs.

3 Know that the LORD is God.

It is he who made us, and we are his;

we are his people, the sheep of his pasture.

4 Enter his gates with thanksgiving

and his courts with praise;

give thanks to him and praise his name.

5 For the LORD is good and his love endures forever;

his faithfulness continues through all generations.

This Psalm states what it is all about. The Psalm speaks of praise, joy, true acknowledgement of the creator, thanksgiving, and a promise of faithfulness to continue through all generations. Worship is much more than just singing unto the Lord, but it is important to join in the singing and praise at your local church. The Lord inhabits the praises of His people. It does not matter how many people are halfheartedly singing, sitting in the pews, or standing there thinking about lunch. We cannot judge anyone. I challenge you to get involved as the Lord leads you. Focus on Him. Allow Him to cleanse you with the power of the Holy Spirit. Do not be afraid of crying, singing, raising your hands or of anything else. *"Repent, then and turn to God, so that your sins may be wiped out, that times of refreshing may come from the Lord"*- Acts 3:19. I have had several refreshing times of worship, some that changed me forever.

Many times, God has given me peace or comforted me in times of trouble during worship. Other times, He has spoken something to me that I needed to do or say to someone, and He has revealed areas I need to make right in my walk and life. It takes boldness and maybe some time to get comfortable to worship. Keep your heart open to Jesus. Do your best to allow Him to have His way in your life. *"Peace I leave with you; my peace I give you. I do not give to you as the world gives. Do not let your hearts be troubled and do not be afraid,"* says John 14:27. Praise Him with your whole heart, listen for His voice. He still speaks.

Worship is not only a corporate gathering of believers but a private meeting with the Divine as well. Praising God on the mission field, I was single but never alone. I used to listen to The David Crowder Band's *Illuminate* disc at bedtime. I would play the last six songs on the album, and I would usually be at peace or sound asleep by the time the song "Stars" ended. I was more than six thousand miles away from home. There were times that I was homesick or lonely, but the Lord let me know that He was there with me. Through even the difficult times that I have experienced most recently, I have been able to raise my hands with tears in my eyes and worship the Lord both in private and in corporate worship. When the walls are falling around us, God is unchanging. I have learned that God is bigger than my situation no matter what it looks like to me. He is working things right to the good of those who love Him. Worship is not about a feeling, an emotion, or your favorite song. It is about Jesus. It is for Him. It is bringing Him an offering of praise. It is acknowledging Him on His throne. What people think really does not matter. Worship is between you and God. God is so big he can speak to us all individually or at the same time.

Worship is life. It is getting up and picking up your cross and following him daily. Perhaps it's holding our tongue when we could go off on someone. It is learning and applying many of the things discussed in this chapter. The way we live our daily lives says more to God than anything else. Walk in love. Learn to forgive others and yourself. Seek God. Stay pure, be thankful, and choose joy. All that may sound like an impossible task, but Luke 1:37 says *"for nothing is impossible with God."* When I have stumbled, this scripture has helped me. *"If we confess our sins he is faithful and just and will forgive our sin and purify us from all unrighteousness"*-1 John 1:9.

*SEEKING GOD'S WILL

Many people attend a moving church service, accept Christ and his forgiveness as assurance, and quickly get bored. The peace of a normal life can make some people anxious or complacent. Sometimes God speaks in a gentle voice. He may reveal that you need to start giving and tithing. He may tell you to ask your pastor, "What can I do?" In reality, the pastor or leadership of a healthy church should be encouraging you to seek God and ask Him, "What can I do for you Lord?" The fruit and blessing of your walk will depend on your obedience to His voice. Living a life that shows you are a person of faith speaks volumes. We all need to be prepared to share our faith, says Philemon v6. Sharing your faith will move you into a place where the Holy Spirit can work through you. It will also put the true joy of the Lord in your heart. I have never left any ministry activity without feeling uplifted or challenged in some capacity.

At this moment, it may be extremely difficult for you to step out of your comfort zone. The blessing will always outweigh the fear. I can promise you that. You may be led to sign up for a class, go on a mission trip, cut someone's grass that is unable, or serve in any way needed. Follow the voice of the Holy Spirit. A person often has to try a few different things before finding his niche. Even after, a true servant will continue to help wherever the need lies or get involved in what God is already doing. Rest assured, you will get closer to God's will by stepping out towards Him rather than sitting around watching television complaining about being bored. There is fine line between grace and potato chips. The Lord knows your heart. *"You will seek me and find me when you seek me with all your heart."* - Jeremiah 29:13.

One of the most frequent questions that I get asked is, "What is God's will for my life?" The answer lies in 1 Thessalonians. It clearly outlines four things that are God's will for your life. They are simple in nature but difficult in execution.

"It is God's will that you should be sanctified: that you should avoid sexual immorality."
1 Thessalonians 4:3

Be pure. That is not an easy standard, nor is it fashionable in today's world. However, sexual sin is serious and has consequences. There are more dangers than disease and unwarranted pregnancy. Ungodly "soul ties" can form and link us to people in a very negative way. I strongly encourage you do a little research on "ungodly soul ties." Personally, I have felt like I have thrown pieces of my heart into a pond or stream only to find that no one cared about the ripple that slowly faded away. There will always be consequences to our sin and choices. The struggle is real. We must avoid rationalization and justification of our desires and choose to meditate on the Lord's standards. Let the Lord prepare you for the relationship that will flow like a river not fade like a ripple in the stream. This choice will help keep your temple clean so the Lord can speak to you and use you. In this battle, we all need accountability, support and prayer.

"Be joyful always, pray continually; give thanks in all circumstances, for this is God's will for you in Christ Jesus."
1 Thessalonians 5: 16-18

Be joyful. Keeping your head up is not easy. Maintaining joy can be a difficult struggle. For me, sometimes the enemy, situations, others, or my own choices can rob my joy. At times, I am a very serious person. There is always a great deal of responsibility on my shoulders. I can never go back to my old ways. In order to have real joy, one must choose to tap into Jesus before stepping out of the door. Ask the Holy Spirit to fill you, use you and guide you. It is a choice. Sometimes I have to press the reset button throughout my day to keep the enemy at bay. If he cannot get us to do things that we once did, he will make every effort to steal our joy. Make the choice to be joyful. Learn to occasionally laugh at yourself and lighten up. I keep a small cross on my doorstep which reads a verse from Nehemiah 8:10 "*The joy of the Lord is my strength*". This is a reminder so that when I come home from "doing good," I do not get lost within myself or my circumstances. I choose to get into the Word early and get involved in His work. "*Shout for joy to the Lord, all the earth. Worship the Lord with gladness; come before him with joyful songs*"- Psalm 100:1-2.

"*Pray without ceasing*"
1 Thessalonians 5:17

Pray continually. The Lord desires fellowship with us all day. It's hard to comprehend just how much He loves us. He is a jealous God. Remaining in a heartfelt mindset of prayer is not easy. I recently graduated from McNeese State University in Lake Charles, Louisiana. I have worked in the construction industry, the food service industry, the oil field industry, the automotive industry among various other jobs. Even after I had developed the discipline of waking early each morning to pray and read the Holy Bible, I still missed the mark. Often, I only allowed God to be with me until my day truly began. Other times, and still to this today if I am not careful, I began doing things in my own power or wisdom. God is for us not against us. He wants to help guide us in all our tasks. I used to wish my day would end so I could spend more time with Him. I was missing the point. The people around us (work, school, and the community) need us to always be in tune with Him. We need fellowship with the Lord to aid us in our tasks. Our lives should serve as a witness to the world around us. Rather than getting things done our way and repenting later, we must all make it a point to communicate with Jesus throughout our day. There was only one that was perfect. He understands our struggles and wants us to talk to Him and spend time with Him throughout our daily lives. I have had much more success in prayer through understanding that this relationship is a privilege, not so much a discipline.

"Give thanks in all circumstances…"
1 Thessalonians 5:18

Be thankful. Being thankful is paramount in walking with Jesus. In my youth, I was influenced by the world and others around me. My mother worked a difficult job to provide for my sister and I. She bought me a Ford Ranger so I could work and get around. Instead of being thankful, I was jealous of others who had nicer cars. I never seemed to notice that there were many kids who had no car. It never even crossed my mind to use the gift she gave me to work hard for a couple years and buy the car that I wanted. I had no idea how to take care of a vehicle nor did I understand the importance of preventive maintenance. I was a spoiled product of the entitlement generation. When I came to know Christ in my late twenties, I gradually learned to be thankful for not only material blessings but for my health, my real friends, my family, my salvation and even the pain which brought me to Him.

Every Good Gift is From Above

Your next breath is a gift from God. He has a plan for your life that is good. His will is perfect. We must all understand that God is the source of all blessing, and every "good gift" is from above (James 1:17). You may think, "I am a self-made person" or "My hard work or talent gave me this." He made you and knows the number of hairs on your head or lack thereof. He gave you that work ethic and those talents. Acknowledge Him. Be thankful. Things do not always go our way. Life can be tough. Find things to be thankful for even on the hard days. Work at putting these four principles into practice. You will hear God speak, and He will draw you closer as you diligently seek His face. He designed us to need and worship Him. I will close this chapter with an encouraging promise from the Psalms that a mighty woman of God prayed over me before service one day... *"Delight yourself in the Lord and he will give you the desires of your heart"*-Psalm 37:4.

CHAPTER 3

Storms and Trials

It is my hope that all who read this chapter will increase in understanding, blessing, preparing, equipping, and strengthening concerning the storms and trials we will all face in our lives. What does the Holy Bible say about storms and trials, heartache and pain? By looking to the Word, we can formulate a plan on the biblical way to handle difficulty. I'd like to share a few key scriptures that have helped me overcome the storms of my own life. By following a few simple spiritual steps, I pray that your eyes may be opened to a pathway to peace in the midst of the storm.

"Blessed is the man who perseveres under a trial, because when he has stood the test, he will receive the crown of life that God has promised to those who love him."-**James 1:12**

There is good reason to keep pressing on. There is a payoff, a reward and a blessing. Every time you "learn your lesson," you grow and mature in some way. In every admission, in every fight, in every press forward, and in every instance where you do not quit, you will find blessing. When the fires of hell want nothing more than for you to quit or give up on the cross, surrendering to defeat isn't an option. We may mess up, but we cannot quit. For me, many of the lessons I learned were in the storm and facing trials. Unfortunately, it is during the hardest times when we learn and grow the most. In the valley, there is growth. God will use whatever it takes to encourage you to pray. Simply put, His desire is for us to always look for and turn to Him. Every major event or crisis is going to either push you away from or draw you closer to God. In 2 Corinthians 7:10, the Bible says, *"Godly sorrow brings repentance that leads to salvation and leaves no regret, but worldly sorrow brings death."*

Always be mindful that you don't react to a situation without first taking a step back to reflect. Before you get mad at God, ask Him for peace and strength to overcome the situation through Jesus Christ. Pray that you will be open to learn a lesson or deeper truth and become a stronger and wiser individual. Sometimes just getting through the day without digressing is enough. <u>The fact is that He wants us to learn to trust Him regardless of our circumstances.</u> Too many of us waste enormous amounts of time trying to understand or figure out "What is God trying to teach me?" Sometimes faith does not make sense. Could it be that Jesus' desire is for us is to trust Him regardless of the circumstances? Ultimately, trusting Him will give you hope and peace in the midst of tribulation. You will not have more placed before you than you can handle. One phone call can change any of our lives. Being angry at God or others is, in truth, a normal reaction. The detrimental and costly part is staying angry. This can develop into bitterness. Bitterness can destroy the soul and other personal relationships. Matthew 6:34 says, *"Therefore do not worry about tomorrow, for tomorrow will worry about itself. Each day has enough trouble of its own."*

Peace and Joy

"1) Therefore, since we have been justified through faith, we have peace with God through our Lord Jesus Christ,2) through whom we have gained access by faith into his grace in which we now stand. And we rejoice in hope of the glory of God. 3) Not only so, but we also rejoice in our suffering, because we know that suffering produces perseverance; 4) perseverance, character; and character, hope. 5) And hope does not disappoint us, because God has poured his love into our hearts by the Holy Spirit, whom he has given us."- **Romans 5:1-5**

Before I accepted Christ, It was said of me that "I was a character"; it was seldom said that "I had character." Perhaps I did, but it was buried far behind walls of pain and regret. The culmination of the trials and storms of my past, which were never properly addressed, simply had taken their toll. Therefore, I had no peace. As I grew spiritually, the Book of Romans showed me from where lasting peace comes.

Verse one- We are justified and made right with God! How? Through faith in Jesus and all he has done.

Verse two- We gain access to Christ. How? By faith! Into where? His Grace! Brother or sister, once you understand that, it gives you hope!

Verse three- Christ suffered the ultimate suffering for you. We must learn to embrace His suffering on the road to peace. Paul said he wanted to share in the suffering of Christ. By doing this, you will be made stronger! Through the process of sharing the suffering of Christ, you develop perseverance!

Verse four- Perseverance in the storm or trial forges character. Character brings forth hope!

Verse five- Hope in Jesus Christ will not disappoint. That is a promise! Why? When you accept Christ, you receive the Holy Spirit and gain power over death. "Real love" comes from God! All the fighting you could ever muster in the flesh will not help. The ultimate blessing comes when we allow the Lord to fight our battles. You can walk in love standing firm in faith.

Thinking point: If you were to take a closer look at Romans Chapter 4, you will see that faith is the catalyst that makes overcoming anything possible.

Where does one find peace in the storm?

"One day Jesus said to his disciples, "Let's go over to the other side of the lake." So they got onto a boat and set out. As they sailed, he fell asleep. A squall came down on the lake, so that the boat was being swamped, and they were in great danger. The disciples went and woke him saying, "Master, Master, we're going to drown!" He got up and rebuked the wind and raging waters; the storm subsided and all was calm. "Where is your faith?" He asked his disciples. In fear and amazement they asked one another, "Who is this? He commands even the winds and the water, and they obey him."- **Luke 8:22-25**

"If Christ is in you, He is also in your circumstances"
Graham Cooke

There is more than one lesson to be learned from these Scriptures. Jesus told His disciples "Let's go to the other side of the lake," and they followed. In obedience, they got in the boat and set out. As the body of Christ, we are in the boat too. Jesus was setting them up for an opportunity to develop their faith. Though Jesus was with them, the disciples woke him from resting when they encounter trouble. The Bible says he got up and rebuked, or prayed against, the storm and brought peace into the situation. His immediate reprimand was "Where is your faith?" I often ask the same question to myself. I am still learning to trust and exercise faith each day. Even having seen Him heal the sick and turn water into wine, they still said, "Who is this?" It is the name of Jesus. It is in His name that we receive the power to still the storms. A working relationship with Christ and God's amazing grace will bring peace regardless of the storm's size or intensity.

The Book of James wrote about a promise. This promise gives us encouragement and enlightenment into the way we view trials. *"Consider it pure joy, my brothers, whenever you face trials of many kinds. Because you know that testing of your faith develops perseverance. Perseverance must finish its work in you so that you may be mature and complete, not lacking anything"*-**James 1:2-4.** We are to welcome trials and consider them a joy? This is easier said than done and comes with spiritual maturity. Why are we to welcome trials? We are to welcome them because testing your faith develops perseverance. Once perseverance through faith is developed in you, you will become mature and complete lacking nothing. It is noteworthy that James did not say "if" you face trials, he said "when" you face trials. Trials will come. These trials often come to develop or activate the gifts or divine purpose that the Lord has placed inside you.

Unknown to me, God had a perfect spiritually progressive plan for my life that later equipped me to combat the storms of life. He first led me to my mother's church, where I accepted Christ with a pastor I trusted. The Lord then led me to a UPC church where the Holy Spirit revealed himself to me during the course of the service and the remainder of the night through the laying of hands and the resistance of temptation (James 4:7-8). From there, I was led to join my home church. The Lord then sent a man who would help mentor and teach me. I would then take my first missionary trip to Lithuania. I am deeply thankful and cherish all of those experiences and people, but after accepting Christ, I feel the biggest difference maker for me was reading the Holy Bible and having fellowship with the Holy Spirit. This progression helped me learn truly what the Word means and is and thus grew me and continues to grow me in the understanding of God's ways. You will never know this understanding until you embrace all that Christ was and still is and read the Bible with God's eyes. It will empower you in more ways than I can explain. The process of renewing your mind and heart can not only begin but continue (Romans 12:1-2).

Understanding the grace of God and what he did for us provides peace where there was none. My advice is, "do whatever it takes". When you hear something that makes you stronger …write it down, put it on the fridge, above the toilet, over your vehicle visor, anywhere you will see it often. Take the time to read the word. You will not make it far until you are tested. Just like we have read so far; you will not pass many tests unless you build your spirit man. Don't worry if you understand it or not, take it in. The time will not be spent in vain. Pray before you read the Bible. Pray "Holy Spirit please, help me understand, remember, and apply what I read" In Jesus name, Amen!

Thinking Point: Read Romans Chapter 8 and meditate on the grace of God.

When you find yourself in the middle of the storm, here are some steps to fight back.

1) Recognize you are in the storm

Before any lasting joy and peace can be achieved, you must first be able to see the clouds for what they are. If one or more of these issues plagues your life, there is a good chance you may be right in the middle of the storm: addiction, depression, anger, lack of responsibility, divorce, marriage struggles, lying, guilt, argumentative parenting, shame, overspending or bankruptcy, sloth (laziness), gluttony (compulsive eating), fear, inability to give or receive love, or inability to recover from your past or the death of a loved one. Blaming others for your hurt or pain is a sign of denial. There is a great deal of relief that comes with admitting that we need the Lord. Now is the time to fully accept and surrender to Christ, to seek inner healing, and to stop running from God. Many of us must learn to "walk it out" while Jesus is doing the work inside us. Recognize, identify, and admit what the problem or situation is. More than likely, the problem runs deeper than the surface. You will NEVER have a breakthrough until you face your fear, admit your faults, and confess your need for Jesus. This is known as honesty and humility.

Thinking point: If you do nothing, you have made a choice.

2) Make a course of action, and then execute your plan (address the situation and yourself)

For some people, being honest with themselves will be the hardest part. For others, consistently putting in the work is the hardest part. There are people who have signed up for discipleship classes for ten years, yet never completed one. The class isn't taken seriously, and their study guide is not filled out or partially complete. Their attendance is subpar. Is there any wonder why they have experienced little growth, revelation or breakthrough? Be aware of the enemy's tactics. Humbly choose life, and be willing to do whatever it takes! It is between you and God now. Listen for the direction of the Holy Spirit. His direction may be as blatant as writing on the wall, or it may be the still small voice of direction and reason. After the disciples called His name, Jesus calmed the storm with a few short words. He was with them, is He with you?

3) <u>Seek wise counsel</u>

If you know the most about Jesus in the circle of friends that you hang-out with, guess what? You need to expand your circle! Find spiritually mature people who have overcome the same struggle that you're dealing with. They should be grounded, live by example, and who can pray for you and with you. Step out of your comfort zone. You will be blessed. It was not easy for me. Understand this- though no one is perfect, not all people who profess to be Christians really are (or they have a shallow relationship with Jesus). Use discernment. It isn't wise to seek marriage advice from a person who has been divorced three or four times, unless they are telling you what not to do. Someone may have the "praying hands" tattooed on their chest and still be totally clueless about Jesus, much less have a functional relationship with Him. I have nothing personally against tattoos. I even have one myself from a previous life. However, it's what's tattooed on your heart that matters the most and not outward appearance. Finding someone to sulk and sit with you is not the answer either. Everyone needs a listening ear, true, but we also need a loving but swift kick in the right direction at times. Friends like that are not easy to find. They are to be cherished!

Learn to receive correction without taking offense. This will save you a lot of wasted time being angry. In most cases, the Lord will give you confirmation through people about things in which we are already aware. Accountability provides strength and wisdom to deal with the subject, issue, or area where we may be lacking. Keep in mind the goal-

don't just have friends, be one! Love people! Help people!
Give back! Real love should always be reciprocated. Learn to
actually listen and provide unselfish, wise, and Godly advice
and presence. One of the greatest ministries people often overlook is being there with a hug, prayer, listening ear, or genuine
encouragement.

Further Study: Proverbs 12:5, 12:15, 19:20, 20:18

4) <u>Keep pressing and do not give up!</u>

Make your mind up that no matter what comes against
you that you will not quit. The Holy Bible says, "Seek me
with all your heart and you will find me." Without Him, you
are missing peace, hope, joy, strength and comfort. These
blessings could be closer than you could even realize. The
best explanation that I can find about why we experience pain,
suffering and trials is "*Praise be to God and Father of our
Lord Jesus Christ, the father of compassion and the God of all
comfort, who comforts us in all our troubles, so that we can
comfort those in any trouble with the comfort we ourselves
have received from God*" **2 Corinthians 1:3-4.**   In other
words, your struggle, storm, trial, or loss can become a testimony, a testimony you can use to comfort others. The Lord
wastes nothing. In a nutshell, this is what the Body of Christ,
the true church, is supposed to do. We were created to reach
out, help, and love hurting people, all people, lest we forget
the words, the red letters, of Jesus Christ?

"A new command I give you: Love one another. As I have loved you, so you must love one another. By this all men will know that you are my disciples, if you love one another."
John 13: 34-35

I would like to share a personal essay in which I wrote in college. In it, are some examples of insight I gathered from my own life's storms. Because it was designed for a collegiate atmosphere, I was trying to sprinkle some salt and stimulate thinking in a liberal environment. This was my attempt to become all things to all people so that I might win some.

Holbrook Park by Sean Barron

Holbrook Park has been and will forever remain a sanctuary and refuge. There have been few changes made by man or nature to the park. In today's modern world, it is a good thing that the park remains close to its natural state. Lightning struck the giant tree across the river where we frequently jumped from. In the last decade, hurricane winds and lightning have torn the high branches on the top of the tree down. Now, it is no longer "safe" or possible to climb high into the tree. Although it is tattered and torn, perhaps more distinguished, the tree still stands. The park roads are now paved and family gatherings are encouraged. There are no more "rites of passage" or "free-for-all" parties held there anymore. The park attendant often surfaces and a sheriff's deputy will regularly pass through. I am thankful there is little known documentation of the things I used to do. There are a few pictures, but mostly spotted memories remain.

The park has always been open to the public. However, in the early 90's, it was reserved for a rugged crowd. There is a road that runs through the park. The road coming into the park is very much like many southern roads. It is lined with cypress trees loaded with moss. There are also several places for bank fishing. The moss seems to hang from the trees in such a way that it always seems to have been there. It is always soothing when a light breeze blows through on a warm sunny day. The left side of the park holds the boat launch, camping area, and several places to cook. If you were to immediately turn right after the entrance, the road forks. Follow this road around the camping area, playground and bathrooms, and you will find my refuge. Here the road circles around, and you will see the Houston River, cypress trees, and an old concrete table. The old concrete table, that has been a fixture in the park for as far back as I can remember, remains. I smiled upon my return to the park when I saw the table was still there. To this day, the table holds its place on the parking side of the river. I always liked putting my things or myself there in between swimming sessions. Depending on what I was up to, I would usually park in this area.

Back in the day, I would drive recklessly around the corner, fishtailing down the hill, park by the table, and quickly establish a perimeter. This place would be the area my friends and I would "hold down" for as long as we wanted. There were also more discrete times in which I would bring only my girlfriend and establish a different vibe altogether. On several occasions, I have retreated to my sanctuary alone to ponder life's mysteries and make important decisions. I enjoy turning my phone off, taking the view in, taking my dog out, or taking a quick swim.

The giant tree across the river was always the main attraction. There was a rope swing which hung from a strong branch about thirty feet up the old tree. Many people perched up on this branch and visited before they jumped. Several people would never even climb to the top and see the view and access the jump. The highest point in the tree, where the branches split, was a sacred place. This is the place where several "rites of passage" were held. It was only a 90 foot drop into the river. The jump proved to test ones "nerves", thus proving if you had the heart to take the plunge. There was no hanging or safe ladder for climbing. The only means to the top was a few old, rotting wooden boards tacked firmly with rusty nails. I remember the ridicule people received for climbing up, looking down, then, in fear, climbing back down. The fear of embarrassment and peer pressure far outweighed any consequence "the jump" may hold.

I braved the tree at 15 years old. The crowd I was hanging with enjoyed adrenalin rushes. Therefore, I quickly adapted. The drive out to the park and everything it encompassed was danger. It was rather common to take these types of chances. With plenty of false courage in my system, I scaled up the tree. When I looked back down the tree, with those angles and rotten boards, I knew it would be more dangerous to climb back down than to jump. This was what I kept telling myself anyway. Perched up on those top branches of the tree, I assessed the park. Next, I observed my peers drinking, hanging out, and, yes, wondering if I had the heart to make "the jump." After one quick look down into the river, spotting the cypress stumps, I knew it was time. I halfheartedly mumbled a prayer to God and quickly launched myself into the river. A portion of the way down I screamed; the rest of the way held an awkward silence. I considered it strange because, in actuality, music was blasting in the background. This "awkward silence" only comforted me for a second. Immediately, I felt the crushing impact of the jump and not landing correctly. I rose above the water as fast as possible. Lastly, I inhaled what air I could muster and casually floated out of harm's way. I did receive a few cheers and high-fives. I then attempted to catch my breath and return to "enjoying" myself at the party.

I looked up to the older guys who invited me to these parties. They had all the connections, sexy girlfriends, money, and reputation. These people seemed to have figured out the meaning of life- to enjoy it fast and hard. I quickly adopted the majority of these philosophies. Cheating on your girlfriend, for example, was one view I never agreed with. I caught hell for this but learned how to stand my ground. I sought and received mentoring in the drug trade from two of my older cousins. They were more connected, dangerous, and exciting than anyone I knew. It was not long before I was organizing the parties and making the money. Before I reached my twenties, I obtained everything I desired. Life rapidly became more serious. Even during this time, I missed those parties at the river and their nostalgia.

These parties at the park were usually wild. There were a few different types of gatherings that took place. The first

and less rowdy kind of party was the after party or the contin-
uation of the night before. The second was a much more fes-
tive soiree. These parties would set the tone for the holiday
weekend and be the tune up for the bar, house party, or club.
It was commonplace that someone would have a vehicle with
a high dollar sound system. Depending on the crowd, the music may have varied. However, one thing remained un-
changed, it was loud.

The idea was to go early and establish the perimeter
around the concrete table with tailgates down. It was nice to
be surrounded by friends with the same mind set. A few things
needed to be in place but several activities were always going
down: drug deals, binge drinking, ice chest loaded, music
blasting, girls dancing, smoke in the air, and the occasional
fight. The park was public, but, clearly, these parties were
not. Unless it was a carload of girls, outsiders were not welcome. We were not out there to make friends. Simply because: our friends were already there. Most would-be swim-
mers or people hoping for that sweet spot in the park, on those
days, were sadly out of luck. I would watch people drive
around the road, look our way then keep going.

Similar to the park, my life was soon hit with several
storms. Not only did hurricanes come, life seemed to be
changing. I guess, deep inside my heart, I did not like that
idea. Who exactly would I be if I moved on? Unlike the tree I
jumped from, my life was not rooted on solid ground. In retrospect, my house was built on the sand. When the storms
came and the seasons changed, everything came crashing
down. Throughout this time, I would return to the park. I

would try to enjoy myself in the same fashion. There was a state of confusion in a place where belonging used to dwell. It was like trying to drive a square peg into a round hole. It was similar to returning to a well that used to provide water, only to discover it had run dry. Surely, it was everyone else who had changed. Maybe the loss of a dear friend had disturbed and altered Camelot forever. I searched high and low, but there was no peace to be found. I visited the park alone one day. All at once, I noticed something strange that I seemed to have missed during my youth and other visits to the park. While it was the same, it was improved. Suddenly, I saw sparrows frolicking, leaves falling, and children playing. The scene was serene, yet I was at war with myself and ghosts of my past. Waves of emotion and revelation crashed all around. Soon, I came to the bitter revelation: I was the problem.

There were many factors and decisions that pushed me into that place. The death of family members and friends, broken relationships, an arrest record and many other pressures always seemed to mount. The anger I had in my heart toward everyone and everything had eroded my soul. I did not understand several things: How was I alive and free and so many I knew were gone? Even when the world was my oyster, I always had the gut feeling "there has got to be more to life than this." The storms of life had taken their toll. Through these difficult experiences, I learned a great deal about storms, people, and how precious life is in general.

In life, it is a guarantee all living things will experience storms. Nature provides several storms; some are even deemed "acts of God" on insurance policies. These storms include typhoons, tsunamis, tornadoes, floods, earthquakes, volcanoes, wildfires and hurricanes, just to name a few. While nature provides many storms, life provides storms in two basic ways. The first being when "life happens". Ultimately, this covers all things one has no control over. Sometimes these are the natural storms of life, death, and such. Other times, however, people rain storms on us for no apparent reason. A spouse leaving another for no good reason is an example of this type of disturbance. The other major class of storm is those we bring on ourselves. If one makes a bad investment, overspends, or has an affair, one day the consequences will be experienced. Almost everyone knows some type of pain. If you have not experienced it, ready yourself, one day it will come. Sometimes it comes in spades. There are many things one cannot control; however, there are a few you can.

The "moment of clarity" at the river eventually sent me on a journey of healing, forgiveness, and eventually purpose. Literally, I have traveled around the world and lived in the nation of Lithuania for two years telling people there is hope. Throughout my life experiences and travels, I learned the only things I can control: my choices and my reactions. The people you surround yourself with will determine the direction you are headed. One may be able to stick and move for a season, but most people get some crap on their shoe or some baggage they carry for life. During my young adult years, it was, in fact, "the blind leading the blind." I have learned to truthfully watch how people live before I listen to their counsel

.

Recently, I experienced some storms I had no control over. I felt the pressure mounting and the tension rise. Therefore, I chose to drive out to the park to seek refuge and direction again. This time, I enjoyed driving down the winding backroads. It was an overcast day with light and dark clouds in the sky. There was chain lightning in the distance splitting the evening's dark clouds. I entered the park and rounded the curb. Thankfully, there was no one there, my concrete table was open. Quickly, I perched up on the table Indian style. My goal was to read my Bible and wait for the storm to roll in; that is exactly what I did. I closed the Bible when the dark clouds covered me and thunder drew near. Then, I stood up on the table and watched the rain whisk across and cover the river from one end to the other. Before I retreated to my jeep, I looked at the old tree across the river. I thought to myself, there are a few things the old tree and I have in common. We both have survived the storms of life, and, by the grace of God, "we are still standing".

"Therefore, everyone who hears these words of mine and puts them into practice is like a wise man who built his house on the rock. The rain came down, the streams rose, and the winds blew and beat against that house; yet it did not fall, because it had its foundation on the rock. 26 But everyone who hears these words of mine and does not put them into practice is like a foolish man who built his house on sand. The rain came down, the streams rose, and the winds blew and beat against that house, and it fell with a great crash." -
Matthew 7:24-27

I hope with all my heart that this has offered insight into the serious topic of storms and trials. With Jesus Christ as our solid foundation, we can face, overcome and deal with anything. With maturity comes lasting growth and new perspectives. The wonderful reality is this what you learn through intense storms and trials, the world and enemy cannot take away. During these times or seasons The Lord may give you a verse that manifests as truth in your life. You will have a heavenly green light to share the verse and story in the form of a testimony (Revelation 12:11). The clean oil and good wine come only through the crushing process. The best encouragement I can give is choosing to stay on the potter's wheel (Jeremiah 18) and do not resist the process.

CHAPTER 4

Against the Grain

Everyone, to some degree, is a product of environmental systems; however, each person within the system has the ability to make free will choices.
Sean D. Barron

That choice is the very thing Jesus died to give us. We have the freedom to become something greater than the world produces, and that is a life changing force indeed. The cross that was thought to shame Jesus brought us victory. The forces of darkness thought they had manipulated Jesus into a situation that would wipe hope off the planet. Thankfully, He finished the process, took all our punishment unto death and on the third day, arose from the grave! This victory which brought salvation, the Holy Spirit, and eternal life for believers came at a horrible price. Jesus prayed in Luke 22:42 to His father that "*if you are willing let this cup pass from me; yet not my will but yours be done.*" He knew the amount of suffering that lay ahead and that the road was not going to be easy. In spite of everything and against the grain, Jesus pressed on to endure the cross with the strength the Lord placed in Him. Prepare yourself because what I would like to teach you in this chapter is not a popular opinion.

The world of today is in search of a quick fix. Some circles refer to this mindset as the "micro-wave generation." When it comes to truthfully following God, denying one's self (Luke 9:23), serious commitment to anything, or removal of selfish, destructive behavior, many "Christians" fall short. Sadly, many do not even seriously attempt to love or live like

Christ. The enemy has placed fear, complacency, and many other obstacles in the path of the believer and the modern church. Jesus was born of a virgin, lived without sin, died for us all, and rose again to display the Lord's power! The life that Jesus Christ died to give us all is worth diligent effort on our part to truthfully pursue. It is His desire that we overcome all, just as He did. However, we first have to receive and experience God's amazing grace in order to express it toward others.

The world, society, or whatever you would like to refer to the various systems that impact us daily, do not care about your faith. That's correct. The system does not care if you vote, get an education, serve God, have a family, or do anything productive with your life. You will pay taxes and consume, that much is clear. The show will continue and the machine will grind hope out of the strongest believer until you die or Jesus returns, but Jesus did not come to this earth so that we can mope around until we die or until He returns. He desires us to have a life of love, victory, and peace. It is unfortunate that many believers suffer and struggle with double-mindedness (James 1:8 and Psalm 119:113-115). The vast majority of people attending church are going through the motions, stuck in religion, or deceived by the enemy. Consider yourself deceived if you live a double life or feel no conviction of sin that leads to repentance. Often, we ignore the conviction toward righteousness, and it eventually becomes guilt. This guilt is subdued by distraction and covered by denial. People form their own doctrines on life and the Bible instead of seeking Jesus and learning what the Word really says. This explains much of the confusion we see in modern times. Have you said or heard any Christians make these "Kool-Aid" statements?

• "Why should I vote, they're all crooks, right?"

• "Everyone has affairs or flirts outside of their relationships, don't they?"

• "I can't get up early and read my Bible, I might be tired all day."

• "That discipleship class happens on the night of my favorite TV show. Maybe next time."

• On recovery programs- "I'm not one of 'those people', I can quit anytime."

• "Why should I pay attention to who my kids hang out with? Boys will be boys?"

• On spending time with the family- "I bought them all the entertainment they need".

• "I just can't learn the Scriptures. It is too difficult to remember."

• On physical exercise- "I will start tomorrow."

• On sleep- "I'll rest when I'm dead."

• On emotions- Vent every aspect of life, including personal problems, on Facebook (or Vague-book).

• "Everyone keeps up with past lovers after they are married. It's the technology era."
• "I will listen to my wife, right after the game ends."

• "Sure, I make love to my husband. Once a month."

• On intercessory prayer- "I think I'll see a shrink (or doctor) first."

• "Tithe? Are you crazy? I can barely make ends meet now."

• "World missions? Yeah, I am on a mission…to the night club this weekend."

•"Hypocrites! Ole' boy that we work with goes to church and does same things we do."

• " My grandpa had anger issues. So does my dad, and so do I. It's just who I am."

• "God forgives, I don't."

• "I have too many problems right now to go to church,… maybe later when I work this out."

• "My denomination is the best. You should join us or you're wrong."

• "It is boring being a Christian."

• "I'll honor my husband… as soon as he changes his ways."

All the above statements are common in both the general populace and Christian community. How many sermons or church services must we attend before understanding that selfishness destroys? The Bible says Hosea 4:6, "*My people perish for lack of knowledge….*" The harsh reality is that we can only play dumb for so long. Galatians 6:8-9 says, "*Whoever sows to please their flesh, from the flesh will reap destruction; whoever sows to please the Spirit, from the Spirit will reap eternal life. Let us not become weary in doing good, for at the proper time we will reap a harvest if we do not give up.*" Sooner or later, there will be consequences based on the seed time and harvest principle (Galatians 6). If a man takes no responsibility for his government or relationships, both will just continue to decline. Jesus lived, died and rose again so that you and I can impact everyone in our sphere of influence. This means in our families, community, work place, church, nation, and, yes, the world. It is very easy to get caught up in your own personal funk or drama that you lose sight of the big picture. Try to keep your life simple. Simply walk with Jesus every day.

It was my initial intention to address each statement on the bulleted list. However, the underlying problem with each of those statements on the list can be narrowed down to pride, selfishness, apathy or ignorance. These "mindsets" are brought on by the enemy, flesh, or conditioning. My paw-paw Barron would say, "They are just ignorant." Depending on his tone and if he shook his head while he said it, he was more than likely calling someone stupid. Ignorant does not mean stupid; it implies one does not know. There is power in humbly admitting we need Jesus. Would you like to have a successful relationship? Learn to get over yourself. Try truly doing it God's way. The structure for the family and all other relationships are laid out in the Word of God. Keep in mind, not everything the Lord shows you about your spouse and loved ones is supposed to be shared with them. Often, He shows us areas in their lives in which to pray for them. This is why wisdom is so important. Love covers a multitude of sins (1 Peter 4:8). Study upon and ask the Lord to show you what it means to be humble. Pride can hold us in stalemate and squash spiritual growth in a heartbeat. Over time, prolonged selfish behavior can produce guilt, which will destroy all life's meaningful relationships.

Religious pride can be detrimental to our capacity to love. When you know the right way to behave and are perhaps living a calm Christ-centered life, the trap is set to believe that your lifestyle is always right, and it can be no other way. I am not referring to absolute rights and wrongs here such as adultery or blasphemy. I am referring to the little conflicts that can steal our joy and slowly create a void in our ability to care. Your heart may easily become hardened to those who are lost and struggling. Do not forget Jesus says, *"It's not the healthy who need a doctor, but the sick"* (Mark 2:17). Though your dog may have dug in the trash can off and on for the past ten years, you still love him when you come home from work without reminding him of his previous mishaps. Sometimes people need a hug or sincere encouragement, even those who have hurt you. Yes, even those who have struggled off and on the last ten years. Why? The Book of Romans says that we who are strong should bear the short comings of the weak, always in love, and not in a condescending fashion (Romans 14).

I find it healthy to "check myself" from time to time. It's beneficial to the kingdom to periodically examine our own hearts. Stay humble, and do not let the enemy mold you into a modern-day Pharisee. What happened to the real love and grace that Jesus expressed to a "sinner like you?" We cannot control people or let people hurt us so deeply that we lose faith. It is dangerous to get consumed with church growth, side doctrine, programs, and our own spiritual ego at the expense of our witness. Here is a friendly reminder - Jesus loves everyone. Even if you're so holy that you only watch Little House on the Prairie, the next sentence still remains true. You are not better than anyone else; you're simply better off.

Please Lord, let us be a generation that never loses sight of Jesus. Do not let us be luke warm Christians satisfied with our dated golden tickets to heaven. In Jesus name, amen.

Questions to ask yourself
1) Is the Holy Spirit free to speak and deal with me?
2) Is the Holy Spirit free to move in my church?
3) Am I still listening and willing to submit to any direction God would lead me?

If you have tasted that the Lord is good and slipped back into toxic behavior, the enemy will attempt destroy you with inner guilt and use people to condemn you. The road is difficult, and the enemy is crafty. Therefore, it is paramount to have a humble heart that is willing to learn new things and listen to the Holy Spirit. It is not God's will for us to keep suffering in any sin or life issue cycle. Romans 8:1-2 says, *"Therefore, Now there is no condemnation for those of us in Christ Jesus, because through Christ Jesus the law of the Spirit of life set me free from the law of sin and death."* Let Jesus set you free from anything holding you back. This includes the law of man, condemning words of others, and self-inflicted wounds as well. We have to grow up in our understanding that spiritual warfare is not for a few elite people. **Spiritual warfare is, quite simply, a way a life.**

The divorce rate is climbing, and families are being destroyed. The vows at weddings do not seem to hold as much precedence as they used to. The reality is that we all have choices in our relationships. Many times, we give up to soon, or, worse, adapt to the world's philosophy of please yourself first. A very popular phrase of the 90's was "I gotta get mine." When couples do not communicate, they often end up splitting up. After doing so, the divorcee often gives a stranger or a new partner the exact affections that their former partner was longing to receive. They may start to get in shape and take much better care of themselves. They may suddenly be affectionate or sweet to a new partner where before they were cold or indifferent. The inability to maintain a long-term, healthy relationship in order to know if "I still got it," is a reflection of a larger pain within. These are all symptoms of brokenness and feeble attempts to fill a God shaped void in our hearts.

There is a popular phrase "going through a divorce" used in modern society. In reality, you are either married or you are divorced. Period. Point blank. There is no middle ground as it pertains to adultery. In a recent 1990's pop culture star's book, she explained how old fashioned it was for her mother to wait until her divorce was final to "officially" start dating. All I can say is that it is a shame that some of the values her mother possessed did not seem to have been passed on to her daughter. Sometimes, it is not the way that we see the scriptures insomuch as what they actually say? Most people that repeat this pattern have never taken the time to heal, repent, or even access why their relationships always end broken. I can personally testify there are always consequences to our choices. However, there is always forgiveness. There is a better way. Only the Lord knows how we can save and guard our relationships. It's never too late to turn to Jesus. God is for us, and He is love.

All the statements mentioned in the above list are common in both the body of Christ and society as a whole. If you have heard someone that doesn't know Jesus or is new to the faith make any of the statements then pray for them! If you have heard anyone in leadership or a supposed "grounded believer" make any one of those statements then pray for them! If you have made or thought any of those statements are correct then repent, simply turn, confess, and ask the Lord to guide you in the truth. The Word is the truth! Jesus' life is the model for all believers to follow. The world and the enemy have a plan to destroy and distract us from Christ. The above comments are examples of common statements of believers and non-believers who, in fact, may be missing the point. While everyone has a bad day or a tough season employing laziness, pride, selfishness, greed, jealousy and disrespect explains the good fruit we see in many people's lives: little or none. Predisposed doctrines about life coupled with a "know it all" attitude make following Jesus seem foolish. However, once the body of Christ can grow up in love, the world will truly see the power of Christ!

The struggle that believers face daily is difficult to overcome. First, we have the battle inside us and our self-will. Simply put: we don't understand the power that's within us. God is on the throne (Revelation 4:9). Jesus is the same yesterday, today, and forever (Hebrews 13:8). You will receive power when the Holy Spirit comes upon you (Acts 1:8). Furthermore, the same power that raised Jesus from the dead lives in you (Ephesians 1:18-23). There are no new temptations or sufferings that Christ cannot handle. His Holy Spirit lives within us, and we need to humbly open our hearts and allow the Lord to guide, minister, heal, and renew us daily. The Holy Bible says (Psalm 136), His [Jesus'] mercies are new every day and His love endures forever. Those are profound statements and promises which I have been learning and meditating on since I surrendered my life to Jesus Christ as my Lord and Savior in 2003.

We have the power of the living God inside of us! (Ephesians 1:19-20 and Romans 8:11) He is for us and not against us! Therefore, it is past time for us to "man-up" in our understanding and the living out of those promises. Perhaps it is actually growing in our understanding of who we are in Christ that will take us to the next level. You and I may be the only Jesus someone sees or experiences. The Holy Bible says it's the love of God that brings people to repentance (Romans 2:4). Things change when we shift into the mindset that we must do "whatever it takes" to position our self, overcome, and press onward to the call in Christ Jesus. I hope this section opens your eyes to the simple fact that though it is not easy, the struggles and pain we face in daily life along the path to peace may, in fact, be "normal."

I believe that pain can be a great motivator for positive change. I also know that if you surround yourself with selfish and negative people, it will affect your attitude consciously or subconsciously. Therefore, be on guard. We cannot control the people around us or what they believe, but we can control the people that surround us! With that said, it is important to know the truth so that you can discern people and their intentions. Romans 10:17 says, *"That faith comes by hearing and hearing from the word."* It is of utmost importance that we take in the Word like our life depends on it. The Lord's plan is good and following Him and spending time with Him is a blessing. He wants us to be people of faith, hope, joy and love. More importantly, He wants us to know him in a personal way through prayer, meditation, fellowship with believers, worship, and study of the Holy Bible.

The blessings may not only come when we start to comprehend how much He loves us, but also when we share our faith and serve others. In the book of Philemon, verse six says, "*I pray that you may be active in sharing your faith, so that you will have a full understanding of every good thing we have in Christ.*" Examine the book of James. It is one of the bluntest, in your face, books of the Bible. It calls believers to be "doers" (James 1:22-25) of the word and points out that "faith without works is dead" (James 2:14-26). The problem with many self-proclaimed Christians is that they don't get busy serving, sharing, connecting with other believers, studying or stepping out in their faith. As a result, God lovingly waits for His children to "get it" instead of crying "I'm bored." Rest assured, if the Lord is asking you to do something simple and you ignore His voice it is no small wonder why you are bored. If the Holy Spirit tells you "Pick up that piece of trash in the parking lot," you ignore Him, how can you expect the Lord to trust you with a ministry when you will not obey His voice? I can honestly say that I don't know anyone who is truthfully walking with Jesus who is "bored." I am not talking about a works-based theology. I am speaking of a functional relationship with the Lord. You learn to embrace peace and rest in seasons because the Lord has plenty work to be done in this broken and hurting world.

There is a fine line between receiving and believing grace and potato chips (sitting on the couch). The point of this rhetoric is to promote thought, which will hopefully touch hearts, open eyes, and promote change. While there is nothing we can do besides open our hearts to receive Jesus (by grace through faith) to enter heaven, there are many choices we must make daily that will impact our lives and the lives of others. In Proverbs , the Holy Bible says that wisdom is more precious than rubies and wealth. We need Godly wisdom in all our choices and reactions. Earlier, I referred to the frustration or pain many of us experienced (or are currently experiencing) as "normal." It is true that sometimes hardheaded people who refuse wise counsel must take their lumps (Proverbs 1:7). Our Father knows that pain, lack, disappointment, and loss all can either push us to our knees or push us over the edge. It is our choice, but know this: The Lord is not in heaven watching us suffer and enjoying it. If that's what you believe, then think about the cross and what Jesus suffered through for you. God is for us not against us. There is no condemnation for those of us in Christ Jesus.

It is a cold, hard, fact that churches across America are dying. Some are hanging onto tradition, religion, or fading membership. The farther the church body's focus is off sharing the true Gospel of Jesus, the more confusing its message will become. People do not need confusing. They need a Savior! That savior is Jesus Christ. The Bible is very clear on the truth. In John 14:6, Jesus says, "*I am the way the truth and the life and no one comes to the father except through me*", and Acts 4:12 says, "*There is one name under heaven by which we are saved.*"

Guess what? Let me tell you a profound secret. It is not about being Baptist, Catholic, Pentecostal, Assembly of God, or any other select denomination! Jesus did not die so we could live in separate factions and criticize each other. Therefore, it is past time that we get over ourselves and become one body. How hard is it to respect another's belief and grant them their right to their opinion? If the way you believe is so absolutely correct, then you should not be so easily flustered by the belief of another. Do you think disrespect will more quickly convert someone over to your belief? There should be no fear in our love for one another. Brothers and sisters, there are so many people who have never heard the true Gospel of Jesus or felt His love. Isn't that what we should be focused on? We have allowed the "speaking in tongues" debate to hinder ecumenical ministry for far too long. I know that is a hard pill to swallow. The other option is just close the blinds and live in your "pod-person" bubble while CNN successfully paints Evangelical Christians as hateful, fairy tale believing nuts. Queue up "I'll fly away", and sit undisturbed until Jesus comes back or unite with the love and power of Jesus? You decide.

Denominations need to learn to not only co-exist and stop downing each other but to work together. Recently, there was a rally for religious freedom and first amendment rights in my home town of Sulphur, Louisiana. The Catholic Church helped organize the event, several community leaders were set to speak, and the entire community was invited. The rally also had a tent where people could register to vote and receive free copies of the Declaration of Independence with the U. S. Constitution. Sadly, in a community of 22,000 people, where many of that population claim to be Christians, attendance was fairly low. What was more painful than the attendance level was the fact that very few differing denominations or fellowships were there to support religious freedom and exercise their first amendment rights. Even if you don't agree with the speaker's every word, shouldn't the community of believers care what is said? Many people in our town missed a great opportunity to connect, learn, grow, and teach our children to love one another through positive interaction and the importance of voting, freedom, and unity in Christ. Let's put an explanation point on this with one last example. In the mayoral run-off later that same year, less than four thousand people participated. The large majority of even this small town in the Bible-Belt simply had other things or more pressing matters on their minds. How do we expect our community to change when we don't care about its leadership or spiritual health? If the government slams the freedom of the Catholic Church, how long until the rights of the Protestant are restricted? We are all in the same boat and supposedly serving the same Jesus. All over the world, it's time to stop the bickering and love one another!

This is our world today. Churches are all over- some dying, some stagnant, and some growing. People are "church hopping" because they lack the capacity for strong community or do not desire accountability. Denominations and fellowships are present on every corner in almost every town in the Bible-Belt. However, nothing changes- the lost suffer and go to hell as churches argue doctrine and worry about attendance and tradition. In 2001, 390,127 people, almost 0.8% of the population of Britain, stated their religion as Star Wars Jedi on their Census forms, surpassing Judaism, and Buddhism, and making it the fourth largest reported religion in the country. As we argue doctrine, the world looks for any belief that fills their void. The only attendance any of us should be worried about is the roll call in heaven.

An essay I wrote in college titled *America: Land of the Free, Home of the Slave* expresses our state perfectly and echoes the heart of this chapter:

In 1964 Bob Dylan proclaimed, "The times, they are a changing." That statement and cultural observation still rings true. One could argue that the moral fiber of America was set afire, like many men's draft cards. Sometimes there is need for change. There must be some course of action to right the wrongs of a "civilized" society. The civil rights movement is an example of this type of action. There will always be conflict when people are forced to address social ills. Many issues have now been swept under the rug. Traditional family values are mocked and downplayed by the media. Now the term "planned parenthood" is associated with abortion not common sense. Big business and the government dumb down the masses through mainstream media. Individual responsibility and respect seem to be a thing of the past. But, what difference does it make? People loathe seeing the ugliness of their forlorn soul, or the evil that lies within it.

What has happened to our once great nation? Was it really ever great at all? How is it possible that a "Christian" nation could virtually destroy the American Indian? Most young-adult Americans have no comprehension of the "Trail of Tears" or the inhumane treatment Indians received. In love, there were some missionaries that tried to reach out to the Indians. However, most of the population viewed them as savages. This is interesting considering it was us infiltrating their land to begin with. It seems that prosperity always comes at the expense of others. People of color have been discriminated against since the inception of our country. The masses always seem to fear what they do not understand. Where are the answers to these types of dilemmas? Shall it come from the far left, the far right or perhaps from above?

There once was the "Greatest Generation" of Americans. They put heavy emphasis on many of the values that made this nation great. Contrary to popular Liberal guise, our nation was founded on or around Biblical principles. These values include hard work, family togetherness, political participation, community involvement and respect for your fellow man. The divorce rate was not nearly as high as it is today.

Perhaps people placed value on actually honoring their commitments and living inside their means. During this time, voter turn-out was much higher. This held politicians to a much higher standard of ethics. It is clear as America prospered from the hard work of the "Greatest Generation," political participation declined, as well as morality. Today our nation faces a crumbling economy and rising social problems. How did "We the People" get into this situation? Whose fault is it anyway? It seems that somewhere down the line, we have lost something.

*From 1991 to 1993, I played high school soccer. Our coach, Mark Duhon, was a former semi-professional player. In his day, he was an intense and fearless striker. He was a balding welder who **chose** to give us his time. There was no explanation as to why he would work all day and then coach soccer practice Monday through Friday. Coach came from a different generation. He ran us like dogs for three weeks before we ever touched the ball. Seldom did he ever have to cut players from the team. The kids with no heart would quit before the cardio-sessions ended. Duhon tried to teach a bunch of disrespectful boys a "team" sport. Many of the boys on this team came from broken homes. We all thought he was a complete jerk and showed him little respect. Therefore, we missed some valuable life lessons that he was trying to teach us.*

Coach knew something we did not: life is tough. He tried to push us to our limits. When we did what he said, seldom did we lose. However, most of us missed the point. Duhon wanted us to be able to outlast our opponents. He wanted us to "lay it on the line" every practice and every game. In retrospect, his philosophies were correct. But, when he challenged me my senior year, I quit. The rigorous cardio

aspect of the training was over and I felt I had earned a start-
ing mid-field position. Then coach said, "You have to win the
position." This made me furious! I knew I was better than
the underclassmen. My game was not world class, but it had
improved from the previous season. That was my last day as a
member of the team. I went on the pursue wine, women and
song for the next twelve years. But, why did I quit? Because I
had felt entitled to that position and was afraid to work for it.

The Republicans blame the Democrats and vice versa.
The media distracts and spins all information. Big business
and government run the entire establishment. Political educa-
tion is limited to half a year of civics in high school. Most
students graduate high school believing that all politicians are
crooks, therefore count their votes worthless. Lust, sloth,
greed, materialism, dishonesty and ignorance dominate Amer-
ican culture. The majority of this shallow influence is by de-
sign. Legislation is passed with the interests of big business
and government while the masses watch Oprah, Dr. Phil and
Jersey Shore. Sadly, reality TV is just an outward sign of the
inward rotting of American values. Prosperity and abused
government handouts have spoiled and distracted several
generations of Americans. The recent presidential debates are
a clear example that courtesy and truth are of little impor-
tance to society anymore.

Technology has many benefits, such as global com-
munication. But, what have all these advances done for our
youth's interpersonal communication skills? Of the small per-
centile of families that do eat together, it is normal to see them
all with electronic devices at the table. It is common that
modern men have no nerve to look a woman in the eyes to see
if there is any chemistry. It seems they would rather just join

chemistry.com, click "like" on picture and flirt indirectly. Instant messaging, texting and "chatting" have replaced actual interaction. Many of this new generation are very informed and intelligent, but they are also socially retarded. These new-age couples have no real communication skills or healthy support systems in place when trouble arises. The mentalities of doing everything possible and dying to self have become lame and "old fashioned." All of these factors contribute to the broken homes, addiction, depression and apathy that rot our society today.

Many morally sound "Christian" people suffer from pride, ignorance and arrogance. There might be forty-five different churches in an area populated by fifty thousand. The sad part is that very few are working together for the greater good of the community. This is not the lifestyle of love and victory Jesus died to provide us. John chapter seventeen states the he loves and prays for "all believers" who would call upon His name. America has lost sight of what has made this nation special. The corruption and erosion of our nation must be stopped. The far right is as guilty as anyone else. Republicans hide behind "Christian issues" while they justify war and do not desire to properly educate the poor or implement programs to amend the recidivism rate. Abortion is murder but the death penalty is justified. Censorship plots have backfired and now Christians, prayer and the Bible are constantly attacked. Publicly burning rock bands albums, like the Nazi's burned books, has not worked to the benefit of one wayward soul. The time has come to do a true heart check and see where we stand.

Everyone has their own life containing blessing and pain. One may claim to love God, country and family. Where is the proof? Coach Duhon made a choice. After a 12-hour workday, he would attempt to do something good for the community. The measure of what you love can be determined by two factors: time and money. Where you spend these shows where your heart lies. The same twenty-four hours a day and seven days a week is given to all. We are blessed to be in a country where we have a choice on how to spend our time, money and efforts. How do you spend yours? Are you involved in the community? When is the last time you voted? When is the last time you donated to a charitable organization? When is the last time you helped someone with time that you did not have to spare? When is the last time you saved money? When is the last time you called your parents or someone dear and told them, "Thank you, I appreciate and love you."?

These activities used to be more American than apple pie. Keeping your word should be normal not unusual. Faith, morals and respect are desperately needed. I had to learn everything the hard way. Pain and adverse situations pushed me into a place where all I could do was look up. Now, I take nothing for granted. Coach Duhon may have failed to reach me when I was a teen, but later his principles echoed true. In life, there is little margin for error. Therefore, all an individual man can do is "lay it on the line" each day. Every day, as individuals, we have a choice to make concerning how we will live. These choices will in turn impact the lives of everyone around us. I see every day as a gift and a chance to make a difference in the world that desperately needs it. Only after several things were taken from me, did I see that freedom and life are precious gifts. After I visited several other countries and cultures, I saw that in spite of America's flaws: she remains a blessed nation. The time has come for us to work together, agree to disagree and move on for the greater good of our nation and all of mankind.

John F Kennedy (D) once said, "Ask not what your country can do for you, but what can you do for your country". As a nation and a people we must return to this creed. The government was not designed to take care of the people. Citizens of the United States of America are supposed to control the government. This has been the underlying problem for quite some time. "Government is not the solution to the problem, government is the problem", Ronald Reagan (R) proclaimed in the 1980s. The further we get from the U. S. Constitution: the more freedom we lose. It matters not what stance you take on government. The fact remains our nation was founded on Biblical values and principles. The freedom to choose your own belief system is part of what makes America great. However, to deny our nations heritage is foolish. No matter what you believe you still have a choice. If "we the people" continue to do nothing proclaiming, "they're all a bunch of crooks" then we have already decided to remain ignorant. With all my heart I believe the following statement to be true. The problems and solutions to America's problems lie in one place: the mirror.

The question we should be asking ourselves is "Did I do my part to truthfully love people?" In Chapter 17 of the Book of John, in His longest recorded prayer in the Bible, Jesus prayed for all believers. He did not just pray for the Baptist, Catholic, Pentecostal, Methodist, Non-Denominational, Calvinist, traditional or hipster churches. This may shock you, but Jesus prayed for us all! So, forgive me if I really don't care what brother (Deacon, Priest, Pastor, etc.) so-and-so told you. There was only one perfect church body, and He was put on a cross by angry "religious" people. When Jesus preached and taught, He did not address a certain type of fellowship. He addressed the lost, sin, and hypocrisy. He met "sinners" and "religious people" exactly as they were without judgment, and lovingly and bluntly shared the truth. This is a dying art in today's broken world. When they were praying in the upper room, it was a body of believers gathered, not a denomination! It grieves the Holy Spirit to see God's people unable to get along, much less work together. The walls have to come down, and the church, who are all supposed to be believers (the bride), must step up, love one-another, teach, admonish, lead by example, and evangelize the lost world. I will share this message until the Lord calls me home. I truly know that if we don't do our part in this commission then the blood will be on our hands.

Jesus was, is, and forever will be the example believers in Christ or "Christians" should follow. Knowing and having a personal relationship with Jesus Christ is the most important thing, period. Once that is established, it's time to start listening and allowing the Holy Spirit to minister, teach, heal, and guide you. The obstacles and strongholds believers face are gigantic. The world and the enemy have a plan to steal, kill, destroy, distract, and rob your joy. It is our duty and calling to truthfully get over ourselves and our denominations. It was my heart's desire, in this chapter, to turn a few tables over. This is a dog-fight until the end. The struggle to deny self and the pride that most men possess is heavy. It is a good thing the price has been paid. Jesus showed us how much He loves us for while we were still sinners, He died for us (Romans 5:8). That is a beautiful act of worship and obedience on His part. That should not only inspire us to pick up our cross and follow him but also strengthen us to sing a joyful song along the way.

CHAPTER 5

Agreement or Truth?

It is human nature to want to feel approval and love. In fact, it is a deep-seated need and desire of all people to seek fulfillment in their lives. I miss "hangin' with my boys" and playing soccer, softball, and backyard football. The competition and laying down my best, often sacrificing myself in the process, made me feel alive. What I don't miss from my past is the foolishness of excess and the male conquest. My sense of worth is now in Christ even though much value is still placed in family and friendships. When emotions, desires, and "self" get involved with defining who you are, it can become dangerous and fatal depending on how we meet and fulfill this need. Everyone needs people to trust and confide in. These days, it is not easy to find such people. As you grow older, you begin to see that a real and genuine friend or caring family member is something to be cherished.

When I was younger, I was completely fed up with life, being told what to do, society, my family, and God. There were a few people that I looked up to that harbored those same rebellious beliefs. On the surface, it appeared that these people were happy rolling along with these mind sets and "smiling through the pain." I did my own thing, for the most part, but I adapted these toxic mindsets. There were times when I completely surrounded myself with these like-minded people, and at times, I completely isolated myself (by choice) with my book of CD's. In one form or another, most of my music collection was extremely hardcore. For twelve years, I sought agreement in dark places because I could not handle the reality that I was the problem, and I had no understanding of the truth. People used me and, for the most part, encouraged my wild behavior, if nothing else than for their own entertainment value. All of my friends sought agreement and were all going through their own personal storms. We were all hurting, brokenhearted, on drugs, in trouble with the police or running from something.

What did these choices cost me? - Everything but my life. It is only by the grace of God that I am alive. All but two of the original people that I looked up to are dead or in jail. I have lost many close friends and family members in the dark. Eventually, I spent four years with serious depression. It was a time in my life where I honestly did not care whether I lived or died. Granted, I am an extreme case, but the facts are clear. I was immature, selfish, and looked for what made me feel good at the time. I did not understand that my life impacted others. I did not believe that other people's mindsets influenced me at all. A constant bombardment of extreme heavy metal and gangster rap was good for the soul, right? The worst part is that I had no desire to face reality or understanding of the truth.

What is the truth? In order to understand truth, you must first understand agreement. Agreement is simply looking for someone, anyone, who will give harmony or accordance to your opinions, beliefs, or feelings. Seeking agreement from others can quickly lead to more problems, more mistakes and more depression. If you are going through a hard time with any situation, be careful from whom you seek counsel. Counsel should only be sought after watching their lives and beliefs closely and verifying alignment with the Word. Most people act like they are happy and project only what they want you to see, and I dare say that most people likely don't have your best interest at heart. For example, if you are having marital problems and seek counsel from another unhappily married person over a few drinks and complain about your respective spouses, how can that help the situation? If you accept the invitation to become the running mate of a recently divorced friend who wants to go out, get some drinks, and mingle and you are married, are you being true to your family? What if that person just misses you or the good ole' days? It is possible that they honestly don't care about your current life, spouse, kids, or the consequences of your bad choices. By seeking agreement, they may be blind to the consequences and only care about their own pain, or the masking of it.

Thinking Point: It is impossible to be a true friend to others when we are not yet friends to ourselves.

By using this model and substituting any hard time, difficult situation, or toxic influence, it isn't difficult to see what can destroy you. You must understand that some people simply do not have the capacity to be a real friend. Why? Because the veil has them blinded and they are not yet friends to themselves. A good rule of thumb is to compare advice given or how you are feeling to the Word of God. Life and death are in the tongue; therefore, be careful who you let whisper in your ear and what you say about yourself. It is easier to hate than love. It is difficult to break old, destructive, hurtful, behaviors and do what it right. Doing the right thing may not come natural when deception has always been the norm. Make no mistake, all our choices and reactions matter. This is why it is said, "In the end, it will be you, your life, and the face in the mirror that you live with." It is time that we are responsible for the well-being of the person who looks back at us. Perhaps seeking a new path and mindset is the answer.

Now that we understand agreement, what is the truth? The truth is this- we all need God through Jesus. "*He is before all things, and in him all things hold together,*" says Colossians 1:18. We need each other, and we need hope. No matter how bad your situation is, and it could be drastically worse, do not lose hope. Do not let the world, family, friends, or anyone else keep you from the truth. I am a flawed man that still makes bad choices at times. However, for a decade and then some, I was my own worst enemy. I have learned, more so in the last few years, that I cannot make it in this bruised and hurting world without Christ. Do not focus on what your situation "looks like." No, I might not understand your exact situation, but I know the One who does. Jesus can immediately change your heart and your situation, but, often, it is a long, hard road full of difficult choices. He will not leave you or forsake you. "*If we are faithless, He will remain faithful,*" says 2 Timothy 2:18. We need to hold to our faith and support and encourage one another (Hebrews 10:23-25).

The choices that you and I make on a daily basis impact the lives of the people around us. It is paramount to have other people who can pray for you, hold you accountable, and love you, in spite of whatever you may be facing. Who we listen to, hang out with, and look up to should be thought through carefully. Proverbs 4:23 says, "*Guard your heart: it is the well spring of life.*" During the course of the lives of everyone on this planet, the day will come when Jesus will be all you have. The choice is yours. In the end, it will be just you and Him. The question will be asked- "What did you do with His Son, who died for us so we can be free?" It doesn't matter where you are, what you have done, or what you have been through. He is as close as a few heartfelt prayers. If you are alive then there is hope. *"Anyone who is among the living has hope- even a live dog is better off than a dead lion,"* says Ecclesiastes 9:4. It is never too late. Every step of faith you take toward Him, He will bless you.

Wisdom in Relationships

Life can hurt, and it can hurt the most when it comes from those closest to us. Why does that always seem to happen? Because we entrust and give power to those most near to us to hurt us. This does not mean that we need to build walls around us and let no one in, but it does mean that we need to use wisdom in our relationships. The following model will teach us healthier ways to structure our relationships based on Solomon's temple. The Lord gave Solomon clear vision and instruction on its building. Paul would later reference our bodies as living temples.

"Do you not know that your bodies are temples of the Holy Spirit, who is in you, whom you have received from God? You are not your own; you were bought at a price. Therefore, honor God with your bodies"-**1 Corinthians 6:19-20**

"Above all else, guard your heart, for it is the wellspring of life." -**Proverbs 4:23 (NIV 1984)**

"Guard your heart above all else, for it determines the course of your life." -**Proverbs 4:23 (New Living Translation)**

The Bible is full of such examples of personal relationships based on the Solomon's Temple outline. Understanding this concept will help you to gain perspective on the placement or structure of who has access to your heart. I heard Pastor Ron Carpenter mention this in one of his sermons, and it instantly gave me revelation into the reason I was getting hurt so deeply and so easily. I recognized that for a large part of my life, I had allowed people who did not deserve access into the deep places of my heart. There were times in my life where I was much too liberal with sharing delicate pieces of my heart. This understanding really helped Proverbs 4:23 become a heart verse, or life verse, for me. Using the wisdom God provides through the Holy Spirit, it is possible to protect yourself by understanding the context of relationships. Hopefully this will be as much of a blessing for you as it was for me. This is just the structure of what the Holy Spirit showed me. It may be slightly different for you, but that is ok. Now let's check it out.

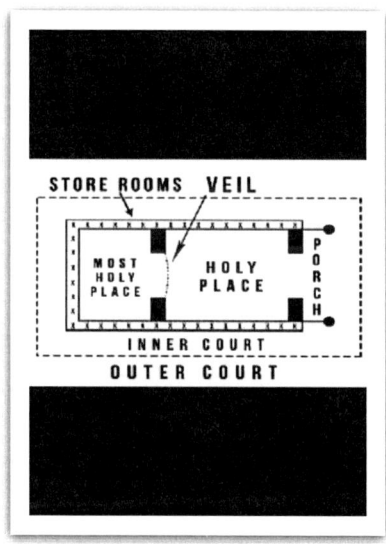

Below are flexible explanations or definitions to the personalized parameters of the temple. I encourage you to identify and personalize your own.

1) **Outer court** - People you went to grade school with; people you may have had a class or two with in college; people you just met; the clerk at the store you see often; a friend of a friend of a friend etc.

2) **Inner court** – Estranged family; co-workers: people you had several classes with; people you played sports with; acquaintances or people you hung out with at the bar, club or other casual gatherings on a very regular basis; people you shared life with though common interests. The degree of bonding would depend on the depth or intimacy of each individual relationship.

3) **The Porch**- friends and family; possibly distant or extended family; seasonal friends; people with whom at some point you bonded deeply with. This would also include accountability relationships and seasonal mentors. Understand this. These people need to **earn the right** to even be sitting on "The Porch" of your life.

4) **Holy Place**- spouse, children, extremely close true friend(s) or family. All important and intimate lifelong   relationships that are carefully nurtured would be in the Holy Place. Note: there will not be a large number of people in this place, for only a few should deserve access. Chaos and brokenness will often be found in life when many are granted access into this place.

5) **Holy of Holies (or Most Holy Place)** - The Lord our God, his son Jesus, and the Holy Spirit. This is the deepest

most important relationship one will ever have. Keeping this relationship healthy and growing will assure and guide you in all other relational areas. Often, it boils down to truly receiving Jesus's finished work on the cross.

6) **The Store Rooms**- the private areas of lives that most of us conceal such as broken relationships, abuse, lust, perversion, guilt, shame, regret, grief, anger, lack of forgiveness, pride, selfishness, and any other thing that hinders your relationship with God or others. The toxic waste in the storerooms causes cancer in all meaningful relationships. Sadly, often we do not see or want to face these rooms or clean them out because of denial or the enemy's tactics.

If any of you lacks wisdom, you should ask God, who gives generously to all without finding fault, and it will be given to you.—**James 1:4**

It is of utmost importance that you believe when you pray. We should all be working to remove all forms of double-mindedness. Pray, meditate and ask, "Lord, give me wisdom in all my relationships. Help me to have the discernment that comes only from you so that I may see who is for me and who is against me. Help me to make good decisions to guard my heart but, yet, continue to love others. Help me honor the relationships that I have and establish healthy boundaries so that I can better serve You. Thank you that I am on the road to healing, forgiveness, and positive change. In Jesus name. Amen."

Scrambled or evenly yoked?

Do not be yoked together with unbelievers. For what do righteousness and wickedness have in common? Or what fellowship can light have with darkness? What harmony is there

between Christ and Belial? Or what does a believer have in common with an unbeliever? What agreement is there between the temple of God and idols? For we are the temple of the living God. As God has said:
"I will live with them and walk among them, and I will be their God, and they will be my people." Therefore, "Come out from them and be separate, says the Lord. Touch no unclean thing, and I will receive you." And, "I will be a Father to you, and you will be my Sons and Daughters, says the Lord Almighty." **2 Corinthians 6:14-18**

"*If you are not evenly yoked in close personal relationships, your life will get scrambled.*"-**Sean D. Barron**

"*If someone determines if they are "evenly yoked" because the other person says they are saved: that is a shallow interpretation of those scriptures*" –**Ron Carpenter**

Are you a true believer in the Lord Jesus Christ? If you are, then that makes you a person of destiny. This simply means that God has a unique plan for your life. This plan will reach, teach, love, and serve a people group that perhaps only you can reach. The Lord's desire is that we make a positive impact on everyone within our sphere of influence. Most assuredly, you could reach these people with the power of the Holy Spirit, pressing forward in God's will. Understand this: the enemy will not sit back and watch you fulfill God's plan. You will be attacked in every way that you can possibly imagine. One of those ways is through relationships. God is not the only force who will send people into your life.

Ephesians 6:12 says, "*For our struggle is not with flesh and blood, but against the rulers, against the authorities against the powers of this dark world and against the spiritual forces of evil in heavenly realms."* While many of us want and desire healthy relationships, we must learn to be careful. The most important thing in anyone's life should be his or her relationship with Jesus. It is from this relationship that all "good things," blessings, wisdom, and comfort flow. It may seem harsh, but this relationship must be guarded at all cost. Proverbs 4:23 encourages us to *"guard your heart. It is the well spring of life."*

Evenly yoked pertains to all relationships, not just dating or marriage. *"If anyone is in Christ, he is a new creation; the old has gone and the new has come,"* says 2 Corinthians 5:17. It is necessary that we recognize that everyone is on different levels with Christ. Many claim to be "Christians" simply because they were born into their family's religion or denomination. You are not a believer in Jesus because your grandmother was a "strong woman of faith." That may have been true; however, your grandmother cannot get you into heaven. Please be careful that you do not miss this point. "A good person" may be safer to hang out with than a dangerous person, but, regardless, the yoke will be uneven or different. If you are a believer in Christ (old or new; it doesn't matter), you should be training yourself to "set your mind on things above, not on earthly things" (Colossians 3:2). In a nutshell, you should have or be developing a "kingdom mindset."

The world does not comprehend the selflessness of a true Christian life. Why would someone think less of himself and more about the needs of others? Why would anyone be into denying himself? Why would any working-class person give ten percent of his income to the church? Why would someone take his vacation time to go on a mission trip to share the gospel and "serve" people? Why would someone avoid extensive fellowship or hanging out with non-saved individuals who are just "good ole' boys" or "really laid-back women." Sadly, many real Christian believers think that they are bullet proof or have not been taught these concepts. The church and society have watered down wisdom, and family values seem "old fashioned," "traditional," or, even, lame. It sickens my heart that some pulpits dilute the Word to increase attendance in fear of political correctness. Please do not drink the Kool-Aid. This is why it is about Jesus and His plan for your life; nothing else matters. By seeking and honoring Jesus, one finds that everything else will eventually fall into place. Walking with Jesus does not remove adversity, but it does interject peace. This occurs when the wisdom He gives us is actually applied to our daily lives.

Through my various life experiences, I have seen many people compromise in relationships. Sooner or later, they all end up in a drama-related mess. I know some very tough individuals that work hard and will back down from no one. In fact, one person, in particular, is as tough and wild as anyone I have ever known. However, there is one weakness in this person that I have noticed throughout our extended friendship-He will not go without female companionship. I have seen horrible separations repeatedly happen occasional eruptions of drama on all levels. Within a few weeks of one break-up, he has another girl he met at a bar now cooking in his kitchen, sitting in his lap, and saying "I love you." The first couple of times I witnessed this I was in awe. However, upon looking deeper into this cycle, I see the reality of his behavior. It wasn't to be envied or glamorized because the same result will inevitably happen. The time frame may be shorter or longer with extreme drama and unfaithfulness sprinkled in the mix.

At this time, my friend does not have peace within himself. He keeps searching, working, partying, and bouncing from relationship to relationship always with the same result-heart break and pointless drama. Very often, I see women doing the same thing with slight variations. They flirt and offer themselves through texts, sexting, social media, emotional cheating, or having affairs while in a relationship. Often, men and women will date someone that they know they will not marry while weighing their options. What drives these behaviors? Could it be a God- shaped void or perhaps fear? This fear of being alone, the power of controlling people or situations, or the need for attention will ultimately destroy all meaningful relationships when the house of cards falls.

If no one admits their wrongs or truly asks for forgiveness there is just a trail of destruction left behind. Simply, because it easier to "opt out" of a relationship then find a new group of people to snow with charm, a destructive pattern emerges. This pattern occurs in both male and female relationships. Some people accept this as "just the way it is" or "just the way I am." In reality, it is a cycle in which the enemy entraps us. There are, of course, lots of different situations in life, and things unfold quickly and painfully at times. The enemy will use feelings of being "bored" or "alone" to drive us into horrible situations. This is why we must learn who we are in Christ! Spend some time with the Heavenly Father. Allow Him to make you whole.

There is one principle about the above paragraphs that I would like to point out: The need for constant attention, excitement, manipulation, companionship, or the fear of being alone. These behaviors, desires, and emotions are signs that salvation through Jesus or "inner healing" may be needed. We keep unaddressed issues and roots of bitterness (Hebrews 12:15) in our storerooms. Where there is an extreme element of chaos, the enemy will always have a presence. The fact also remains that life can be extremely difficult at times or for a season. Becoming real and accessing where you are and what needs to be done is usually the first step. For some, there may just be a few heartfelt changes that need to be executed while others may need drastic lifestyle changes and spiritual deliverance. It is all just part of the process.

Seek out your next steps in prayer by asking for wisdom and direction from Jesus. Broken or unhealthy relationships can destroy our spirits. This makes us unfruitful in the kingdom of God and miserable in daily life. This is what this chapter is all about. I pray the message goes straight from Jesus to you. If the wisdom from this section can save one person from entering or rushing into a toxic relationship, give someone the courage to end one, or enter the road to healing, it is all worth it to me.

It is important to grasp the fact that God desires to make you whole in Christ. Jesus wants to know you and be more real to you than any other relationship in your life. Ironically, it all starts here, with Jesus. I understand that many people are afraid of total surrender and the depth of spiritual warfare it may require getting free. Until we allow Christ to save and heal us and our lives hold lasting fruit, we are just spinning our wheels. The Lord Jesus wants to put two whole believers together in dating and marriage relationships. This means a great deal more than "are they saved" or "or they my denomination." I do not care what gifts you have, how strong willed you think you are or the size of your bank account, the cold hard fact is that you cannot change or fix anyone.

There is no person walking who can validate you or make you whole. As a believer in Christ, you are a person of destiny. Please do not yoke yourself even casually with unbelievers because you are "bored" or "lonely." Always apply wisdom. Your life is not just your life. It has been bought with a price and for a purpose. In that purpose, you will find everything you have been seeking. Therefore, do not trip out! It takes time. In no way am I condemning anyone who has made bad decisions or had relationship struggles. I have made my share of mistakes before and after I made my choice to follow Christ. He has always been there for me, and He will do the same for you.

Everything I just shared is not understood by the world's system. If you are looking for approval from people, look out. Your faith and service will be built on sand. How many "likes" your selfie gets should not determine any level of your happiness. It is possible to drive yourself crazy seeking the approval of others. Therefore, it is paramount that you discover who you are in Christ. This can be a lengthy process, but it is essential in discovering your purpose and becoming comfortable with God's amazing grace. This grace provides victory not just a mere ticket into heaven! Learning to take a step back or pausing to take a deep breath in order to hear God's voice takes time. It is about maturing in Christ and learning His ways (understanding His nature). There are elementary things of God and then there are deeper levels of anointing and intimacy. If anything, understand this point-who you are "yoked" with will always play a factor in where you are with Christ and the direction you're headed.

In the earlier section, we discussed some concepts about seeking wise counsel and peer groups. The dictionary cannot truthfully define what "friendship" means. I once had to ask the Lord to show me the characteristics of a true friend. In Christ, the standard of friendship should be higher than the world's standards. Why? Jesus lived, died, and was resurrected as the example. He provided our basic guidelines and standards, and it is through Him that we receive our true power! Jesus died so that we may be justified but also because He was a true friend. Such a friend that He died in our place. *"Greater love has no one than this, that someone lay down his life for his friends,"* says John 15:13.

Friendship

Having gained some perspective about the structure of relationships, let's look at what it means to be a friend. I will spare you the insertion of the world's definition of a "friend" here. In the 1980's, a rap group named Whodini released a song called "Friends." In it, they did a pretty good job of describing life and how people are prone to treat each other. The message of the song was actually designed to be a thought provoking message about friend selection. The song names various kinds of people that we let into our lives, including seasonal friends. Further into the song, they suggest that some people are not really "friends" at all. They are right! Some of my friends I have not seen in years, but we still hold respect and love for one another. Circumstances, goals, and values change in life, and some "friends" will not encourage your new-found interest in following Christ. In fact, you may be made the butt of a few jokes. Regardless, the friend you have in Jesus will never leave you or forsake you! Eventually, the Lord will show you who your true friends are and give you new brothers and sisters in Christ. Through the power of the cross, you will let your light shine for Jesus.

Every person has a few words, an idea, or a picture of what the term "friend" means. Over the years, I have heard, and continue to hear, from the Lord on the topic of friendship, and I would like to point out some characteristics of a "Godly friend." You can reference this as a "true friend" if you would like. The intention is to understand that there is a standard and guide laid out in the Word. It cannot go without saying that no one is perfect. Therefore, this section is not a check-list. Rather, think of this section as a guide to challenge yourself to love deeper. Perhaps it will help you see who has been in your corner all along? Perhaps it will help you to see whom you should consider moving from the "holy place" to the "porch" or maybe even the curb. God's grace, wisdom, mercy and forgiveness should be present in all our relationships.

Characteristics of a true friend

1) They honor the "Greatest Commandment"

"Hearing that Jesus had silenced the Sadducees, the Pharisees got together. One of them, an expert in the law, tested him with this question: "Teacher, which is the greatest commandment in the Law?"

Jesus replied: "'Love the Lord your God with all your heart and with all your soul and with your entire mind. This is the first and greatest commandment. And the second is like it: 'Love your neighbor as yourself.' All the Law and the Prophets hang on these two commandments."
Matthew 22:34-40

The Greatest Commandment is well known by people conditioned around church goers or true Christian homes. Even people who do not believe Jesus is the Son of God are somewhat familiar with these verses. I will go so far as to say that if people have never heard these verses at all, they still understand the principle. At the very least, most people grasp "do onto others as you would have done to you." Several people have taught or heard this lesson in Sunday school. However, very few actually live these verses out daily. I was not "raised in church" so when I read those verses for the first time, I thought, "Man, that's deep."

If one truly loves the Lord, he or she will learn to trust and obey Him. In Christ, we find peace, blessings and fruit. Those far outweigh anything that the world could offer. This also implies that there will be forgiveness and healthy relationships. When attempting to expand your understanding of the second law (Mark 12:30-31), know this: it goes deeper than the surface. In an indirect way, Jesus is suggesting that we should learn to love ourselves. If we are ever going to love other people for the "long haul," we must learn to love ourselves. This means that it is essential that we have peace and contentment with ourselves.

What does all that mean? Perhaps it means we should love God and ourselves enough to establish healthy boundaries. Before my walk with Christ began, I did not feel like I deserved to be happy or even content. I experienced so many wonderful things yet could not hold onto any of them. I did not love myself first even though I gave of myself with no regard. At one point, I had people living in all the bedrooms of my own house, and I slept on the couch! Even then, I struggled to do the right things in my own life while doing good things for others. No matter what your past experiences are, Christ wants you to know Him in a personal way. He is waiting for us to ask for His wisdom and seek His ways. Psalm 14:2 says, *"The Lord looks down from heaven on the sons of man to see if there are any who seek God."*

If the body of Christ lived out the Greatest Commandment, the Great Commission would take care of itself. The light of the love that He has shown us should radiate unto others and overflow into our daily lives. When this starts to happen, it will touch the lives of those around you and all over the world. Once you get a true taste of that Jesus' love, you will go!

2) **They extend a Hand**

"This is a trustworthy saying. And what I want to stress these things, so that those who have trusted in God may be careful to devote themselves to doing what is good. These things are excellent and profitable for everyone." **Titus 3:8**

How will a lost and dying world ever see the love of God in Christ if we stay hiding in the fellowship hall? There is no doubt that we need to be careful and guard our hearts; however, get two or more brothers and sisters in Christ together and start serving your community. Love and help your difficult family and friends with the strength God provides. Learn and practice the habit of turning the other cheek. Do these good deeds with no expectations of a positive response or returned favor. Jesus has already blessed you. There is no service, giving, or encouragement sown that will not be rewarded.   The book of Hebrews says in chapter 13:2-3, *"Do not forget to entertain strangers, for by doing so some people have entertained angles unaware.   Remember those in prison as if you were their fellow prisoners, and those who are mistreated as if you yourselves were suffering."* These verses cover a huge amount ground.   Prison ministry, missions, feeding children or the homeless, freeing girls from sex slavery, and helping people you do not really know are all things that the Holy Spirit will lead you to do.   When you answer the call, God moves in a special way!   It is after surrender to the call that He can, in fact, make a way.

The book of James says in 1:27, *"Religion that God the Father accepts as pure and faultless is this: to look at orphans and widows in their distress and to keep oneself from being polluted by the world."*   Ministering to the elderly and the orphans are tremendous areas of service.   Our society is very fast-paced, and the wisdom that we are losing by disregarding our old and young will indeed cost us dearly.   The love of Christ supersedes any of today's trends!   Open your heart, and seek out what the Lord is calling you to do!   You will feel lasting warmth and start to see life is about more than your own selfish desires.   There is no hangover or negative side effect from experiencing and sharing God's love.

"Do not forsake your friend and the friend of your father…."
-Proverbs 27:10

"A friend loves at all times, and a brother is born for adversity."-**Proverbs 17:17**

This is not always easy.   Can you be a real friend?   This may require extending grace, mercy, and most definitely forgiveness. It may mean that you get woken up in the middle of the night. It may possibly involve giving someone rides to church or work until he or she can get on their feet. The hard part is when tough love through wisdom comes into the picture. You cannot let your friend borrow the rent money when you know that he or she is headed to the Casino or to call his or her dealer. In these situations, pray and use wisdom. You can go to the store for them or pay the landlord yourself. The fact is that if you continue to be manipulated, then you are enabling the person to stay in the "cycle of abuse." A real friend can provide accountability. Quite simply, it's a firm kick in the rear. Yes, it is a fact, we all need one occasionally. Speaking the truth in love will always point a person towards Christ. This can be a prophetic opportunity to call out hidden potential. It entails more than just hammering them with accusations. You will need facts, especially if the enemy keeps minimizing the severity of the situation.

Some people need a little extra love or grace. I recommend that you pray to become more in tune with God's voice. Make sure that you are honoring your time with Him. In this way, it will be easier for you to discern or know what you should do in each situation (1 John 4:1). The enemy's attacks in the Christian and "normal" life can sometimes attempt to crush our hope and faith to pebbles. We have to be careful not to judge, but listen carefully, use wisdom, and inspect the fruit. I know testimonies of people who struggled for years in and out of church and are now free in Christ Jesus. Do not allow the enemy to get you so angry that you will not pray for the hurting. Sadly, the army of God (the church) is one of the few armies where we shoot our wounded. The reality is that pastors struggle too. Sometimes things have to truly get broken before they can be fixed. This process is different for each individual. The length of time required often depends on our own willingness and choices made during development.

Let us keep on loving each other, loving hurting the broken, and even loving the "difficult" religious people. There is power in submitting another's prayer request to other "prayer warriors" when you are discouraged. We all need each other's support whether we agree on things or not. Love is the foundation. Keep this in mind: it may be your prayers or act of kindness that finally helps set someone free. This is why every deed in service must be done in the love of our Heavenly Father. James 5:19-20 says, *"My brothers if one of you should wander from the truth and someone should bring him back, remember this: Whoever turns a sinner from the error of his ways will save him from death and cover over a multitude of sins."*

Thinking Point: This is why we all need relationship with Jesus-in order to hear and distinguish His voice from the noise of manipulation. There is no cookie cutter advice when it comes to helping people and personal boundaries. However, I will suggest going as far as the Holy Spirit tells you to go. It would be wise to use your accountability partner to pray with you. Quite frankly, no one wants to make emotionally charged decisions or vows.

3) They lay it on the line

"Greater has no love than this, that he lay down his life for his friends." **-John 15:13**

"Perfume and incense bring joy to the heart, and the pleas-antness of one's friend springs earnest counsel"
-Proverbs 27:9

"Wounds from a friend can be trusted..." **-Proverbs 27:6**

It is repeated three times in the gospel "deny yourself, pick up your cross daily and follow me." The core of Jesus' statement is the basis for this section. Sometimes we do not understand how many people are watching our lives and possibly counting on us to reflect Christ. I am not trying to be legalistic here; however, in the power of the Holy Spirit, we can reflect more of Him and less of ourselves. Is it possible to forgive, to not hold grudges, or to talk respectfully in modern times? The Bible states in Psalm 119:9, *"How can a young man keep his way pure? By living according to your word"*. The goal of learning who you are in Christ will set you free: free to be the same person around everyone in your life. This means more than putting on a show or a "church face" and truthfully "keeping it real" with your relationship with Jesus. This does not mean perfection, but it does mean to be genuine in all things, even your mistakes.

This may mean you stop smoking or drinking (in God's time) with strength from Holy Spirit. You may occasionally have to cancel going to the gym or going to a barbecue in order to help someone move. The real measure of a friend is giving a listening ear. The Lord may lead you to lovingly hold someone accountable. I suggest praying and using wisdom, setting the stage for a heartfelt talk. In several cases after prayer, the people I was concerned about reached out to me! We must be careful not to fall into the "people pleasing" trap (Ephesians 6:7).

The world is full of people who will tell you what you want to hear. The vast majority of those people have an agenda or an angle. A predatory man seeking a woman will tactfully listen to her distress. He may be quick with a compliment or offer to buy her a drink. It is a pretty safe bet that the man described here has interest in only one thing. A woman who has no place to live falls "in love" quickly in the south. Many people are just looking for a port in the storm, not the solution. It takes the discernment from Jesus to know who is for us and who is against us. Many of us just need some of Jesus' love so that we can care about ourselves enough to care about others. Very few people, women included, ever told me that I might need to slow my lifestyle down. Most people were just along for the ride until the party was over. After all the lively gatherings, I would again find myself alone. In retrospect, I was also guilty of emotionally pushing people away or closing them out.

To "lay it on the line" is to be the best friend that God calls you to be. In order to achieve this friendship, we must get over ourselves. We all need wisdom and boundaries so that we can fluidly function. Moreover, if you learn to obey the voice of the Holy Spirit, you will eventually have peace, simply because you have done everything the Lord asked of you. Sometimes, we are supposed to offer counsel. Other times, we are to guard our hearts and pray! (Proverbs 4:23) A real friend knows how to give a listening ear. Never minimize the ministry of "being there." One of my mentors is a master of asking questions that help me find the answers myself. I confess; I am still learning and growing each day.

Thinking Point: We must be careful NOT to allow codependent relationships to form.

4) Use what God gave you

*"Share with God's people who are in need. Practice hospitality." -***Romans 12:13**

All that you own, including your gifts and your talents, are really not yours. They're God's. Once you arrive at that revelation, you will unlock the door to peace and blessing. Your home should be used to build the kingdom. Yes, it should be a place of refuge and peace, but the reality is that you can host a Bible study or serve dinner to build relationships in Jesus name. Oh, you're not comfortable teaching or sharing? Do not be surprised if the Lord will provide someone to come teach and lead prayer on your behalf until you're ready. It is important to use wisdom and discernment about selecting the proper person and time. I have received many blessings and made new friends in these "cell group" type gatherings. Developing a healthy Christian community is of upmost importance.

It does not stop here. Your car can be used to give people rides to church or the grocery store. In the south, your truck **will** be used to help people move. You might as well help with an attitude of being a blessing. This means that you will do it without complaining (Philippians 2:14). Your boat can be used to take someone fishing in order to encourage them or spiritually connect with them in a time of need. This is a great way of building or restoring relationships. Once someone is in your boat, he or she cannot get away even if they wanted to. Even so, always share Christ with wisdom in love and without judgment. Things do not have to get weird in order to bless people.

God has given us each passions and talents. We are to use them to build kingdom relationships. Hobbies such as working out, cycling, MMA, football, tennis, golf, video games, the arts, and having coffee can easily become an avenue to meet new people, deepen relationships, or encourage others. There is nothing wrong with being passionate about what you're into. The Lord knows that some days I enjoy training alone to center my spirit. However, my life is not about me anymore. Therefore, when He puts someone in my path or on my heart, I honor that. Life is made to be shared and enjoyed with others. Only in the last thirty years has technology and creature comforts pushed us away from real human interaction. I'm sorry, but "chat" on social media is not heart-to-heart interaction. It can be a good way to stay in touch or encourage someone, but there is no substitute for real, genuine communication. Think about it. Time is your greatest asset; it is not money. I encourage you to "invest wisely." I may never make a million dollars on the stock exchange, but I will never be broke from investing in people. When you love God's people like Jesus does, it is honored by God.

5) Follow the Holy Spirit in Obedience and Prayer

"Whoever has my commands and keeps them is the one who loves me. The one who loves me will be loved by my Father, and I too will love them and show myself to them."
–John 14:21

When God tells you to do something, do it! The quicker you can become in tune with God's voice, the better off you will be. That is only the first part. The second part is to obey: in small things, in big things, in relationships, in giving, and in all areas of life- period. This also pertains to when to walk away and when to protect yourself. The blessing will outweigh the cost, especially when you become mature enough to trust the Lord. You may not get out of debt immediately, but blessings will come when you tithe, give, and become faithful with the things you own. First and foremost, Jesus wants you. He wants a deep personal relationship with you. When you learn to trust Him, you will gain something more valuable than riches: peace in your heart. From that peace and wisdom, all other blessings will flow. The Lord knows where you are, and He knows your heart.

When you feel the urge to pray for someone, do it! Do not hesitate! When the Holy Spirit makes you aware of someone's struggle, follow your heart. What do I mean by that? Maybe it means that you should pray, text, use social media, call, or visit someone. Only God knows, but the idea is following the Lord in obedience and love. There should be no selfish motivation behind the text, message or call. Here are a few examples: "Hey, I was thinking about you today, wanted to say hello, and to let you know that I'm praying for you." When in doubt send an encouraging Bible verse. While it is not our job to "rescue" people, it is our job to love them and snatch them from the fire (Jude v22-23). Always be careful not to get drawn into sin by recklessly doing "good" (Galatians 6:1).

The Lord rescued a friend of mine, Norwood, a few years before I responded to His call. Norwood heard that I was now a Christian, and he knew my struggle. He lived two hours away, but he would call, visit, listen, and encourage me. Even after I would do good for three months and then horribly mess up, Norwood gave me a listening ear, kingdom resources (CD's with teaching, music and books), and prayed for me. This came at a pivotal time when I needed it. God used him as a trailblazer to show me that change is possible. He was following the Holy Spirit's prompting by "speaking life" and encouraging me.

Thinking point: Sometimes, the Lord may tell you to "get out" of a certain situation. When you have continually bent over backwards for someone who continues to hurt you, lie, consume your time, produce worry, and refuse to change harmful behavior or listen to loving, Godly council, it has become time to remember to be a friend to yourself. Take a step back and establish a healthy boundary. The enemy does not play fair, and helping (loving) people can become challenging. That is why we must learn who we are in Christ. In some cases, people will not respond to loving, Godly counsel by repenting or admitting to anything. In fact, they may get mad, minimize, deny their problems, or even curse you out! Through the deception of the enemy, some will even try and reverse the situation and blame you for their actions. Again, this is why it is important to know who you are in Christ. Godly advice and counsel is not nagging nor will it compromise the truth of God's word. That is why it is done in love and obedience to Christ. Sometimes, you have to obey Christ and bounce the ball into the other person's court. The results will then be on Jesus and not you.

CHAPTER 6

Trust and Obey

Before I was a Christian, I was guilty of assuming the Holy Bible was a collection of restrictive rules and regulations on living. At that time, I was proof positive of what the Bible calls a "double-minded" man. I knew what the Bible said about sexual relations only with your spouse and about drunkenness. Those two things I remembered from my youth. I liberally interpreted its instruction according to the season I was in. My convictions faded the more I fed my fleshly desires. Once I was high or "loose," I could release darker sides of myself that otherwise were held in check. Coming from an environment of street thugs did not help my perspective. When I was dating I altered the Word's rules of monogamy. I thought, "Well, what does it matter that I am in a sexual relationship before marriage? I am faithful to whoever I am with at the time. This is just a test drive to protect my investment. It's not nearly as bad as most people I know." Somehow, I did manage to grab that being faithful was of value-to me if no one else. However, when I was single and emotionally damaged for a season or two, I was not quite as chivalrous. The Lord often reminds me that "who has been forgiven much loves much." Another misconstrued view of life I held was that my drug use and drinking only affected me. I formed my own life's doctrine, and I honored the "code of the street" over my family and Jesus Christ. My mentality was, "It's my life, and if you don't like it, there's the door." Yes, I had a lot to learn. I had no idea what being a good man was about. I didn't know that a good man was righteous, of good character, and possessed integrity. Slowly, I grew further away from God.

My poor choices and daily lifestyle eventually eroded my soul. I spent four years in a state of serious depression. I didn't care if I lived or died. In Jesus name, I hope the next few paragraphs help to keep someone from suffering as much or as long as I did. For me, life was like riding a rollercoaster for a very long time. I thought of myself as a 'Rocky Balboa' type. Go ahead and knock me down. Sooner or later, I will get up to fight again. I was driven by pride of self and self-determination for years. The only reason that I didn't take my own life, I thought, was because I did not want my enemies to be able to say that my life was about nothing. Pride, grief, bitterness and resentment were the roots of my problems. As I grew spiritually, God used my pride to my advantage. Now, I do not flatter myself at all. It is only by God's grace that I am alive. The Bible says in Psalm 136, "His love endures forever."

Today, the real problem with most of us is that we want to do things "our way." Most people simply cannot take constructive criticism well. It took me many years to accept that there was even such a thing as "constructive criticism." I freely admit that, at times, I still do struggle with this. When you live life with a chip on your shoulder, it is hard to learn anything. Many of us have listened to no one. Ironically, we often expect others to hear us out or accept our opinion as the only correct view. The principle of honor comes in to play here. How can we lovingly confront or correct anyone when we, ourselves, have never received correction?

Someone I love dearly once came to me and said, "My child just will not listen and appears to be going down the wrong path." The person who shared that with me was extremely rebellious throughout most of her life and still struggles with rebellion. She has disrespected her parents and still has difficulty with Godly authority. An old song comes to mind when presented these situations "The Cats in the Cradle." Grandma may have said, "You made your bed now you must lie in it," but that is not in the Holy Bible. That statement leaves little room for repentance and grace. What the Bible **does** say is, *"God cannot be mocked, as a man sows he also reaps"* (Galatians 6:7-10). The principle of seed time and harvest must be considered in these situations. Traits, such as generational rebellion, will only get stronger unless they are put under the blood of Jesus. Sometimes, we have to experience things ourselves before we can truly understand what others have endured or are currently experiencing. It is a good thing for us all that in Christ we can become humble and teachable, can repent, and can start sowing new seed to reap a new positive harvest! No matter what our defects of character are, it is never too late to become humble and teachable.

Much of the general population is familiar with at least some of the teachings of Jesus. We've all heard "Love the Lord with all your being," and "Love your neighbor as yourself." This sounds simple, right? Sadly, the children in Sunday school class understand this better than the Sunday school teacher. Many of us act like we understand and even have some of the basics of Jesus's teachings down pat. However, few of us actually put these teachings to practical use on a daily basis. Jesus says in Matthew 6:14-15, *"For if you forgive men when they sin against you, your heavenly Father will also forgive you. But if you do not forgive men their sins, your Father will not forgive your sins."* If the church alone honored this teaching, it would change local communities and, consequently, the world forever.

In our daily walk with Jesus, forgiveness is the key, and it is essential for freedom. Jesus lived, died, and rose three days later to provide freedom from guilt, shame, abuse, hate, and any other impediment to a fulfilled life. We should settle for nothing short of total healing. If we are to love our neighbor as ourselves, we must first learn to love and forgive ourselves. For most, this forgiveness concept is not easy to grasp. This process was extremely difficult for me. My life was an instrument of destruction- focused both toward others and toward myself. Destruction turned into guilt which allowed addiction to take control of my life, and guilt compounded grief and normal life transitions. I thought I loved Jesus, but I sure was not even close to honoring or loving Him with all my heart, soul, and mind. The real problem was I had not received grace in its fullness. I did not have the power of the Holy Spirit working in my life. There were times when I would allow the Lord to sprinkle little pieces of healing or good fruit into my life, but then I would eventually return to my "old ways."

Unfortunately, there were days that I lost my mind. I had to completely hit bottom **several** times before I would completely surrender to Him. What I did not see was that the Lord positioned me for that very moment. Ironically, I was right where I was supposed to be in the exact state required: brokenness. I was completely broken and thus moldable clay in His hands. After I rededicated my life to the Lord (as a grown man), it took a period of time, lots of prayer, Bible study, the laying of hands, stepping out in faith, and stepping out of my comfort zone to bring healing into my life. I had to learn the Word. Finally, I had to learn to trust the Holy Spirit and follow His guidance with obedience when taught. Changing our lives to be like Jesus is a process; it is also a lifetime experience and journey. I have had to learn to receive God's blessings and grace. I occasionally still struggle to hold onto my joy. James 1:2-3 says, "*Count it all joy, my brothers, when you meet trials of various kinds, for you know that the testing of your faith produces steadfastness.*" This I am receiving because, "The joy of the Lord is my strength" (Nehemiah 8:10). In Jesus name, I pray we can all trust God to work in our "troubled areas."

"Our way" or the "way we see it" is often the exact opposite of what the Word of God says. Romans 12:1-2 says, "*Therefore, I urge you, brothers and sisters, in view of God's mercy, to offer your bodies as a living sacrifice, holy and pleasing to God—this is your true and proper worship. Do not conform to the pattern of this world, but be transformed by the renewing of your mind. Then you will be able to test and approve what God's will is—his good, pleasing and perfect will.*" This renewal process is referred to as sanctification. The importance of reading the Word daily or often should be as essential as morning caffeine. This, in turn, grows our faith. Where does faith come from? Romans 10:17 declares, *"Faith comes from hearing and hearing from the word of God."* We must arm ourselves with the Word then allow God to change us.

There is no doubt that I experienced love in relationships in my life before Jesus. However, I also experienced tremendous hurt, loneliness, pain, lack of forgiveness, and guilt. One could say it was just God's timing for me. On the other side of the coin, one could also say that I was selfish and did things my own way. Many times, I would say the most hurtful thing that came to my mind in an attempt to "win" the argument. I most often acted this way when I was hurting inside or when things weren't going my way. Unknowingly, I had built walls and would lash out as a defense mechanism. Almost all of my relationships with women were sexual, even though I thought I was chivalrous for being with one woman at a time when I was dating. I was clearly not hearing God, and to be truthful, nor was I truly honoring the women I was with. Honoring her would have been cherishing her as a person and offering her a safe covering through the covenant of marriage. Society tells us to please ourselves. This kind of behavior often leaves a trail of destruction and one or more parties picking up the pieces.

There are some things in the Holy Bible that are not clearly "spelled out." Denominations have even divided over some of these areas. However, sexual immorality is not one of the areas. Several times, the Word is clear on this subject. A few examples include:

- *Flee from sexual immorality. All other sins a person commits are outside the body, but whoever sins sexually, sins against their own body.* (**1 Corinthians 6:18**)

- *But among you there must not be even a hint of sexual immorality, or of any kind of impurity, or of greed, because these are improper for God's holy people.* (**Ephesians 5:3**)

- *It is God's will that you should be sanctified: that you should avoid sexual immorality.* (**1 Thessalonians 4:3**)

The reason for these parameters is not to stop us from enjoying life. The reason is to instruct us to do things God's way. The principle is this: 1 Corinthians 6:19-20 states, "*Do you not know that your bodies are temples of the Holy Spirit, who is in you, whom you have received from God? You are not your own; you were bought at a price. Therefore, honor God with your bodies.*" I don't think Paul was referring to having a beer at the bonfire here so much as he was referring to a higher principle of reverence. We were bought for a price. The enemy is the accuser, and he will use any sin he can to trap us and to make us feel guilty or unworthy to be in God's presence. Some of the worst pain I have ever experienced in my life is knowingly engaging in sexual immorality and compromise as a believer. No one is perfect. I am not trying to condemn anyone: the fact is that if we want God's blessing on our lives, families, and relationships, then we must learn to honor Him. This, in turn, will teach us to honor each other. It all starts with Jesus and His love and purpose for us all.

In all honesty, this has been the most difficult struggle for me. Personally, I know that I will settle for no less than God's best for me. I confess that I do long for the togetherness and bond with my future wife. It will be something pure, beautiful, holy, and a bond unlike which I have never known. The people in my life who have put Christ first are blessed. They will testify that it is worth the wait. There are several couples I know that would not be together apart from the grace of God and power of Jesus. Restoration is possible. Jesus is our unchanging hope. Keep this verse in mind: *"Jesus looked at them and said, "With man this is impossible, but with God all things are possible."* – Matthew 19:26

The Holy Spirit will give us wisdom and strength. The Word says that we are the righteousness of God in Christ (Romans 3:22). We need to be willing to trust God and do things His way. If we want Him to sustain and bless our relationships, then we need to put God first. I know this is not fashionable in today's world. It may make sense to very few people around you. However, I ask you to join me in prayer and seek the Holy Spirit's wisdom to show us and give us the power to honor Him in our daily lives. In reality, we need to be willing to receive what Christ has already done! Once we understand that we are now seated with Christ in heavenly realms (Ephesians 2:6) and are now part of a royal priesthood (1 Peter 2:9), victories start to come easier. Knowing your position is of great importance. Furthermore, how, what, and where you focus will always be a factor in your success.

Obedience is the key to most blessings and, quite often, spiritual growth. When God speaks to you about anything, learn to obey. Do this sooner rather than later and always in love. He may tell you to give an offering beyond your tithe to the church, pay for a child's youth camp, give someone a car, and visit someone in prison or the hospital. It may be something big, or it may be something as small as giving your old clothes to the poor. Whatever it is, I suggest that you do it. Many times, our hard heads or rational minds keep us from walking in the fullness of Christ. Jesus is not looking for willing candidates for "Christian make-overs" or behavior modification to create "boring pod people." He simply wants us to get to know Him and His goodness.

When God speaks, do what He asks. The Holy Spirit may be telling or tugging at your heart to do various things such as cleaning your house, exercising, eating better, tithing, stopping smoking or cursing, loving without fear, opening up, submitting or removing stubbornness. Humbly admitting that we need His power to do these things is the catalyst to activate Holy Ghost power. In Celebrate Recovery, they teach us to address one "issue" at a time. Unless the Lord zaps you with the power all at once, it will be a process-a process of learning that requires hearing His voice and then actually doing what He says. It is largely about trust, but it is always based on love. The Lord will not leave you hanging. If He asks you to say your testimony for the first time, He will be with you. Your simple obedience may be withholding someone's blessing or be someone's answer to prayer. Someone may need your help or to hear your testimony. He will also help us and teach us. Keep in mind that your testimony and love walk is not just for you. It is used to touch and reach others for Christ. Keep this verse close to your heart.

"Teach me your way, Lord,
that I may rely on your faithfulness;
give me an undivided heart,
that I may fear your name. - **Psalm 86:11**

CHAPTER 7

Faith, Hope, and Love

There are entire books written on each of these subjects; however, it important that I expand and touch on each of these topics. Honestly, none of us should ever think we know so much about a Biblical topic that we stop learning or seeking a deeper understanding of its truth. This is known as pride. Danger begins to creep in when we repeatedly think that this sermon or that book would have been great for someone other than ourselves. We say things like "Yeah, Aunt Sally sure did need to hear today's message" or "so-and-so should have read that book." Sometimes, that may be true. However, at other times, we need to slow down long enough to open our own heart and receive a word meant for ourselves. With that said, let's take a look at faith.

Faith

We all believe in or have faith in something. As one of Bob Dylan's songs said, "You gotta serve somebody." To some degree, we all have faith in, believe in, and serve something.

I used to put my faith in other people, music, drugs, and myself. My hope was that if I fought hard enough, then, sooner or later, I would come out "winning" again. The extreme ups and downs of living that way almost destroyed me. I was selfish, misguided, and extremely afraid of reality. To put it another way, my faith was focused on the world and on self.

Even after I felt God's presence and His calling on my

life, I often lacked the faith to pursue Him. After four years of running from Him and battling serious depression, I began to hear Him talking to me again. Because I am hard-headed, I responded slowly, and I used what little faith I had to move toward Jesus rather than away from Him. By taking one small step at a time, I was eventually able to fully embrace Jesus and His amazing grace for me. Each small step I took moving from my own comfort zone to His light required faith. The enemy held fear, insecurity, and lack of trust over me like a black cloud. It was, literally, a walk from darkness to light. Over time, I repeatedly learned that the blessings far outweigh the fear and cost.

The Holy Bible defines faith in Hebrews Chapter 11. *"Now, faith is being sure of what we hope for and certain of what we do not see."* –verse 1. In a nutshell, faith is to believe and trust in God's sovereign power in all things. We accept Jesus Christ by faith. Ephesians 7:8-9 says, *"For it is by grace that you are saved through faith. Not from yourselves, it is a gift from God. Not by works so that no man can boast."* Salvation comes to us by faith. We can't physically do anything to bring salvation to us. The only thing we "do" is to choose Jesus. This clearly demonstrates our faith. The Lord can use a submitted and humble heart. Maybe you have accepted Christ and gotten off course. Perhaps you have become stagnant in your walk with Him, or you've recently accepted Christ as your Savior. By faith, God will restore you and guide you. Hebrews Chapter 11 is the Bible's "Hall of Fame" of faith. I plead with you to read this chapter with an open heart and a mindset of prayer. Notice how many verses start with the phrase "by faith." The fact that each of these individuals were flawed "regular people" should inspire us all. We should not need to watch inaccurately made comic book movies for inspiration or encouragement. The word is alive, and the promises are for you. History was written according to the faith of those with a good report, and worlds were changed because of it.

Not only in Chapter 11 of Hebrews but throughout the Holy Bible, which is the Word of God, He used ordinary and flawed people-people who had the faith to trust and obey Him. He has the power to turn your weakness into His strength (Hebrews 11:34). Be patient and stay the course; It takes time to develop faith. Do not let the world, people, or actions deter your faith or steal your hope. Life can and will be tough. Despite what many think, most people are not cheering you on, even if they click "like" on your social media posts. The enemy does not fight fair. As soon as you get a "word", he will attempt to steal it, demean it, or refute it. He can even use someone in your life who means well to throw cold water on your dreams. We call these people "dream squashers." Let these words of warning and your own difficult moments become the things that make you stronger in faith. If you choose to hold to the faith and the "word" God gave you, you will be reap a harvest. Be aware, a good mentor may also douse someone's dreams or ideas in order to see the degree of belief or faith the person has about a particular vision. Often, we need faith that Godly integrity is worth possessing and that, in fact, good things do come to those who intently wait.

Hebrews 11:6 states, *"And without faith it is impossible to please God because anyone who comes to Him must believe that He exists and that He rewards those who earnestly seek Him."* Every step you take towards God, He will bless you. The enemy will try to discourage even the strongest believer's faith. That is one of the many tactics he uses. John 8:44, *"when he [speaking of Satan] lies, he speaks in his native language, for he is a liar and the father of lies."* There is a battlefield, and it is in our minds. Joyce Meyer coined an expression and wrote a powerful book called the "Battlefield of the Mind." If you haven't done so already, I truly recommend it to all believers, regardless of where they are at in their walk. When our heads hear the lies that come from within (self-condemnation), from the enemy, or from others, by faith we do not have to receive them. The Bible makes it clear in 2 Corinthians 10:5, *"We demolish arguments and every pretension that sets itself up against the knowledge of God, and we take captive every thought to make it obedient to Christ."* How then is this possible? Simply put- by faith in Jesus and the authority we possess in the name of Jesus.

There is a phrase that all believers in Christ should know, and it should be our battle cry. That phrase is this: "in the name of Jesus." Sounds simple, right? It is simple, but it is also powerful and effective. When spoken in faith, it is our greatest weapon as a child of God. The church has overlooked and underused this truth for far too long. Throughout daily life, we are bombarded with negative thoughts or accusations such as "I'm a loser," "Things will never change," "I hate [anything]," "It's too late," "I'm too young or too old," and insert any toxic or fear-based thought here. Focus on this because I really want you to get this part: When the thoughts come, pray out loud, and fight back! Invoke the power of His name! In His name lies the authority over any situation. <u>One must have a humble repentant heart filled with the love of Jesus to succeed in battle.</u>

So how does this all go down? Here is an example of

what to say when the enemy begins to battle in your mind: "I do not receive that, in the name of Jesus. I know you died so that I can be free. I know Your word says, "No weapon formed against me will prosper." Thank you Lord for your word says that I have authority over the enemy, and he must depart from me in the name of Jesus! I can do all things through Christ who strengthens me. I am fearfully and wonderfully made by you. I will cast these thoughts down and take them captive as written in Your word. Thank you Lord that there is no condemnation for those of us in Christ. Thank you Lord for this work you started in me, a work you will finish! Thank you that nothing can separate me from You, and I am in your hands. In Jesus name, amen!

The power is not just in speaking it out loud. I am not sharing some new age message of positive thinking. The above paragraphs are real examples of spiritual warfare. Notice that the words spoken are directly from God's word. His Holy Word, coupled with faith and the given authority in His name, is the ultimate weapon. Hands down, that is the game changer. When the enemy comes to attack, he does not play fair. Some of you may be thinking that sounds like a lot to handle or thinking "I am no Bible scholar," guess what? If all you did was say "Jesus, Jesus, Jesus..." over and over, you are still fighting back! (If you believe by faith). Throughout this book, I have shared Romans 10:17 which says, *"Consequently faith comes from hearing the message, and the message is heard through the Word of Christ."* It does not matter how or when, but we each need to spend time daily in God's Word reading the Bible. I can promise you that if you humbly and prayerfully take the Word in, sooner or later, it will produce good fruit. The mind and the heart will come into agreement with the Holy Spirit and produce Godly characteristics. Eventually, through building a relationship with God, the shift from Godly behavior (occasional acts of obedience) into Godly character (a natural way of life) can occur. This is the natural progression when a healthy, loving relationship with Jesus deepens.

You may say "That all sounds good on paper but, I can't remember the Scriptures." Allow me to get in your face for a second. Some sports fanatics that play Fantasy Football can name every starting player on all thirty-two NFL teams. Why can he not remember, "I can do all things through Christ's power." Avid fishermen know both freshwater and saltwater baits, color choice according to water clarity and time of year, what size hooks are used for each fish species, barometric pressure effects, spawning dates, and the location of secret "honey holes," yet they cannot make time to take in a few verses to meditate on and put to memory? Sports athletes know about nutrition, work-out regimens and supplementation as a lifestyle, but they cannot memorize a few verses a month? Some ladies can tell you all about the latest fashion trends and what celebrity is wearing it, whether the occasion calls for flats or heels, the best make-up line on the market, and what colors to wear and when they are acceptable but cannot learn a verse a month? Give me a break. Personally, I can remember the verses of a number of songs from when I was in high school and younger. Small town radio replayed the same songs over and over; therefore, I know a lot of songs I would rather forget. How do any of these people learn about their passion or hobby? They learn it by dedicating time, repetition, desire, and effort to their passion. First, get the Word into your mind, and it will then trickle into your heart. We should all desire a passion to learn and a revelation in our understanding of the Word.

This is a war. There will be opposition, and the enemy is real. However, we must always be mindful to, *"Fight the good fight of faith. Take hold of the eternal life to which you were called when you made your confession in the presence of many witnesses."* Timothy 6:12. In this verse, the Apostle Paul is encouraging Timothy to move forward by faith. We must learn to take hold of our salvation, which we confess by faith. If this is the case, then where does faith come from?" Remember that Romans 10:17 says, *"Consequently faith comes from hearing the message, and the message is heard through the Word of Christ."* The more of the Word of God you consume, the more of God that you allow inside of you. *"In the beginning was the Word and the Word was with God, and the Word was God."* This is declared in John 1:1. The sole purpose of reading the Bible and honoring the principles in this book are to help build and strengthen your personal relationship with Jesus. You will get further faster if you approach it with this mentality. It is all about Jesus, which means it is all about God's love.

The Holy Bible is not just a book of instruction or wisdom. It is the Word of God. The Christian faith has been mocked, persecuted, copied, and oppressed since Jesus walked this earth. Why is this so? *"For the Word of God is living and active. Sharper than any double-edged sword, it penetrates even to dividing soul and spirit, joints and marrow; it judges the thoughts and attitude of the heart."*-Hebrews 4:12. When a person is confronted with conviction of sin, moves toward righteousness, or sees a need for salvation, the next action always requires faith. The choice must be made to either obey Jesus or to continue on a destructive, selfish, or worldly path. The conviction of righteousness is an internal prompting from the Holy Spirit to change your life for the better. That feeling or nudge to change is a good thing. With the power of Jesus all things are possible. For too long, Christianity has been condemned as an unattainable life full of rules and regulations. How far from the truth that is! Jesus simply wants you to enjoy all that He paid for on the cross for you, and all that He requires is your faith.

"Heavenly Father, I pray that you strengthen our faith. Help us to understand how much you love us, and that your plan is good. Grow us to maturity in all areas of our life, and that by faith, through your power, we learn to trust and obey your Word. Help us to hear your voice today and increase our measure of faith. Through faith in You, help us to believe and to receive all that your word says! Guide us as we seek, pray, share, and believe the truth! Increase our fellowship with You. In Jesus name, AMEN."

If you are new to the Christian walk of faith, you may be wondering, "How much faith do I have?" Take heart. When Jesus was instructing the disciples He said, "*Because you have so little faith, I tell you the truth; if you have the faith as small as a mustard seed, you can say to this mountain, 'Move from here to there', and it will move. Nothing will be impossible for you.*" --Matthew 17:20-21. We need to become grounded in the Word in order to have faith. There is no way around that fact. Allow the Holy Spirit to open your heart. Your pastor or parent's faith cannot save you when the storm arises. This is why a close, personal relationship with Jesus is essential. The Word that you have etched in your heart will continually strengthen your faith. When the storms come, the Holy Spirit will take this engraved Word and return comfort and peace. This life we live is the battle ground. Our faith grows when we use it, trusting Jesus in every area of life. Knowing Jesus is something special that the world cannot take away from you. He will always be there for you. Jesus gave us a promise in John 10:27-28 when He said, "*My sheep listen to my voice; I know them and they know me. I give them eternal life, and they shall never perish; no one will snatch them out of my hand.*"

Hope

"*Let us hold unswervingly to the hope we profess, for he who promised is faithful.*"
  -Hebrews 10:23

Most people's understanding of hope has been sadly distorted. The world's common use of the definition of "hope" is not the true Biblical hope Jesus offers. When someone purchases a lottery ticket, they say "I hope I win." Chicago Bears fans say they hope that one day the team will go back to playing smash mouth football. Many hope this is the job they've always wanted or the relationship they've dreamed of. Where I come from in the south, the older generation even have a saying, "You can hope in one hand and spit in the other and see which one fills up faster." We all have "hope," but it truly matters where your hope rests. This fact will largely determine your behavior. If you never grasp the Lord's "unchanging hope", your moral compass will constantly be moving.

The revelation I pray that you receive is this: If you

put your hope in Jesus Christ, you will never be put to shame. Jesus Christ is the only free gift and sure thing in this universe. A promise is written in the Word that nothing can remove you from God's hands. The hands of_God are much better than All State. The hope Christ offers us all is real and unchanging. Once you gain true depth in your relationship with Christ, you will become unshakeable. Real life- changing hope does not disappoint. There is a spiritual procession moving towards Godly hope which begins with faith.

"Therefore, since we have been justified through faith, we have peace with God through our Lord Jesus Christ, 2 through whom we have gained access by faith into this grace in which we now stand. And we boast in the hope of the glory of God. 3 Not only so, but we also glory in our sufferings, because we know that suffering produces perseverance; 4 perseverance, character; and character, hope. 5 And hope does not put us to shame, because God's love has been poured out into our hearts through the Holy Spirit, who has been given to us."- **Romans 5:1-5**

In Ecclesiastes, we find an interesting verse speaking of hope.

"Anyone who is among the living has hope—even a live dog is better off than a dead lion!"-**Ecclesiastes 9:4**

This verse always gives me perspective when I feel overwhelmed. The reality is that today is the only thing we have. Yesterday's victories may serve as markers or stepping stones, but they will not win today's battle. There is no need to take the bait, worry to death, be anxious about what tomorrow holds, or live in past regret. There is no fruit in that, and it serves you no good. What will you do today with the air you breathe? Where does your hope rest? I encourage you to give it to Jesus. No matter where you are or what you are facing, it is never too late. There may be present consequences of seeds sown in the past to overcome; however, it's your choice concerning how you will sow seeds today. Speaking life into, praying and worshiping with, serving beside, seeking alongside, and fellowshipping among God's people could be the wisest choice you will make. Let your faith and hope rest in God alone.

Thinking Point: The above verse from Ecclesiastes should give us all some perspective. In the sense that if you are breathing, God has granted you the time you have today. It is your choice how you will spend it. Your faith will determine how you perceive it. You can sit there and wallow in your situation for whatever reasons you are allowing it to hold you captive, or you could choose that today I will be thankful. I will seek Jesus by faith. I believe that no matter what- He is with me. Whatever time I have left on earth, my heart's desire is to make it count. One of the deepest things the Lord has ever taught me is that we are all just passing through. Often, we allow pain, betrayal, hardship, or similar tactics of the enemy to become our focus. The devil magnifies its reality (blows it up) and tries to make the situation your downfall. I am not implying that the pain is not real, but the fact is God's love is so much greater. These momentary afflictions cannot hold a candle to the joy, peace, and love that is Christ Jesus. This will always hold true, in this life and in heaven with Jesus forever. He wants us to have victory now. Hope in Jesus is the only sure thing in the universe.

Love

"What's Love Got to Do With It?" –**Tina Turner**

Everything!

When it comes to love, most people are familiar with terms such as:

Love life	Love Hurts
Love child	Love Bites
Love nest	Love song
Love triangle	Free Love
Love struck	Love Connection
Love sick	Unconditional Love
Lovebird	Unrequited Love
Love seat	Lovelorn
Lovely	Loveless
Love making	Love letter
Loving	First Love
Lover	Lovey-dovey
Love handles	True Love

Most dictionaries literally define "love" as:
(1) a very strong emotional and/or sexual feeling for someone
(2) The feeling of liking and caring for someone such as a member of your family or a close friend.
(3) Someone you have sexual or romantic relationship with
(4) Something that is enjoyed very much (example: I love music)
(5) British –someone you like very much because they are kind
(6) Used at end of a letter (a term of endearment)

Is it no wonder there is something wrong with the world today when two of the five definitions of love are defined sexually, two use the term "like", and one is a generically used suffix? Which means that none of these definitions actually scratch the surface of what love truly is. The Holy Bible defines love in 1 Corinthians 13. This is often read at weddings, but I feel it is seldom understood.

"(1)If I had the gift of being able to speak in tongues (or languages) of men and angels, but have not love, I am only a clanging cymbal. (2) If I have the gift of prophecy and can fathom the mysteries and all knowledge, and if I have faith that can move mountains, but have not love, I am nothing. (3) If I give all I possess to the poor and surrender my body to the flames but have not love, I gain nothing."- **1 Corinthians 13**

Before moving on, let's take a closer look at those verses.

Verse One- Paul makes reference to speaking in the languages of men and angels (heavenly) and mysteries

Verse Two- Paul makes reference to the gifts of prophecy (aka: Greater Gift), knowledge, and faith

Verse Three- Paul makes reference to giving all and surrender.
In verses 1-3, Paul is referencing spiritual gifts and giving. These are the things that he says are to be desired "Gifts from God."   However, he clearly distinguishes that without **love**, these things are nothing.

"(4) Love is patient, love is kind. It does not envy, it does not boast, it is not proud. (5) It is not rude, it is not self-seeking, it

is not easily angered, it keeps no record of wrongs. (6) Love does not delight in evil but rejoices with truth. (7) It always protects, always trusts, always hopes, always perseveres."

Let's look at this closer before we move on. At first glance, this sounds like a fairy tale in the natural. However, these words are the standard of what true love is and, thus, the authentic definition. This was written more than a thousand years before the dictionary casually links love to sexual encounters and your enjoyment of a song. Our world and media has lied to us and drastically lowered the standard. Biblical love may seem unattainable, but it is something to strive toward. Someone once said to me, "Sean, you believe in fairy tales." Not exactly, but I do believe in miracles. I'll admit that I did enjoy the fantasy film "The Princess Bride." The fact remains: I have personally witnessed "fairy tale" restoration and the blessings of honoring God in the lives of many. Make sure you read the testimonies featured the back of this book.

I have traveled the world, and it is quite unfortunate what I have seen. Over the last twelve years, I have personally witnessed some of the worst cultural aspects of nations in Europe, third world countries, and America. However, regardless of where I have traveled, most people love and have a desire to be loved. Before I could truly love others and become comfortable in my own skin, I had to experience the love of Jesus. His love is something we should all receive first before attempting to truly love others as Christ intended. In fact, without the Holy Spirit being active in your life, this type of love is unattainable. It goes way beyond natural comprehension. This is Jesus' agape love we are referring to-the love that surpasses all understanding. Having a hard time comprehending a love such as this? Think about the cross. He died to heal our relationship with God, the Father. He stood in our place and bridged the gap between man and God. He bared all of the shame of sin for eternity so that God could look at us as sons and daughters. Peace on earth and goodwill toward men (Luke 2:14) encompasses more than just the holidays.

Let's finish chapter 13…

(8)Love never fails. But where there are prophecies they will cease; where there are tongues they will be stilled; where there is knowledge, it will pass away. (9) For we know in part and we prophesy in part,(10) but when perfection comes, the imperfect disappears. (11) When I was a child, I talked like a child, I thought like a child, I reasoned like a child. When I became a man, I put childish ways behind me. (12) Now we see but a poor reflection as in a mirror; then we shall see face to face. Now I know in part; then I shall know fully, even as I am fully known. (13) And these three remain: faith, hope and love. But the greatest of these is love.

Let's take a closer look at these verses........

Verse eight starts with a promise, that love never fails. Does that mean life works out like a romantic comedy where everyone gets back together in the end? I can tell you first hand that the answer is "no," but, in the end, love remains. When you experience the love of the Holy Spirit, it sheds light and truth on what is good, perfect, and genuine. Verse eleven is very special to me for I had many childish ways to walk away from. Only His mercy and grace gave me the time to turn to Him in order to see the truth. It was God's love that brought me to repentance. God's love shining through others helped then and still helps me every day. Throughout my journey as a minister, I have witnessed miracles of restoration. It began with and it will end with Jesus' undying love for that which He created. It fuels His grace, and it compelled Him to give up His life so that we may truly live.

To understand the context of verse twelve, you must understand that Paul didn't enjoy the same comforts that we do today. Mirrors had poor reflections two thousand years ago, often nothing more than polished metal. Definitely not modern day clean bathroom mirror "selfies". Sometimes the Lord speaks, and we do not quite understand, but one day we will all see Him and talk to Him face to face. My advice is ready yourself. Why? Simply this: Paul is most likely making reference to the return of Jesus Christ. In that time, you must know fully where you stand with Him. In Verse thirteen, Paul again makes it clear that **LOVE** is the most important thing. The veil must be removed from our hearts so that we can truly experience God's love and step into His plan.

Most of us have heard that Jesus commands us to love our neighbors as ourselves, but how do we do that? The verse is found in Matthew 19:19 within the story about the rich young man, and it states, *"honor your father and mother and love your neighbor as yourself."* Upon deeper reflection, we get to the heart of the matter. How can we truly love our neighbor or brother if we do not love ourselves? If you do not have peace in your life, how can you reflect the true love of Christ to others? Discover and receive who you are in Christ! It will help you love, serve, and forgive the people around you. Many people think love comes easy, that it comes and goes, or that it's "all about me." Jesus Christ gave His love for us as a free gift, but Jesus has earned that right. His gift of love for you was bought for with a price. What was the price? It cost Him His life.

"For God so loved the world that he gave his one and only Son, that whoever believes in him shall not perish but have eternal life. For God did not send his Son into the world to condemn the world, but to save the world through him."
-John 3:16-17

In order to increase your understanding of these verses, I recommend that you read all of John Chapter Three. God sent His Son, Jesus, into the world to save it. *"He has come to seek and save that which is lost,"* says Luke 19:10. Jesus states in Mark 2:17, *"On hearing this, Jesus said to them, "It is not the healthy who need a doctor, but the sick. I have not come to call the righteous, but sinners."* When people get plagued by "religious" devils or the enemy gets people to miss the point, things can get ugly. I have even heard people speak the truth but with hurtful intentions, and that is not the love of Jesus. The motivation must be pure and the prompting from the Holy Spirit. I know people who mean well, but they have lost the ability to just simply love others and humble themselves. Jesus is a relational Savior. He died to be our friend and our Father. Jesus loves you. He loves that wayward child. He loves the friends who make light of your situation. He loves the homeless person you see on your way to work in the morning. He loves people of all ethnicities. Can you stand with Him in love for all of those around you without being weird, argumentative, and constantly condemning or judging people? Is my influence used in a selfish, codependent, or self-righteous manner? Is my heart's motivation pure? Have I developed kingdom mindsets in my daily life? My prayer is that we can take on and live in the nature of Christ through the power of the Holy Spirit.

An even deeper question is "Can you even love those who hate you? Few people actually practice this verse, but, like it or not, it is in red letters (Christ's own words); therefore, it deserves our attention. *"But I tell you, "love your enemies and pray for those who persecute you.""*- Matthew 5:44. Jesus commands it. He does not ask. He doesn't say "it would be nice if you did." Think about it! He says to do it! Your first prayers for those who have hurt you may come through gritted teeth. Honestly, I think that is ok. Keep choosing and speaking forgiveness. Pray for those people and release them to God. Keep doing it until all malice is removed from your heart.

Tucked away nearly at the end of the Bible is a small but powerful book called 1 John, and it talks about God's love and much more. An excerpt from it says:

(16) And so we know and rely on the love God has for us. God is love. Whoever lives in love, lives in God, and God in him. (17) In this way, love is made complete among us so that we will have confidence on the day of judgment, because in this world we are like him. (18) There is no fear in love. Perfect love drives out fear because fear has to do with punishment. The one who fears is not made perfect in love. (19)We love because he first loved us. (20) If anyone says, "I love God", yet hates his brother, he is a liar. For anyone who does not love his brother whom he has seen, cannot love whom he has not seen. (21) And He has given us this command: Whoever loves God must also love his brother."
- 1 John 4:16-21

God is love. Get right with Him, and you will not

have to fear judgment. This comes by accepting Christ into your heart and getting to know Him. There is no fear in love; perfect LOVE drives out all fear. The love of Jesus is perfect. He loved us first. These basic but deep truths are worth our meditation. Before you knew who He was, He loved you. When you walked away from Him, He loved you. When you were at your worst, He loved you. No matter where you are now, He loves you. Make amends with those who have hurt you or whom you have hurt. Offer FORGIVENESS, and accept his or her sincere apologies. Be genuine, and give it your most sincere effort for God cannot be mocked or fooled. Love each other; this is how the world will see His light. This is how hearts are softened and people are led to repentance.

Thinking Point: Have I truthfully received Jesus Christ, His love and the power of the Holy Spirit? Perhaps I need to allow, receive and rest in Jesus. Maybe it's time to allow the Holy Spirit to graft God's Word's into my heart so it can become part of me.

In John 14:21-23, there are a series of verses that are hard pills to swallow. They are often quickly glanced at, more often passed over, and lose some readers in the first sentence. Preachers and T.V. evangelists seldom mention them, some pastors may never preach on them, and a handful of preachers use them to slide into an entire works-based doctrine. However, if you are ever to understand love then you must also understand obedience. The amazing part is that really knowing Jesus instills in us a heart that desires to obey Him.

(21)"Whoever has my commands and obeys them, is the one

who loves me. He who loves me will be loved by my Father, and I too will love him and show myself to him."(22) Then Judas (who betrayed Jesus) said, "But, Lord, why do you intend to show yourself to us and not to the world?" (23) Jesus replied, "If anyone loves me he will obey my teaching. My Father will love him, and we will come to him and make our home with him."-**John 14:21-23**

Love is more than just words. It is action. It is dying to self, sacrifice, time, work, forgiveness, listening, mercy, and grace. Loving people can be difficult and downright ugly at times. Real love goes so much deeper than mortal understanding. No one naturally enjoys discipline, submission, or selfless living. There was only one perfect, sinless being. However, obeying Christ' commands and doing the good Christ has put on your heart will set you free. You will be blessed. Condemnation is not from God. Conviction toward righteousness is from God (Holy Spirit). It makes you grow when you follow the driving force that is making you more complete. This comes through the understanding that it is a conviction towards righteousness and not guilt. When you mess up, do not give up, because 1 John 1:9 says, "*If we confess our sin he is faithful and just to forgive our sin and purify us from all unrighteousness.*" Confess to whom? Christ! Why? Jesus is the only one that can purify us from unrighteousness through His blood. The Bible reminds us in Hebrews 9:22, "*Without the shedding blood there is no forgiveness of sins.*" It is only possible through His blood. Jesus is the one true mediator! Jesus was ordained as the one true high priest. His sacrifice on the cross makes us sons and daughters and heirs to the Kingdom of God. We can therefore pray with Godly confidence and assurance.

"14 Therefore, since we have a great high priest who has ascended into heaven, Jesus the Son of God, let us hold firmly to the faith we profess. 15 For we do not have a high priest who is unable to empathize with our weaknesses, but we have one who has been tempted in every way, just as we are—yet he did not sin. 16 Let us then approach God's throne of grace with confidence, so that we may receive mercy and find grace to help us in our time of need."-**Hebrews 4:14-16**

Thinking Point: Jesus' love, blood, and sacrifice will **completely** save us if we choose Him. Not only is He the Lord of your life, He is the High Priest of the new covenant.

22 Because of this oath, Jesus has become the guarantor of a better covenant. 23 Now there have been many of those priests, since death prevented them from continuing in office; 24 but because Jesus lives forever, he has a permanent priesthood. 25 Therefore he is able to save completely[c] those who come to God through him, because he always lives to intercede for them. 26 Such a high priest truly meets our need— one who is holy, blameless, pure, set apart from sinners, exalted above the heavens. 27 Unlike the other high priests, he does not need to offer sacrifices day after day, first for his own sins, and then for the sins of the people. He sacrificed for their sins once for all when he offered himself. 28 For the law appoints as high priests men in all their weakness; but the oath, which came after the law, appointed the Son, who has been made perfect forever."
-Hebrews 7:22-28

Thinking Point: Men, yes, even priests, pastors, and preachers, can, and, sadly often do, fail us, but Jesus will never fail. Do not let the shortcomings of man dictate or dilute the love of the Father. Remember, Paul says follow me as I follow Christ (1 Corinthians 11:1).

Paul's prayer for the Ephesians (church and people) reflects Christ love.

(14) For this reason I kneel before the Father, (15) from whom his whole family in heaven and earth derives its name. (16)I pray that out of his glorious riches he may strengthen you with power through his Spirit in your inner being,(17)so that Christ may dwell in your hearts through faith. And I pray that you being rooted and established in love, (18) may have power, together with all the saints, to grasp, how wide and long and high and deep is the love of Christ, (19) and to know his love which passes all knowledge -that you may be filled to the measure of fullness of God. (20) Now to him who is able to do immeasurably more than we ask or imagine, according to his power that is at work within us, (21) to him be the glory in the church and in Christ Jesus throughout all generations, for ever and ever!- **Ephesians 3:14-21**

Amen. We, the "body of Christ," are supposed to be a family. Modern religion has turned believers against each other. No matter the circumstances or difference in doctrine, we, as believers, should pray for each other. Unplug yourself from these toxic mindsets and walk in a "more excellent way." Find a way to work together for the Kingdom of God, so others may come to know His love! Paul prays that the Holy Spirit may make you strong! Why? So, Christ may live in your hearts! How? Though faith! Where is faith first started and rooted into your being? "In love" so that we may have power to taste (grasp) the love of Christ. The love of Christ runs deeper and truer than anything we could possibly understand in the natural. It is His desire that we may be filled with the fullness of God (the Holy Spirit, His Word, His love). When this happens (verse 20-21), you can and will do more than you ever dreamed! This will be by His power at work within us! Glory to the Church (those who love, worship, understand, and live in Him, and to all generations whom it is our responsibility to teach. Glory to God! This scripture sums it up and remains the bottom line.

"These three remain: faith, hope and love. But the greatest of these is love."-**1 Corinthians 13:13**

CHAPTER 8

MOUNTAINS AND MOLEHILLS

Don't be surprised if you pray to "move this mountain" and someone brings a shovel to your door. It is not God's desire for you to stay where you currently reside. Whether He gives you a teaspoon, a shovel, a pick axe, or a front-end loader, His plan is to help you work **through** your circumstances and situations. It takes faith and perseverance to maintain a walk with Christ. Learn, read out loud, and speak the word and live out your walk with Jesus daily. It is not how much of the Bible you know that matters but rather how much of it you live. Life can be tough, and the devil and his forces do not play fair. Therefore, take in as much of Jesus as you possibly can. When the storm comes, when trouble arises, and when people turn on you, you can have a real underlying peace knowing that God is on the throne. You will have more success when your relationship with Him is firmly established. God wastes nothing. No matter how it seems to us, He will use even the hardest situation for His Glory. Your testimony of pain and struggle may be positioning you to be the comfort to someone else who desperately needs to know that they will make it through. Keep the faith. Jesus mentions in John 14, *"Do not let your hearts be troubled, be not afraid."*

I will admit that sometimes life can feel downright overwhelming. However, life can also be very beautiful when you are looking through the eyes of Jesus. When you truly become serious, the Lord will increase your faith. You will be writing me to share the amazing testimony of your victories or of His unfailing comfort during the battles. Sometimes, He leads us down a path in order for us to learn and grow. Often, but not always, He does take us down the easiest road. Make up your mind today– I will keep the faith! Receive the power of the Holy Spirit, and stop fighting alone (Luke 3:16, Acts 1:8). Jesus says all that we have to do is ask and sincerely mean it. Stop beating yourself up when you fail. Psalms 37: 23-24 says *"The steps of a man are established by the LORD, And He delights in his way. When he falls, he will not be hurled headlong, because the LORD is the One who holds his hand."* He has you by the hand and is determined to not see you fall. You must become determined that you want to see the victory in and with Christ Jesus. Until we, as His church, consistently do our level best in "walking it out," we will never know what God can do through us. By faith, seek Jesus and place your light on the stand. When the victory comes, simply share who He is and what He has done for you.

I am quite certain that you have heard the expression, "Don't make a mountain out of a molehill." In other words, don't make a big problem out of a small inconvenience. On the journey to become Christ-like, the path is known as "the walk." What can be a very easy area of the walk for someone may be extremely difficult for someone else. For example, the person who struggles with lust may not struggle with anger. This principle works the same way with the gifts of the Spirit. The person that leads worship in front of a congregation of hundreds or thousands may not have the desire or feel comfortable teaching a small group Bible study. In the kingdom, we must learn to be willing to do whatever the Lord asks of us. He gave us the authority to be everything for Him, no matter if we feel "comfortable" or not. It is not required that we feel comfortable to receive the deeper things of God; rather that we believe. Stepping out in faith, over the mountains and on top of the molehills, to advance His kingdom is what He created us to achieve. This is always for your good and for His glory.

Our strengths and our weaknesses differ, but we are the "Body of Christ" together. This is why we need each other. We are not here to judge one another or engage in gossip but to encourage and instruct each other in love. What is a mountain for you may be a molehill for someone else. Our struggles and strongholds may differ, but the war is the same. The war against sin, self, complacency, and apathy is very real, as is the war against the enemy. This world can be a cold, harsh, and cruel place. Competition and the darker side of the "American Dream" have produced divorce, insecurity, and insurmountable debt. Many people are so hurt and broken that they don't know who they are anymore, and people that are hurting, hurt other people. Pain and brokenness can breed a vicious cycle.

When I was fifteen, I swore that I would never be like either of my parents. At times, they seemed so serious and unhappy. Both were living apart from each other and without God at that time. When I was in my mid-twenties and battling depression, I saw my reflection in the mirror and realized that I had become the worst of both of them. All of the rebellious and destructive paths I had chosen until then brought me to that single moment in my life. I had not realized, until it was almost too late, what I had become and how ugly my heart was. My heart was broken, diseased, and hardened. If you or someone you know is suffering from negative behaviors or a "toxic mindset," rest assured that it almost always stems from a heart issue. Pain causes us to build walls or to strive to become what we think people want us to be. Pain can also drive us to not care at all and become apathetic (numb) to other people's needs or feelings. Pain can transform you into a living shell, void of any glimmer of hope or ray of light, and, in this darkness, the enemy thrives.

After much procrastination, seeking, and soul-searching, I rededicated my life to Christ as an adult. However, for a year afterwards, I fought that war in my own strength. The enemy constantly told me that the road was too difficult. I was surrounded by negative influences, and I was skeptical of Christian fellowship. One night while visiting a Pentecostal Church, I responded to the altar call segment of the service. The preacher asked that if anyone needed to accept Jesus Christ as their Lord and Savior to come forward. I said to myself, "I am good," because, without a doubt, I had accepted Jesus. Then, the preacher said, "Maybe you are stuck in a rut and can't break free and need power from the Holy Ghost." I can tell you now that it was not in my plan to stand in the front of the church, but it was in God's plan. I found myself at the altar with my head bowed. Many people laid hands on me, prayed over me, and spoke blessings and life into me. This was the only time that I went forward in a church service, other than to accept Christ. I was way out of my comfort zone.

God was positioning   me to change my life during that service, but it took me stepping out in faith and receiving what He wanted to do. When I checked my phone afterwards, I saw that the enemy had already begun his attack against me. Every possible temptation was laid out before me in missed calls and voicemails-drugs, money, women, and partying. The difference now was that I could see how very real the war was for my soul, life and ministry. I did not give in or return calls, but the enemy wasn't done. Minutes later, through my door, a close friend came to my house with more temptation. I said, "Tonight, I am just going to reflect on Jesus Christ and if I am going to be a Christian or just stop talking about it." Otherwise, was I going to put my money where my mouth is or fold my hand. This person respected what I said and left immediately. As soon as my friend left, the Holy Spirit moved on me and ministered to me for three days! I experienced the Holy Spirit, and that changed me forever. The power, revelation, love, wisdom, and peace blasted into me right there in my living room. Instantly, I rose to my feet. I clearly heard God's voice in such an intimate way that it is hard to describe. I know now that what I received was the Baptism of the Holy Spirit and a prophetic call to ministry. Simply put, I received the power to change my life and, the revelation on the importance of sharing Christ became real to me. It was just God and I. My heart was purified. I threw out my vast pornography collection without thinking twice. He spoke to me about joining the church that I was currently attending, joining the Celebrate Recovery Ministry, taking Discipleship Classes, and more! The Lord revealed to me that everything I had stood for was a lie. He showed me what mattered most in life and how to pursue it. James 4:7-8 became real to me *"Submit yourselves, then, to God. Resist the devil, and he will flee from you. 8 Come near to God and he will come near to you. Wash your hands, you sinners, and purify your hearts, you double-minded."*

Before moving on, I would like to expand more on this testimony. I had accepted Jesus as my Savior almost two years prior to that night. To say that I was struggling would be a drastic understatement. I was reading my Bible and sporadically attending church. There is no doubt that I was seeking Him, and I always knew "there had to be more to life than this." At that time, the longest stretch of sobriety that I could achieve in my own power was roughly three months. Considering where I was and what I came from, pushing every extreme the world offered for twelve years (sex, drug dealing, excitement, binge drinking, and addiction), three months was a good start. However, when I would slip and return to my old vices, it was always on a grand scale and in full view of those waiting to see me to fail. Therefore, to some people it "looked like" I was not trying or wasn't serious about my walk, that I was still the same or an even worse person than before. Even with Jesus, I hit personal lows. These lows and the Word that was in me gave me the courage to "step out in faith." After the service that night, the enemy tried to get me to justify calling those women or getting high with my "friends." Thoughts rushed through my head such as "Tonight's just a Wednesday. You can start over on Sunday" and "Don't you deserve one last night of fun before you give all this up?" This was my cycle for the last three years. Understand this: it would have been easy to give in on just a "regular night." I was determined that tonight wasn't going to be a regular night. I just left God's presence. I knew something was happening. I had seven missed calls in two hours on a Wednesday night. Nothing happens on a Wednesday night.

The enemy over played his hand. For the first time in my life, I could see that my friends and acquaintances were being used by the enemy to destroy me. God was stirring in my heart. Armed with that revelation, I did not return any of those calls. Where he overplayed his hand before, he completely revealed his cards when someone came to my house with some free drugs, drugs I really used to like. At that point, I had another very real choice to make. Nancy Reagan and her "Just say no" campaign didn't work for me my entire life, but the Holy Spirit gave me the encouragement to respectfully decline and the power to say: "Tonight, I am just going to reflect on Jesus Christ and if I am going to be a Christian or just stop talking about it." When that person left and the back door of my house closed, my life was changed forever "on a regular night."

My personal mountain was the fear of the unknown and complete surrender to God. What little experience I had of "living for Jesus" came from a traditional and reserved church background. I had not been to church very much when I was younger to instill in me a solid foundation to build on. The reality was that I was way out of my comfort zone. Having been there, this is my advice. Move forward as you are led by the Holy Spirit. Don't let other people push you off of the path of righteousness because they don't understand where you are going. In fact, you may not even fully understand it, but keep walking. More importantly, don't let anyone discourage you from seeking God. Strive to make right choices regardless of emotion. Though the end of the road is the same, everyone's journey is different, and each is a personal, intimate walk with Him.

I challenge you to honestly follow your heart without fear as the Lord leads you. Remember, the enemy will use anything to keep you from coming to Jesus or to separate you from Him. Don't listen to negative "religious people", family members, enemies, or even friends. We all need creditable mentors but we should only follow where God leads us. This is about you and Him! It is possible to do this humbly and respectfully of another's opinion. There is no need to be rude or disrespectful while seeking. The Holy Spirit will guide you, and eventually, you will know in your spirit that you have arrived at a fellowship of believers to call home. Do not be surprised if it takes a bit of time. There is nothing wrong with visiting and seeking out that place. You should pray, seek and ask for God's wisdom through the process.

Worrying about what people think or "people pleasing" is a mountain for some people. While staking your own joy on another's happiness can be detrimental, there is nothing wrong with wanting to get along with others. Paul writes in Romans 12:18, *"If it is possible, as far as it depends on you, live at peace with everyone."* That is no easy task when you stand up for Christ. You can live "at peace" in your own heart even when others are mad or living a discontented existence. When you begin to consistently do the right thing, you will sleep better and hold your head higher. When you change your friends, your life's objectives, and life style, people will talk about it. Let me be perfectly honest: In most cases, it takes time. We don't just wake up holy, much revelation is needed. It is a process of moving from one right decision to another and eventually Glory to Glory. Don't let this discourage you. I am not suggesting that you turn your back on your family and friends. However, we all need support from other believers if we are going to "finish the race well." We should be dedicated to praying for our friends and family who need a deep relationship with Christ. They need people praying for them and inviting them to church. They don't need to see people whining about their problems on Facebook and living lives that are hypocritical of Christ-like character. In fact, you will have difficult days and many challenges, but your changed life will speak louder than any words you will ever say. What I am saying is that you may feel yourself drifting away from those who negatively influenced you before. This doesn't mean that you don't love those people; it means that you are learning to guard your heart. Sometimes, it takes wisdom from God to walk away, heal, and get stronger. Make it a point to follow God's lead, and try not to let anyone drag you onto that broad highway that leads back to a sinful, destructive, or hurtful lifestyle.

FORGIVENESS

Forgiveness is, quite possibly, the biggest mountain of all to overcome. Each week, Sunday School teachers will teach Jesus' words to children yet they, themselves, will not speak to others in the sanctuary because of some past slight or hurt. Many of us have experienced horrible, unfair, or abusive treatment from a parent, spouse, other family member, or someone we love. Others may remember being tormented in high school over something that is still painful. One of my close friends summarized his entire grade school years as "pure hell." Others of us are "hot heads" or competitors, and it may not take much to set us off. No matter who you are, living deep within every person is the need for forgiveness. The longer "un-forgiveness" lingers, the deeper the scar becomes. By not forgiving those who have hurt you and by harboring the resentment it carries, spiritual doors are opened to the enemy to wreak havoc in your life.

Hurt, pain, abuse, grief, insecurity, fear, apathy and

depression are very real in us all. The degree may vary, but we all have hurt others or have had others hurt us. My heart goes out to anyone reading this. I pray these next sections help us all in our understanding of forgiveness. It is an important bridge to freedom. If we are to walk in love, we must learn and practice forgiveness.

Why forgiveness?

Can we afford to forgive the people who hurt us? The question we really should ask ourselves is, "Can we afford not to forgive?" Jesus is very clear on the subject of forgiveness in Luke 6:37-38 when He says, *"Do not judge, and you will not be judged. Do not condemn, and you will not be condemned. Forgive, and you will be forgiven. Give, and it will be given to you. A good measure, pressed down, shaken together and running over, will be poured into your lap. For with the measure you use, it will be measured to you."* Forgive and you will be forgiven, and the measure of forgiveness you demonstrate will be measured toward you. Therefore, it is paramount that we learn to forgive each other with genuine intentions and actively practice forgiveness with others (choose the mindset of Jesus). Forgiveness does not mean that we allow people to walk over us or remain in an abusive situation, but it does mean that we can forgive the wrongs done against us and move on as best as possible. You are of value, and you were bought with a price. It is very possible to both forgive someone yet choose for them not to be a part of your life.

Boundaries and forgiveness

Living for Jesus does not mean that you instantly become a 'people pleaser." There is a real danger in developing overly flexible or overly rigid boundaries. In general, Christians seem to have a hard time defining their personal boundaries. They will either draw a thin line in the sand and retreat when pressured or dig a moat around themselves and become unyielding and judgmental. It is important that we learn the delicate balance between taking responsibility and ownership of our own lives when we fail, yielding gracefully when it's not worth the fight, and preserving the spiritual direction of our own life and choices. It is a daily battle redeeming proper and healthy boundaries. It is possible to set limits and still be a loving person. It is possible to live free of fear, harm, regret, or indecision. I pray that as you grow in spiritual maturity that you will seek more study on this complex subject. Although we don't like to admit it, co-dependency is just as detrimental and nasty as any type of addiction. *Boundaries* by Dr. Henry Cloud and Dr. John Townsend is an excellent choice on this subject.

Pride and Forgiveness

For me, pride is the biggest hindrance in allowing the Holy Spirit to deal with my heart. God is not free to work in us when we build walls and vent horrible things that should never have come from our mouths. Not forgiving one another destroys friendships, relationships, families, and churches. In fact, the energy I spent hating and hurting others launched me into depression. When I approached Jesus for the first time, the roots of my tree were rotting, and the fruit it produced was toxic. My entire house, that which I had based my life on until then, was built in the sand. In Celebrate Recovery, I learned that my "issues" were not the problem. My inner hatred for authority of all kinds and for those that I felt betrayed me and an unforgiving heart were the core issues. Only Jesus, brutal honesty, and support from a strong Christian brother have set me free.

"Father God, we humbly ask now that You prepare our hearts for true forgiveness of ourselves and others. Help us, O Lord, to be honest and real. We need Your power because we cannot do this on our own. Help us to seek out, and to trust and obey whatever You speak to us. Help us take action and move forward. In Jesus' name, Amen."

"See to it that no one misses the grace of God and that no bitter root grows up to cause trouble and defile many."
-Hebrews 12:15

There is a great deal of wisdom in this verse. Preachers are fond of saying "A bitter root equals bitter fruit." That many sound corny, but it is a fact. Hurting people always seem to hurt other people. They may not mean to, but they do, and those that hurt others are both believers in Jesus and non-believers. It may shock some that it makes no difference. People hurt people. Personally, no matter where I tried to run or what scenery I tried to change, sooner or later, my past would catch up with me. It didn't matter if I started new relationships, changed jobs, or moved to a different neighborhood, it always seemed like I was constantly inviting trouble on myself. If I could stay clean from drugs, the enemy would use a woman to bait me into compromise. At the very heart of the matter, I did not feel like I deserved God's blessings because of buried guilt, deep resentment, and pride that seemingly did not want to die.

We cannot just assume that because Jesus is in us that forgiveness will come naturally or easily. His forgiveness of our sins is free; all we have to do is receive that truth. However, we still must choose to forgive ourselves and others. This is the only path to true peace, freedom, and the joy that Christ has for us. We must not allow negative comments or hurtful actions of others to cause us to "take action." It is natural to want to retaliate. As far along in my walk as I have come, I still struggle with this. Sometimes, it is best to walk away. Never fight a battle when the prize won't outweigh the pain. What prize do you win when you get in the last word? The "last word" is usually spoken alone as a damaged relationship walks out the door. Even if you are absolutely "right," it can be communicated in a way that is "dead wrong." Until the root is removed or dealt with, it will continue to infect our lives and cause problems.

Evaluating where you are is mentioned throughout the Bible. Lamentations 3:40 says, *"Let us examine our ways and test them, and let us return to the Lord."* Journaling my spiritual walk helped me to process it all and to be honest with myself. As I was writing, the Lord would reveal more insight or new remembrances of things that I had not completely dealt with. By resurfacing these insights, He reminded me of the things I had yet fully submitted to Him. Sharing my personal inventory with mentors and solid Christian friends was a liberating experience. It removed a tremendous load off my back. This process brought light into those darker areas. The practice of confession is Biblical, and it can be understood further by looking at what James 5:16 promises: *"Therefore, confess your sins to **one another** and pray for each other **so that you may be healed.** The prayer of a righteous person is powerful and effective."* Your accountability partner or mentor should be able to help you work through struggles and not condemn you. Confession is about healing, not about punishment; Jesus paid the full price. The blood of Jesus truly is what makes a man righteous. Choose wisely whom you confide in. As awesome an experience as that was (my liberation of what was weighing me down), we must learn to evaluate ourselves daily.

Assessing the direction of your spiritual walk and honestly evaluating your spiritual intentions is essential for growth in the Lord. Over the past six years, I have done three in-depth inventories of myself to gauge exactly where I am with God and where I am going. I have several well-grounded Christian brothers that I can call for support; they help hold me accountable. Without this kind of support, the "root" just keeps coming back, much like a weed that grows through a crack in a concrete driveway. No matter what hurtful, abusive, or sinful experience you have been through, no matter what you have done, no matter what lies the world or your family has told you, God is bigger. His ways are better, and through the power of the Holy Spirit, in the name of Jesus, forgiveness is a choice. God's way is the only way to freedom and a new life.

It may be a day by day, hour by hour, or even minute by minute choice at first. I encourage you to choose forgiveness today. Don't just cling to the cross and wait for heaven but, rather, pick up your cross and follow Him.

FORGIVING YOURSELF

Despite my past, I was able to grasp the importance of forgiving others rather quickly. The ability to forgive others did not come easy, but, with His help, it did happen. Still today, as with most people, the hardest part is learning to forgive myself. It is difficult to grasp how much Jesus truly loves us. What He did by dying on the cross paid our debt in full. No matter what you have done or what sin you are fighting to overcome, if you abide in Christ and He in you, you are forgiven. He paid the costs. His blood is what makes us pure and righteous. Today, for me, it is more about receiving entirely what Christ has done. That just brings everything full circle in knowing Jesus. Nothing is more important than discovering who you are in Christ, through the Word of God and the Holy Spirit.

We all need to work toward "being holy" in our daily lives. 1 Peter 1:16 says, *"be holy as I am holy."* His blood is what makes us holy. His blood gives the victory in all areas: life, death, sin, salvation, love, holiness and forgiveness. Psalm 103:12 says, *"As far as the East is from the West, so far has He removed our transgressions from us."* That same promise is found in Psalm 103:2-3: *"Praise the Lord, my soul, and forget not all his benefits—who forgives all your sins and heals all your diseases."* The Lord, through the completed work of Jesus, forgives all of our sins. He desires us to live fruitful lives of victory. If you are like me and struggle with forgiving yourself, start meditating on God's love. Say to yourself, out loud, "I am forgiven; my debt is paid, and I thank you Lord, for victory over self-condemnation." Always keep Romans 8:1 in mind, *"There is no condemnation for those of us in Christ Jesus."* Often, we confuse conviction with condemnation. Sometimes my guilt of not acting on my God given, Holy Spirit inspired "convictions" leads me into condemnation. Continued disobedience brings on guilt or layers of denial. This is why we need to trust and obey whatever God tells us. This should be done sooner rather than later. The Lord will not wait. His plans and purpose will be fulfilled.

Although I may never reach perfection, I try very hard to act when God speaks- big or small, difficult or easy. This gives the enemy less fire power against me and less time to develop a strategy. The power of the blood of Jesus and His Word can help us forgive ourselves by letting go of the past. It empowers us to slowly begin to do what God tells us through a trust relationship with Him. This is where true joy, peace, and purpose will be found. Heart-felt convictions are God's messages from His Holy Spirit or His Word to re-direct or discipline our will and heart. Convictions are designed to bring us closer to Him or introduce us to a new level. In order to steal this intimacy, the enemy's response to conviction is condemnation. Condemnation causes feelings of guilt, oppression, or self-defeat. Condemning thoughts are designed to keep us down or in bondage. We must learn to discern or recognize these feelings and to find healthy ways to react and deal with them.

The way we "see it" is often not anywhere close to the way God "sees it." Exercising this fact is a daily battle of allowing God to transform our hearts and minds into His likeness. This is a very real struggle requiring discipline and the determination to find God's promises in the Holy Bible to help us stand on the word. I am continuously learning that when thoughts of self-hate or guilt creep in, it helps to know Scriptures to fight these old tricks that our adversary uses to keep us down. It states in Isaiah 53:5, *"He was pierced for our transgressions* (unchecked fleshly desire)*; he was crushed for our iniquities* (sins and short-comings that you are naturally bent towards)*. The punishment that brought us peace was upon Him and by his wounds we are healed."* By His wounds we are healed! Through what He did on the cross, we are forgiven and healed. We make this much harder to comprehend than it should be. Read this passage, memorize it, post it on your bathroom mirror, your fridge, or in your car, and speak it out loud. "I am forgiven – I am not guilty." Remember Romans 8:1-2 states, *"Therefore, there is no condemnation for those who are in Christ Jesus, because through Christ Jesus, the Spirit of Life set me free from sin and death."*

We may have a long way to go to truly understand or even feel God's forgiveness, but forgiveness comes to us the instant we accept Christ. If we are in Christ and humbly ask for forgiveness, we are forgiven. We may still need to make peace with people- people we have hurt or people that have hurt us. In the next section, we will address these areas. The mountain of truly accepting Christ and His forgiveness is worth the climb. The Holy Ghost may work slowly or cleanse us instantly. Do not give up. Seek His will, and do not be afraid of tears. Do not be afraid of spending some alone time with God. Allow Him time to show you that you really are a new creation. Give yourself an opportunity to heal. Embrace the process, and focus on your relationship with Him. When the enemy, who is defeated, gets you down, then you must claim your promises. Stand in agreement with the word.

From a psychological perspective, we need to forgive ourselves in order to heal; however, it goes much deeper than that. When it comes to having victory over guilt and self-condemnation, it is spiritual matter. Jesus paid the price once and for all so that every true child of God can be made whole. No matter what angle you examine this concept from, it all boils down to one question we each must ask ourselves-"**Is the blood of Jesus enough**?" Yes, my friends, it is all we need.

FORGIVING OTHERS

This subject is "taboo" and difficult to approach because most people do not want to admit that bitterness holds them hostage. In fact, I purposefully did not entitle this chapter "Forgiveness" because I did not want to scare people away. Despite its difficulty, forgiveness is "key" in our walk with Him. One of the main virtues of the person of Christ is forgiveness. Often, the roots of bitterness have taken over the tree and caused our fruit to become bitter. It's easy to "block" events or hurts from our past. If you find yourself thinking about the person who hurt you and what they did, possible revenge or worse, you will catch yourself acting like them. Then, it is safe to say that the issue of forgiveness needs to be addressed.

Despite what you may have heard, time does not heal the pain from old wounds, but the pain may lessen over time. It is often lying right below the surface waiting for the right trigger to reemerge. For me, it took the power from the Holy Spirit to allow me to forgive myself and others who caused me serious hurt. Trust Jesus – He will be with you during this time. He, through His Word and the Holy Spirit, can help us, comfort us, and give us the strength to forgive.

Often, forgiveness is not only for the person whom you hurt or who hurt you, but it is for you as well. When we invite in hate or meditate on our pain, we, in turn, give power to the people who hurt us. In some cases, they may have no idea of the pain they caused us. It is possible that the enemy has blinded them and they do not see or care, or it may have been unintentional. Sometimes the person who hurt us may already be deceased. These cases further affirm that forgiveness is for us. It is a heart issue that we need to put at the feet of Jesus. It would help if you found an accountability partner or prayer partner that has overcome the same hurt, and who is sensitive to the Holy Spirit's guidance. This person should have the wisdom to not allow or encourage you to "sweep these areas under the rug." In other words, they need to be someone you can trust. This person should be a real Christian brother or sister who walks what they talk as best they can. It would be best if men sought men and women sought women; otherwise, problems could arise. This insures emotional compatibility and eliminates any attempt by the enemy to use the situation to his advantage in any capacity.

In order to forgive and make peace with our past hurts, we need people that can pray with us and teach us to pray. The natural demonstration of someone's relationship with Christ should draw us to a deeper level. This type of individual can help you be honest with yourself and with God. Ask Him to help you write down these hurts (address them). You must start praying daily for God's healing power to touch and soften your heart. We must allow God's healing power to work and move in our lives. Jesus promises in John 8:36, "*If the son sets you free, you are free indeed.*" That is what I hope and pray for all reading this – freedom.

Friends, I don't know what you have been through. In fact, in some cases, in my wildest imagination, I couldn't imagine what you have experienced. However, I just ask you to continue to trust God and to seek Him. Jesus knows every tear we have cried and every pain we have endured and "*…He will not leave us nor forsake us*" Deuteronomy 31:6. Follow the direction of the Holy Spirit, and be willing to do whatever it takes. The Celebrate Recovery ministry helped teach me how to forgive myself and others. However, there are some who have said that they feel more comfortable in one-on-one counseling. I encourage you to speak with someone who loves Jesus. I challenge you to seek out and obey the Lord! Matthew 5:21-24 says, "*Therefore, if you are offering your gift at the altar and remember that your brother has something against you, leave your gift there in front of the altar. First, go and be reconciled with your brother; then come and offer your gift.*" Jesus tells us to make peace with our brothers and sisters. Paul states, "*when it is possible, live at peace with everyone.*" (Romans 12:18)

Forgiveness not only heals you, but it also has lasting spiritual benefits such as:
1. Maintains and establishes a healthy prayer life.
2. Gains or establishes healthy relationships.
3. Develops a greater peace in life.
4. Helps to remove "hinderances" during worship.

Please allow me to expand on these benefits.

1) <u>Maintains and establishes a healthy prayer life.</u> Having a healthy prayer life is essential to victory. This is so very important in doing our part and having our prayers reach the throne. When we can make peace with others, it gives us freedom from the enemy and the guilt he attempts to hold over us. The second part of James 5:16 states, "...*The prayer of a righteous man is powerful and effective.*" Yes, our righteousness comes from the blood of Jesus. We all fall far short. However, when we do our part to make peace with others, it allows God to move and use us in special ways.

I don't know where you are with forgiving others. It may be time to address this now, or you may have already started to make these efforts. Continue to pray, asking God to prepare your heart and show you His perfect timing to do so. Paul writes in Ephesians 4:2-3, "*Be completely humbly and gentle; be patient, bearing with one another in love. Make every effort to keep the unity of the Spirit through the bond of peace.*"

(2) <u>Gains or establishes healthy relationships</u>. Jesus calls us to walk in love. 2 John verse 6 says, "*and this is love: that we walk in obedience to his commands. As you have heard from the beginning, his command is that you walk in love.*" 1 Corinthians chapter 13 defines love. Verses 4-7 state, "*Love is patient, love is kind, it does not envy, it does not boast, it is not proud. It is not rude, it is not self-seeking, it is not easily angered, and it keeps no record of wrongs. Love does not delight in evil, but rejoices in truth. It always protects, always trusts, always hopes, and always perseveres.*" The road to forgiveness and perfect love is the lesser traveled path.

Through the power of the Holy Spirit, all things are possible. Let's keep on the narrow road, never quit, and persevere until the end.

Once we have made peace with others, it is still a choice to maintain peace around us. Jesus declares in His sermon on the mount, *"Blessed are the peace makers, for they will be called sons of God."* -Matthew 5:9. It takes an all-out effort in prayer and in our thought life to keep the peace. Of course, we all will have the occasional difficult day. Life is full of difficult days and even difficult seasons. However, we can reset our bad day with prayer or a grown up "time out."

(3) <u>Develops a greater peace in life.</u> Ephesians 4:26-27 is worth meditating on. It will help in all relationships. *"In your anger, do not sin, do not let the sun go down while you are still angry, and do not give the devil a foot-hold."* Before I knew Jesus, I would go to bed and wake up angry. Why? I did not see that there was a choice in the matter. I didn't realize that I accepted anger as a perfectly practical behavior. A dear friend of mine who is a decorated social worker worded this type of behavior as "having fellowship with darkness." This Scripture calls us to walk and live in the light of Jesus. This is a lofty and tall order, with God's power, it is an order worth working toward.

I once had a meeting with "Mr. Fred" from Don Dickerman Ministries. I was sharing some events in my life and my relational struggles before we got down to business. In this discussion, I came to realize that the enemy had been trying to take me out for quite some time. Often, he tries to turn us against each other. He seeks to destroy the church and all relationships that we hold dear. During the course of this process, Mr. Fred's wife came into the room to get some paperwork. When she left, he made a few profound statements. First, he quoted from the Book of Ephesians, and then he looked me directly in the eyes and said, "I love that woman. Through it all, we don't give the devil a place in our bed." He continued by teaching me something about love- to disagree is normal but allowing a wedge to form gives place to the devil. Mr. Fred has experienced much in his life and would be considered a "tough guy." The way he serves God and honors his wife spoke to me in a powerful way. The love and saving grace of Jesus took this once hardened man and shaped him into a well-rounded, Godly disciple of Christ who loves, honors, and cherishes his woman.

Peace and learning to resolve issues early will save us all much heartache and grief in the end. God's wisdom should be applied in all relationships. May the Lord teach us and show us the blessing of keeping the peace and doing our part through the power of the Holy Spirit. In Jesus name. Amen.

(4) <u>To have nothing hinder you during worship.</u> Worship is such a powerful experience. Will the enemy attack you while you are trying to get in the presence of God? You better believe, my friend, he surely will. He will bring accusations, guilt, your sin, your past, the trouble you had in the morning, and virtually anything else to attempt to detach you from the Father. Because the enemy knows, *"The Lord inhabits the praise of Israel (His people)"* Psalm 22:3. This means that when we stand before God, with our hearts right before Him, we worship Him in spirit and truth. The enemy does not want us to enter into or experience God's glory. John 4:23-24 proclaims, *"Yet a time is coming and has now come when the true*

worshipers will worship the Father in spirit and truth, for they are the kind of worshipers the Father seeks. God is spirit, and his worshipers must worship in spirit and truth." True freedom in worship will come when we get our hearts right, let go, and have no concern of what others may think. This will allow the Holy Spirit to touch, move, speak to us, and cleanse us. It allows the anointing to fall and God to have His way. His presence should be our heart's desire regardless of how we feel. The anointing of the Holy Spirit is what changes us and gives us revelation. *"As the deer pants for streams of water, so my soul pants for you, O God."* --Psalm 42:1

MAKING AMENDS

Making amends is an essential part in the forgiveness process. It is one thing to pray about the situation, but it is another to act on a situation. Putting prayer into action can be a difficult thing. Simply taking the step of saying "I forgive this person and will now apologize for 'my part'" may take some encouragement and prior healing. Through prayer, timing, accountability, and honesty, the Lord will show us who we need to be reconciled with and when. Remember, forgiveness and obedience to "my part" is just as much for your healing as it is for that relationship. The freedom you gain is worth the awkwardness or any embarrassment you may feel. All forms of pride must be swallowed in order to nurture a broken relationship and possibly start the road to healing.

In some cases, it may not be possible to ask for forgiveness, such as in the case of losing contact with or the death of someone. It is still possible to go to a special place, a place of meaning, ask God to forgive you, release that person of their hurts, and just speak what you feel you need to say.

This might sound crazy to some people, but until we address the bitter root, our lives will have bitter fruit.

There are also cases where it may not be appropriate, or be more harmful, to ask forgiveness from someone. Situations such as apologizing to an ex-spouse, a boyfriend, or a girlfriend that may have married or long since moved on or apologizing to those who live in a toxic lifestyle could cause more harm than healing and possibly endanger yourself. In some cases, such as an elderly parent, the Lord may want you to leave it alone. Pray and the Holy Spirit will guide you. Analyze your motivations behind the apology. In most cases, the best and most sincere apology is a redeemed and changed life. Do not let fear stop you from pursuing peace. Seek wisdom from other brothers, sisters, and your accountability partner, and receive guidance from the Holy Spirit.

Last but not least, do not justify the actions you are apologizing for. This is not an apology at all! Justification is a veiled accusation while an apology is an acknowledgement. Justification only serves to make **us** feel better or create a vain attempt to make the other person understand our reasoning for our hurtful actions. An example might include, "I am sorry I cheated on you, but you were always working" or "I'm sorry I punched you in the face, but you were getting on my nerves." These are denial-ridden apologies, and they will not produce healing. We don't need understanding; we need forgiveness.

Please understand that the reaction of the person you are asking forgiveness from might not be pleasant. Always remember, it's not for them. It is so you can do "your part" (clean your side of the street) in obeying God by humbly asking for forgiveness. If you are not ready to tell the truth and possibly answer questions honestly and non-defensively, then you are not yet ready. Think about how you would like someone to apologize to you (Luke 6:31). This and prayer will guide you in making true amends to others. Whenever possible, make right whatever wrongs that were done. If money was involved, pay the money back, even if it requires a payment plan. Facing the things we have done, and making peace with people is no easy or fun task. However, prayerfully use wisdom, seek God's sovereign timing, and *"when it is possible, live at peace with each other"* (Romans 12:18).

There are two predominate mindsets to maintain when making amends. 2 John 6, declares *"Walk in love."* and Matthew 7:12 says, *"So, in everything, do unto others what you would have them do unto you, for this sums up the law of the Prophets."* We've all heard that old adage growing up, but these are the words of Jesus. Honestly ask yourself, "How would I expect someone to apologize to me in this situation?" Be prepared to humbly answer questions and share the honest facts of the matter not its reasoning. It's very easy to assume that you understand some of the "basic" teachings of Jesus. Often, the most difficult part may be getting the teaching from your mind into your heart. Hit your knees at any time and humbly ask for revelation and help in any specific area of need. Be mindful that *"God is love."* (1 John 4:16), and He wants us to be free (John 8:36). 1 John 4:18 states, *"There is no fear in love, but perfect love drives out fear, because fear has to do with punishment. The one who fears is not made perfect in love."* Once we can learn to obey God and follow His lead, the rest is up to Him.

Thinking Point: When making amends, always honor and

remember the words of Jesus when He said do unto others as you would have them do unto you. Forgiveness and trust are two totally different things. Restoration was finished on the cross, but, between human beings, it is often a process. A redeemed and changed life is worth more than a million times saying, "I'm sorry."

RECEIVING AN APOLOGY

How to biblically receive an apology is a hugely important topic that seldom, if ever, gets addressed. We all hear about the need to apologize, but how often do we hear about the need to receive one in love? If you are a child of God, then a price has been paid for your life. Your sins are forgiven and then some. We are granted the freedom to live the "blessed life," and it is truly a blessing to walk with Jesus. However, this does not make us exempt from being deeply wounded. Even while walking with God, many of us, at some point, have been seriously burned. It can come from virtually anyone-the people you try to help, your family and even those we love deeply such as a spouse or parent. These events are the things that can make us or break us in life. How we actually deal with them will determine the next course our lives will take. Keep in mind, you are forgiven. How much punishment would we deserve apart from the grace of God?

There may come a time when you are offered an apology-when the person who did you wrong or "smashed your world" may ask you, "Is it possible for you to forgive me?" You will be faced with a dilemma. On one hand, it would be a great opportunity to hound this person and rub your pain in their face wouldn't it? In some cases perhaps, but that's really not why Jesus endured the cross. On the other hand, will you be able to extend the same grace Jesus showed you? Will you extend that same grace, the same unmerited favor, that you were shown on the cross? I am not implying that you forget what was done, but I am implying that you forgive what was done. Remember that forgiveness and trust are two different things. Nor am I encouraging you to return to a toxic or dangerous situation because of an apology. I am simply encouraging you to forgive or gracefully offer the same forgiveness that Jesus gave you.

Let's look at this parable in Matthew 18:22-35.

Jesus answered, "I tell you, not seven times, but seventy-seven times.
23 "Therefore, the kingdom of heaven is like a king who wanted to settle accounts with his servants. 24 As he began the settlement, a man who owed him ten thousand bags of gold was brought to him. 25 Since he was not able to pay, the master ordered that he and his wife and his children and all that he had be sold to repay the debt.
26 "At this the servant fell on his knees before him. 'Be patient with me,' he begged, 'and I will pay back everything.' 27 The servant's master took pity on him, canceled the debt and let him go.
28 "But when that servant went out, he found one of his fellow servants who owed him a hundred silver coins. He grabbed him and began to choke him. 'Pay back what you owe me!' he demanded. 29 "His fellow servant fell to his knees and begged him, 'Be patient with me, and I will pay it back.' 30 "But he refused. Instead, he went off and had the man thrown into prison until he could pay the debt. 31 When the other servants saw what had happened, they were outraged and went and told their master everything that had happened. 32 "Then the

master called the servant in. 'You wicked servant,' he said, 'I canceled all that debt of yours because you begged me to. 33 Shouldn't you have had mercy on your fellow servant just as I had on you?' 34 In anger his master handed him over to the jailers to be tortured, until he should pay back all he owed. 35 "This is how my heavenly Father will treat each of you unless you forgive your brother or sister from your heart."

Let it go, in Jesus' name. Release your offender even if the apology never comes. If it does come, remember this parable and truthfully and from your heart, extend grace.

Will every person approach you with the sincerest of apologies? Unfortunately, no. This is why we must keep in mind Proverbs 4:23, "*Guard your heart, it is the well spring of life.*" Some people may try to manipulate and "pull the wool" over our eyes to "sweep it under the rug." Use discernment. It is wise to be on guard. Always be careful, but do not hold to hate. Forgiveness is given, and trust is earned. Forgiveness frees your heart and makes you open to be used by God. I know this all can be difficult, but it will always be worth it. Jesus has our best interest at heart. He paid the price so we are "not guilty" in the eyes of the Father. So when possible, let's behave like we know and understand that concept. In doing so, we may be freed from our own prison cells and our Heavenly Father may be glorified.

CLOSING REMARKS

We are all God's special creations, uniquely made with different strengths and weaknesses. We all have our own gifts and our own shortcomings. We must strive to make peace with ourselves, the past, and those around us. Learning to walk in love is a daily process, and this process will continue until Jesus returns or calls us home. He is the God of restoration, healing, comfort, peace and salvation. He has given to us all the ministry of reconciliation. None of this is possible in our own strength. We must fully receive Jesus and the power of the Holy Spirit. Let go of the fear of the unknown, pride, religious superiority, or even denominational belief and seek God. Sometimes, I think that we think we know too much for our own good. Alone on my knees and on my face, the Lord has taught me and touched me deeply. Through the laying on of hands and fellowship, I have experienced gifts and healing. If you get nothing else out of this chapter, grab this concept: seek God. Seek and you will find. Knock and the door will be opened, and when it is possible, live at peace with everyone. Allow the Holy Spirit to guide you throughout this difficult process. Let's move forward, facing our fears, one day at a time. In Jesus' name. Amen.

CHAPTER 9

PRAYER

"Prayer is not something you do before service, prayer is service." -- **Adrian Rodgers**

A statement I always seem to hear is "I don't know how to pray." The "religious" community has over complicated prayer to the point of confusion. It doesn't have to be difficult. Prayer is simply "trimming the fat" and being real with God. Speaking the truth, being honest, and sharing your heart and situations with the Almighty are key to your breakthrough. Likewise, prayer is also about listening to His voice. If you have faith that God exists, you will need to start communicating with Him. This is what prayer is all about. Prayer allows us to talk and listen to the Heavenly Father, through Jesus. Jesus gave us a guideline and instructions for prayer in Matthew 6:5-8:

"And when you pray, do not be like the hypocrites, for they love to pray standing in the synagogues and on the street corners to be seen by others. Truly I tell you, they have received their reward in full. 6 But when you pray, go into your room, close the door and pray to your Father, who is unseen. Then your Father, who sees what is done in secret, will reward you. 7 And when you pray, do not keep on babbling like pagans, for they think they will be heard because of their many words. 8 Do not be like them, for your Father knows what you need before you ask him.

Jesus makes it clear that there is no need to be formal or attempt to sound dignified with fancy words. Use your own everyday speech, groans, or prayer language (1 Corinthians 14:4). Talk to Him as you would a dear and trustworthy friend. What matters is that it all comes from the heart-genuine and real. Praying in a group and having others stand with you (agreement) in prayer is also a great way to pray. Matthew 18:20 says *"for where two or three gather in my name, there am I with them."* If that sounds intimidating then listening to or being a part of a group prayer, or prayer at Bible Study, is a good way to learn and become more comfortable. However, it should be known that group prayer is no substitute for talking with Jesus one-on-one. In Matthew 6:6, Jesus encourages the believer to go in one's room (a place of seclusion) and pray in private. Jesus desires us to spend time with Him. Many people refer to this place as a "prayer closet." The place can be different for each of us. I have a few places I retreat to for serious times of prayer. There are also some other select places I may go in times of warfare or intercession. My regular spot is on my knees in front of my bed, bath tub, or in my office.

When I was going to college and working as the custodian of my mother's church, my regular spot was inside the sanctuary when no one else was around. Scripture records that Jesus also spent time alone and away from others in prayer. Jesus walked this earth in human flesh. Therefore, He knows what it feels like to be tired, "wore out", lonely, disappointed and frustrated. If Jesus, himself, needed alone time with the Father, how much more do we need that time? Examine Jesus' approach to prayer in a few scriptures from Luke:

"Early the next morning Jesus went out to an isolated place..."-**Luke 4:42**

"But Jesus often withdrew to lonely places and prayed."-**Luke 5:16**

"One of those days Jesus went out to a mountainside to pray, and spent the night praying to God."-**Luke 6:12**

HONOR YOUR TIME WITH GOD

In today's fast-paced world, it is difficult to slow down. It can be even more challenging for those nurturing a family, working overtime to make ends meet, or involved in extra activities (including ministry). As difficult as this can be, slowing down long enough to honor your time with the Father is the most important part of growth and establishing a healthy relationship with Christ. This time can be spent in various ways: studying the Word; reading a devotional; attending Discipleship (Equip Class) or Celebrate Recovery classes; praying (for yourself and others); surrendering, praising, and fellowshipping with the Holy Spirit; allowing time to listen to the voice of God; accessing your feelings and emotions (making them submit to Jesus), meditating, and, finally, just clearing your head from the troubles of the day. The Lord will bless, grow and teach you through the time you spend with Him. Psalm 46:10 says, *"Be still and know that I am God; I will be exalted among the nations, I will be exalted in the earth"*.

The enemy has many tactics to attack us such as confusion, busyness, lust, anger, addiction, and denial to name a few. He knows that if he can keep you away from the Word and the fellowship (between you and Jesus and you and other believers) that he will drain you, and a drained person makes an easy target. This is why we need the guidance of the Word, strength of the Spirit, and accountability and support of fellowship. The Word of God can hold you accountable; it is not crafty, new age thinking or a trendy self-help book. The Holy Spirt speaks to us through God's Word and brings the conviction towards righteousness or Godly character.   Self-help books and secular humanist jargon will not mention sin nor do they have the ability to judge the attitudes of the heart. Moreover, secular humanism, by nature, can only address issues of the soul (mind, will, and emotions) rather those of the Spirit. Many of these books will encourage selfish behavior and feeling "good" about it. I am not suggesting that one cannot learn anything from this style or genre of book. I am simply issuing a warning-it is easy to be led astray by what your flesh wants to hear. Many times, we keep seeking books or songs that come into agreement with our emotions or desires. Have you ever heard "I went to a therapist once. They didn't help me at all?" or, better yet, "I love this song. It's exactly how I feel." A selfish spirit seeks **unhealthy** agreement; a godly spirit seeks submission and truth.   Instead of making our emotions and short term wants to submit to Christ (2 Corinthians 10:5), we seek instant gratification of "understanding."   Here is the difference between the Word of God and everything else. Hebrews 4:12-13 says *"For the word of God is alive and active. Sharper than any double-edged sword, it penetrates even to dividing soul and spirit, joints and marrow; it judges the thoughts and attitudes of the heart. Nothing in all creation is hidden from God's sight. Everything is uncovered and laid bare before the eyes of him to whom we must give account."*

Praying and the reading (study) of the Word is of utmost importance. This will always help and guide us on our journey. Likewise, there is also the importance of the need to be humble. The Lord wants us to be dependent on Him. He also wants us to be connected to a body of believers (community). Take your time, and let the Holy Spirit guide you. There are lots of dangers in rushing into anything. When you become serious, the Lord will shepherd you out of your comfort zone. The bottom line is this:

We need each other and the community or fellowship of God's people.

"Let us not giving up meeting together, as some are in the habit of doing, but encouraging one another—and all the more as you see the Day approaching."- **Hebrews 10:25**

BENEFITS OF "QUIET TIME" WITH THE FATHER

1) <u>To know Christ on a personal level</u> and to strengthen the relationship to a more intimate and meaningful level. This also allows us to feel more comfortable reading the Word, praying, listening, worshiping etc. This is a good time to use your prayer language to edify (literally translated as to build a temple) yourself and gain strength. Let the Lord guide you during these moments, windows of time in which should be routinely set into our daily lives.

2) <u>To seek direction and guidance.</u> We all need direction in every area of our lives. Family, relationships, business, work, scheduling, hobbies and past times, our calling or "ministries," using our gifts, and our involvement in service to Jesus all require the need for establishing healthy boundaries. Without them, we would easily become frazzled and overwhelmed.

3) <u>To bring our needs and the needs of others before God.</u> It is ok to unselfishly pray for yourself; Jesus did. It is important to pray for everyone in your life. It is also important to pray for your small group, your family, the church you're involved with, your community, and your nation. We need to band together in prayer because it is an all-out war, and real, honest, humble, firm, and Spirit-filled prayer is the most powerful weapon against the enemy's attacks or grip!

4) <u>To bear fruit and get stronger!</u> Jesus wants your healing and walk with Him "to last." He wants our lives to be strong as the tree mentioned in Psalm 1. He wants our houses built on the rock that is our Lord (Psalm 127:1 and Matthew 7:24-27). As we get stronger, our lives will change and produce positive things like healing, healthy relationships, sobriety, maturity, peace, wisdom, forgiveness, and more good fruit.

5) <u>To give thanks!</u> The Bible says be thankful always (1 Thessalonians 5:18) and count your blessings because you have Jesus! Likewise, the Bible says to enter His courts with thanksgiving and with praise (Psalm 100). We have so much to be thankful for if we only open our eyes wide enough to see.

6) <u>To stay the course.</u> Don't wait until the train is off the tracks to seriously and lovingly talk to Jesus. Relapse, backsliding, or digression can happen apart from addiction. Turning back to your old ways or selfish behavior is always dangerous and unfruitful. Adding depth to your relationship with the Lord is always a good thing. God already knows what's on your heart; therefore, when we talk to Jesus, there is no need for carrying on, "lip service," or trying to sound dignified.

There is nothing wrong with spending as much time as needed in prayer. We should pray until the Holy Spirit releases us or until the time we have allotted Him has expired. I genuinely feel that Jesus wants us to talk to Him from our heart. He takes no pleasure in "babbling" words (false piety like the Pharisees) or beating around the bush.

In today's world, many people are extremely busy, and I understand that completely. However, I have learned the hard way that everything is more fluid once I put Jesus on the throne. For me, I must start the day in prayer. I spend a little time in His Word and pray for His help, wisdom, and strength to guide and use me that day. The discipline of prayer and Bible study will change your life through the power of the Holy Spirit! There is nothing easy about forming these new habits. The blessing of having a set time to spend with God develops a greater fellowship with Him and increases knowledge of His will for your life. This will do you no good if you do not act upon it. Jesus is a friend as well as a Savior, and we should naturally get in the habit of spending time with Him.

My grandmother (Granny) taught me the Lord's Prayer when I was very young. I am thankful for this experience. There have been many times when I have prayed this prayer, but I never learned about freely talking to God until later on in life. The Lord's Prayer is our guideline for prayer. When prayed from the heart with a full understanding of what each line means, it is very powerful.

Look at **Matthew 6:9-13**:

9 *"This, then, is how you should pray: " 'Our Father who art*

in heaven, hallowed be your name, 10 your kingdom come, your will be done, on earth as it is in heaven. 11 Give us today our daily bread. 12 And forgive us our debts, as we also have forgiven our debtors. 13 And lead us not into temptation, but deliver us from the evil one.

Jesus begins praying by openly acknowledging the Father in heaven and giving Him all of the honor. He is acknowledging not only His Father but also the **name** of His father as "hallowed" which means "sanctified," above all, and set apart. He further glorifies the Father by calling all things His-your kingdom, your will. Verse 10 says to give us today our "daily bread." This means to give us what we need today in every aspect-to be freely given all the strength, forgiveness, providence, blessings, compassion, etc. that will be needed for the day. It also means to give us as much of "You" as we need. Jesus referred to Himself as the "bread of life" (John 6:35) and the Living Water (John 14:13-14). Jesus is the source of real life and everything good associated with it. In Verse 12, He reiterates the importance of the need for daily forgiveness and the ability to forgive others. Finally, in Verse 13, Jesus asks that the Father lead us not into temptation and protect us from the evil one. This is our guideline for prayer. It is five simple steps-praising, acknowledging, asking, forgiving, and guidance/protection. He is not suggesting that this is the only prayer to pray. There are many different and specific situations in life in which we need to be equipped to pray about. Whether it is for our own daily lives and needs or the lives and needs of others (supplication), we should bring them before the Lord in the same manner as Jesus did.

KING DAVID

Within the Scriptures, it is hard to find a more perfect example of being honest and real with God than you will find with King David. Apart from Jesus praying, "Let this cup pass from me, but let your will be done" (Matthew 26:39), David is a prime picture of openness with the Lord in Psalm 51. If you are not familiar with it, allow me to set the stage. David, the seemingly insignificant shepherd boy chosen by God to be king and the anointed man of valor of Israel, had completely blown it. We find him at his lowest point, having recently staged the murder of his loyal general, committed adultery, and lost a child conceived through those actions (2 Samuel 12). Though David wrote many of the Psalms, the depth and power of Psalm 51 makes it stand out amongst the others. Through its verses, he is truly repenting with his whole heart. The passion God instilled in him for battle and creativity is now used to repent and turn from his ways. Many of us cannot relate to being king. However, many of us can relate to "blowing it."

<u>Thinking Point</u>: You may reach people with your gifts and strengths, but you will only relate to and build intimacy in relationships through your weakness (or vulnerabilities).

As the Psalm progresses, we get to a few of my favorite verses in the Holy Bible.

"Create in me a pure heart, O God,
and renew a steadfast spirit within me.
Do not cast me from your presence
or take your Holy Spirit from me.

Restore to me the joy of your salvation
and grant me a willing spirit, to sustain me."
-Psalm 51:10-12

King David expressed himself in prayer and song. He was a man after God's own heart. He made mistakes like everybody else does. In this Psalm, he did what we must all learn to do-humbly repent before our Father in heaven, and this is usually done through prayer. Once we can learn to become open, honest, and real with God, healing and restoration is possible. Without being real with Jesus, we can never truly have blessed relationships with others.

WARFARE

Prayer is the most important and powerful weapon in our Christian lives. Spiritual warfare is very real. If you believe in heaven, then you must also believe in the alternative– hell. Therefore, to believe in angels, means that demons are very real as well. Everyone has areas in which they are strong and in which they are weak. Often, the main thing to be considered is "who is the boss of your life?" In Christian lingo, this would be referred to as lordship. Time must be spent in prayer seeking what areas in your life serve as "open doors" for the enemy to attack. Once they are defined, the intricate process of obedience must take place to close the doors and kick the "pigs" or unclean spirits out. How does this happen? The victory, power and authority are given to the believer "in the name of Jesus."

There are many things going on around us in the spiritual realm that we do not see with our human eyes. Your situation, spouse, family, co-worker, boss, or friend is not your enemy. They can be the physical manifestation of the battle happening spiritually. *"For our struggle is not against flesh and blood, but against the rulers, the authorities, the powers of this dark world, and against the spiritual forces of evil in the heavenly realms"* –**Ephesians 6:12**. There isn't a physical battle happening on Earth that isn't also happening in the spirit. There is more going on than meets the eye. Prayer is the equivalent of a blanket of arrows darkening the sky, a cannon booming in the distance, a left hook from Julio Caesar Chavez, or a jab from Muhammed Ali.

The devil, his demons, and this world have taught us that sin is a normal way of life. This mind-set has turned most western societies into self-seeking, selfish, and desensitized versions of Babylonia. It's all about me and what I want. People are more interested in Podcasts, blogs, and looking good than actually serving the Lord Jesus Christ. <u>If the enemy cannot get you to buy straight into the pleasure of sin, he is content with "watering down" the "all-in" message Jesus delivered.</u> The main way he will attack us is in our minds. He plants seeds of destruction and fear in attempts to lead us astray. The enemy will do anything possible to get us to take the "bait." Fortunate for us that, *"Greater is He who lives in me than he who lives in the world"* (1 John 4:4).

In today's world, it can be a struggle to walk upright and with integrity. How is it possible to walk unyielding in times like these? *"How can a young man keep his way pure? By living according to your word,"* says Psalms 119:9. We must learn to meditate on the Word and "soak" in the presence of the Father. Prayer is essential in our daily struggle against the enemy and self-will. This works to help us grasp constant fellowship with God. Simply put, this is to pray without ceasing. Faith is needed to receive Jesus' finished work on the cross. His Word is the way and the truth. The Word of God helps us to see the truth, and it gives us power so that we can put on the Armor of God. It is like a Panzer Tank cresting the horizon against an army of swords and shields. The enemy hates a true Christian warrior.

THE ARMOR OF GOD

"Therefore put on the full armor of God, so that when the day of evil comes, you may be able to stand your ground, and after you have done everything, to stand. 14 Stand firm then, with the belt of truth buckled around your waist, with the breastplate of righteousness in place, 15 and with your feet fitted with the readiness that comes from the gospel of peace. 16 In addition to all this, take up the shield of faith, with which you can extinguish all the flaming arrows of the evil one. 17 Take the helmet of salvation and the sword of the Spirit, which is the word of God. 18 And pray in the Spirit on all occasions with all kinds of prayers and requests. With this in mind, be alert and always keep on praying for all the saints. 19 Pray also for me, that whenever I open my mouth, words may be given me so that I will fearlessly make known the mystery of the gospel."-**Ephesians 6:13-18**

Many books have been written about the "Armor of God." I have heard several sermons that go into great detail and some that only scratch the surface. Each piece of armor plays an intricate part in every believer's walk with Jesus. I suggest that you dedicate some study time to furthering your knowledge of the armor, and let the Holy Spirit show you more truth about wearing it. He will give us all wisdom if we humbly ask. It is most beneficial to do a verse-by-verse breakdown on each piece. The armor represents truthfully knowing who you are in Christ. Paul used this analogy because he knew his audience could relate to it. Perhaps, you already know about the armor and have been walking with Christ for years. Maybe, you just read that for the first time? Sometimes, we get into trouble because we think that we know so much about life or the Word of God. In reality, there is always more-a deeper level in our love and in our walk with Jesus.

Keeping in mind that Jesus is the foundation of our faith, Colossians 2:6-7 says, *"So then, just as you received Christ Jesus as Lord, continue to live your lives in Him, rooted and built up in Him, strengthened in the faith as you were taught, and overflowing with thankfulness."* If you are rooted in Christ, you are rooted in love. If you walk in faith, believing God only wants the best for you, it becomes difficult for the enemy to steal your joy. The major tactic that has been used against me is to tempt me to focus on "what is not good" or "what it looks like." That's where the warfare begins. I encourage you to not take the bait. Find things in which to be thankful! Focus on God's Word or on the direct promises He has spoken or shown you. Stay rooted in Him as Jesus describes in John 15. The walk is a renewing, rejuvenating, and rejoicing process. Out with the old and in with the new (Colossians 3:9-10). Herein lie the keys to not becoming a cold-hearted soldier for Christ. It will also keep you from becoming self-righteous and unfruitful in your life.

THE UNDER ARMOR OF GOD

What I am about to share is something Jesus taught and is still teaching me now. It is a concept that I call the "Under-Armor of God." Paul makes it clear that first we must focus on God and allow Jesus to remove (take off, put to death) toxic mindsets. This will then allow us to successfully put on the Under Armor-the humility of Christ.

"Therefore, as God's chosen people, holy and dearly loved, clothe yourselves with compassion, kindness, humility, gentleness and patience. Bear with each other and forgive one another if any of you have a grievance against someone. Forgive as the Lord forgave you. And over all these virtues put on love, which binds them all together in perfect unity."-**Colossians 3:12-14 (NIV)**

In the King James, it reads as:

"Put on therefore, as the elect of God, holy and beloved, bowels of mercies, kindness, humbleness of mind, meekness, long-suffering; forbearing one another, and forgiving one another, if any man have a quarrel against any: even as Christ forgave you, so also do ye. And above all these things put on charity, which is the bond of perfectness. -**Colossians 3:12-14 (KJV)**

This is where it gets deep. The world and many believers, still today, miss the point. In a paper I once wrote for college, I used the expression "people are no longer willing to **die to self**." The professor put an arrow and a question mark in the margin. Why? Because she, an esteemed literary professor, did not get it either. To die to self means to kill your emotions. In a broader sense, it means making your agenda submit to Christ. The religious terminology would be to "crucify your flesh" or come to the revelation that your flesh is already dead. Jesus did not want to go to the cross, but he did it anyway. Long before He was crucified on a cross, He had crucified His flesh. Paul writes in Philippians 3:10, "*I want to know Christ—yes, to know the power of his resurrection and participation in his sufferings, becoming like him in his death...*" In 2 Corinthians Chapter 6, He also explains the trials in ministry. Everyone who is truly "called" to ministry or to accomplish great things for the Lord should learn to meditate on those verses from Philippians 3:7-14 and II Corinthians 6: 3-13. Life, itself, will not be a cakewalk. Can you still love others and serve when totally betrayed? Can you forgive the gossip, lies, and rumors told about you when you aren't around? What happens when jealousy starts to poison your soul? Is it possible to forgive affairs, foul business deals, disrespect, abuse and other atrocities? Oh, but that burning desire to "set the record straight" we seem to covet so much. The need to defend against the twisted lies of the enemy or retaliate against any abuse burns deep. How much deeper does it burn if you, in fact, have done nothing wrong?

It can strike your heart like a cat of nine tails. For me, personally, there are times that it shakes the foundation of everything I believe for a moment. It reduces pride into pebbles. Paul says, "We are to put no confidence in the flesh/self (Philippians 3:3)." If you're not paying attention, these battles can destroy your sense of self-worth. This happens quickly when we take these spiritual attacks personally. Once this happens, one begins to embrace the lies of the enemy, thus adapting toxic behavior and mindsets as coping mechanisms.

We are not called to be doormats. If I ever get another tattoo, it will not be the word "welcome" on my forehead. However, there remains a fine line between spiritless and Spirit filled, between fainthearted and full of heart. Look to the Under-Armor of God to define your daily attitude and mentality of Jesus.

Love is the polar reaction, not the natural response. In other words, it is normal to desire to retaliate or at least to return the same attitude we are given. The gene pool from my family on both sides naturally takes "crap" from no one. Being "raised up" in the south, we do not take kindly to disrespect, cheating, lying, and the like. Adding to the cultural response, the environments and people that I let influence me during the twelve plus years that I was "out there," all play a factor in my natural response mechanism. When you combine everything in the pot, what I learned was the response of speaking my mind, retaliating, or patiently waiting for revenge. When I hear people talk about an incident on the news say, "How could they do that?" I often think to myself, "Buy me a cup of coffee and I will explain." The reality remains: None of these reactions ever helped me in life.

This is what you must ask yourself, "Is the blood of Jesus enough?" Will I choose to "put on" or "clothe" myself with the Holy Spirit's love (see the above Colossians verses)? Keep in mind that Paul encourages us to take off the toxic mindsets and consciously remove the garbage. This makes room to be able to receive the true Under Armor of God. If it is "no longer you who lives but Christ in you (Galatians 2:20)," then gradually or immediately you should reflect His character. For me, the realization of this spiritual and mental warfare had me on my face in tears. When it happened, I had never felt so weak, shattered, or alone. From engrained natural emotions and the enemy's whirlwind of lies, I honestly felt like I was a coward. The struggle was "on" inside me to retaliate or defend myself. The above burn I explained to "do something" was very real. However, what I was feeling was my flesh (self-will) dying. This was and still is an ongoing process. While at that breaking point, or crossroads, I chose Jesus, by faith, and then slowly became stronger. The irony of it all is that I wasted much of my life fighting my own battles. Now, I am learning to truthfully let the Lord fight my battles for me. Many of my character defects, such as ego and pride, were drastically dealt with. Through these trials and tribulations, my relationship with the Lord has never been stronger. The clean anointing and the richest fruit are often produced by people who can handle the crushing process. Lean into Jesus during difficult seasons, He wants us to trust Him.

Thinking point: Could it possibly be that through attacks the enemy uses to "take us out" that Jesus is just refining us into His image? Can you keep going in life and ministry when the cards are against you and all hope seems lost? Everyone who is serious about their relationship with Jesus should ponder those questions and ask the Lord to show you the truth.

We must choose daily to arm ourselves for the very real battles happening around us and for us. The enemy may be unable to drive you to commit a hostile crime, but he may get you to flirt with a co-worker when your relationship is in trouble or receive the like. Maybe your husband is giving you the silent treatment, but an ex just so happens to text or Facebook message you when your guard is down. These types of events and situations are traps. Satan is crafty and does not play fair. He knows each person's shortcomings and weaknesses, and he will try to expose us or set us up to make it look like we are not trying at all.

The good news is that the Holy Spirit will show you truth and will empower you to do the right thing more and more after you learn to trust Him. God will bless you abundantly as you trust and get to know Him. Jesus says in John 14:21, *"Whoever has my commands and obeys them, he is the one who loves me. He who loves me will be loved by my Father, and I too will love him and show myself to him."*

The more faith, prayer, obedience, and reading of the Word that you employ, the less power the enemy will have over you. Your relationship with Jesus will be grow stronger through your delighting in the Lord (Psalm 37:4). The struggle is real, and we need each other for honest accountability and support. There is no successful "lone warrior" style of Christian. Even the Lone Ranger had Tonto. Jesus assures us that, *"… truly I tell you that if two of you on earth agree about anything they ask for, it will be done for them by my Father in heaven. For where two or three gather in my name, there am I with them."* – Matthew 18:19-20. What an awesome promise that our Lord hears us, and the Holy Spirit will join us. Jesus also declares in John 15:7-8 that, *"If you remain in me and my words remain in you, ask whatever you wish, and it will be done for you. This is to my Father's glory, that you bear much fruit, showing yourselves to be my disciples."* Jesus is simply saying that in order to have this type of power in prayer we must remain in Him. We must get in tune and allow Him to change the "dial" of our lives.

The apostle Paul was a soldier for Jesus, yet he humbly asked for prayer. Ephesians 6:18-20 says, *"18 And pray in the Spirit on all occasions with all kinds of prayers and requests. With this in mind, be alert and always keep on praying for all the Lord's people. 19 Pray also for me, that whenever I speak, words may be given me so that I will fearlessly make known the mystery of the gospel, 20 for which I am an ambassador in chains. Pray that I may declare it fearlessly, as I should."* He encourages us to always pray for God's people, and he then asks or declares others to "Pray for me also." I have heard many people say, "I don't pray for myself," or "I don't request prayer for myself because God knows my needs." Yes, the Lord knows everything. However, He wants us to know that we need Him. He desires us to admit our needs and true helplessness without Him. We need to allow the Father to love us and stop running from His touches, advances, and presence. Many people start to feel God's love or presence and become uncomfortable or even afraid of Him when He draws near. Prayer makes way for our own personal encounters with Jesus, and it may also make way for others.

We all need people praying for us. If your request is too personal for a group setting, you can voice it by saying "unspoken" or request a more private location afterwards with someone you can trust. Never let pride, guilt, or fear keep you from asking for prayer. Jesus prayed for Himself in John Chapter 17. Paul asked for prayer on multiple occasions, and let's not forget the prayer of Jabez in 1 Chronicles 4:10. How much more do you think we need to be praying and humbly asking for prayer? When will the body of Christ begin to understand that praying for yourself is not selfish? If you aren't asking then who is? Do we really want to live life being blessed piecemeal by another person's request? Praying for God's favor, blessing and anointing on your life are essential in a true life of victory!

Prayer is also important for one to remain centered. The narrow path (Matthew 5) is very easy to exit. The wide path that leads to destruction pulls on us all. We need to maintain a discipline of praying continually. It is best to always be communicating with and listening to God. Do not just pray for the hurting and broken. Paul writes to the Colossians and lets them know that "I hear God is at work in your lives. I am praying for you."

Examine the Scripture in Colossians 1:3-14:

"We always thank God, the Father of our Lord Jesus Christ, when we pray for you, because we have heard of your faith in Christ Jesus and of the love you have for all God's people— the faith and love that spring from the hope stored up for you in heaven and about which you have already heard in the true message of the gospel that has come to you. In the same way, the gospel is bearing fruit and growing throughout the whole world—just as it has been doing among you since the day you heard it and truly understood God's grace. You learned it from Epaphras, our dear fellow servant, who is a faithful minister of Christ on our behalf, and who also told us of your love in the Spirit. For this reason, since the day we heard about you, we have not stopped praying for you. We continually ask God to fill you with the knowledge of his will through all the wisdom and understanding that the Spirit gives, so that you may live a life worthy of the Lord and please him in every way: bearing fruit in every good work, growing in the knowledge of God, being strengthened with all power according to his glorious might so that you may have great endurance and patience, and giving joyful thanks to the Father, who has qual-

ified you to share in the inheritance of his holy people in the kingdom of light. For he has rescued us from the dominion of darkness and brought us into the kingdom of the Son he loves, in whom we have redemption, the forgiveness of sins."

These passages show me that we also need to be praying for the people and areas where God is working. Furthermore, we need to pray for our leaders, mentors, and spiritual friends. The more you are doing for the Kingdom of God, the more likely you will come under attack from the enemy. Ask God to bless the people who care about you enough to call out your name before the Most High God. The victory is in Jesus. **Lasting victory and true peace will come when we can just accept that spiritual warfare is a way of life.** The more you understand your position, whom your advocate really is and how much He cares for you, overcoming will become normal. You will receive that being "more than a conqueror" is possible (Romans 8:37). Adding depth to our prayer life helps us discover who we really are in Christ.

Lastly, always give thanks for prayers on your behalf. Paul writes in
2 Corinthians 1:10-11:

"10 He has delivered us from such a deadly peril, and he will deliver us again. On him we have set our hope that he will continue to deliver us, 11 as you help us by your prayers. Then many will give thanks on our behalf for the gracious favor granted us in answer to the prayers of many." Paul gave thanks for prayers which helped grant him favor. We need God's favor in our daily life and ministry. Let us always be thankful that Jesus hears our prayers. Praise the Lord for the people who have been praying for us.

THE POWER OF INTERCESSION

TESTIMONIES

A Struggling Friend

I was once in a situation in which I was being misled by a friend who was struggling. I had every justifiable reason to be angry. I was working alone and pondering the situation. Because it was difficult for me to pray, I grabbed a Bible and read Psalm 23 out loud. The Lord began to soften my heart and stir something in the spirit realm. As I returned home, I ran into my cousin walking her dog. She asked me how I was doing, and I replied, "Not good." She gave her dogs to her fiancée and came inside to talk. At first, we started to vent about the entire situation (the human response), but then the Holy Spirit prompted us to pray (stand in the gap) for the person who was struggling (the spiritual response). We had no idea what was truly going on with this person. In that moment, we chose love over hate, anger, or resentment, and we elected to pray for the person who had been misleading us.

What we could not know was that the person we were praying for would be in a horrible car wreck later that night. Returning from the bar, this person fell asleep at the wheel and crashed into a rock-solid street light. The car was totaled. However, the person we had prayed for had only a bruise on the forehead. Had we fed our emotions or anger, we most likely would never have prayed. Could it simply be that by our choice to pray for guidance, protection, and strength, this person wasn't totally alone that night? The enemy loves to turn us against each other so that we won't speak to let alone pray for one another. These moments have nothing to do with pride, boundaries, hurt, or, even emotions. Rather, they become matters of obedience. When the Lord prompts you to pray: do it! Sometimes we have to grow up and pray for people no matter how we feel.

"Cousin Joe"

Today, my cousin Joe is a "stand up" guy in Christ Jesus. He is a missionary, servant, prayer warrior, Bible teacher, preacher, deliverance minister, church planter, friend, and husband. I consider him a mentor and trail blazer. He is one of the few people on this earth that I completely trust. Period. The Lord molded him into a real, well rounded "Man of God." However, in his young adult life, he struggled with hard drugs, including speed in all forms. He was an iron worker, which means it was normal for him to work "in the air" or in dangerous environments. It is easy to work under the influence or still "feeling it" when that is the life you lead. Consequently, it would blow most people's minds if they knew how many people perform dangerous jobs while using or "struggling" with abuse. Sooner or later, it catches up with most people.

One day, Joe's mother was compelled to cry out to Jesus on her son's behalf. She knew her son's struggles, but it was more than just a general prayer for his well-being. She only knew that now was the time to pray, and, in this instance, it was spiritual warfare. What she could not know was that Joe had fallen and landed on a beam. He could have easily fallen to his death or became crippled for the rest of his life.

Instead, that event was one of the markers that helped him to steady his course with Jesus. His mother's prayers helped save his life. The enemy tried to take Joe out so that he would not fulfill his calling. Had he succeeded, I could have never written nor would he have deserved such a lofty introduction because he would have never had the opportunity to accomplish or experience all he has for the cross. Thank God for his mother's obedience to pray exactly when the Holy Spirit prompted her.

"Aunt Beverly"

I have already mentioned several times of how wild and reckless I lived for twelve years. We all believed in God, but our family did not have a strong foundation. Aunt Beverly is a devout Catholic woman. She loves Jesus, and she has been steady through the years while we were not. During a number of our gatherings for the holidays, my dad and I were guilty of excessively "enjoying ourselves." My dad rarely drove after these occasions (being truly "full of holiday cheer"), but I can admit that on several instances I drove even when I shouldn't have. Often, when talking about grace, we like to say, "I don't know how I made it home." A few years ago, in casual conversation, Aunt Beverly made a profound statement. She said, "Ya'll made me so nervous that when you would leave, I would go pray for ya'll for thirty minutes." I couldn't help thinking to myself, "Wow, that's how we made it home." While I drove home from that visit with my aunt, tears filled my eyes. That is grace, mercy, and love in action. She was faithfully talking to Jesus, when we were still lost. Today, she has been married to my Uncle Garry for thirty-eight years, and their two daughters serve Jesus. The

Almighty now has a strong presence in our family where before there was little.

Restoration Happens

As a Layman and Pastor, I have been doing the work of the ministry or sharing the love of Christ since 2005. The Lord will put people on my heart or reveal a burden of prayer. Over time, I have learned to move in the direction when the Lord asks, reveals, or speaks something to me. Every time that He reveals something to me or "squeezes me," I know the next action is prayer. There are a handful of families that I have been periodically interceding on behalf of for the past ten years. It is easy to become discouraged when you do not see breakthrough, fruit, or even forward motion in the lives of those in which you pray. However, this same thing happened to many of the Biblical Prophets. Therefore, we should not lose hope, heart, or the ability to walk in love, regardless of what natural eyes see. One of these families, I have known since my teens. I began praying for them almost immediately after my prayer life started. This family shares many of my old struggles, issues, and pain. I suppose this makes it easier to develop these "prayer burdens" as you grown in the understanding that God wastes nothing (2 Corinthians 1:2-5).

Over the years, I began to pray as the Lord placed many members of this family in my path. Over time, the Lord moved on many members of this family. I later learned and met a Godly Christian Uncle in this family that was praying for and believing with the same intensity for years. Through "circumstances," the Holy Spirit launched His assault on various member of this family. Many are now saved, have become open to the things of God, and are starting to live lives that bear fruit. Now, I am blessed to serve with many of them in our church home and Freedom Ministry.

A woman I will refer to as "Aunt Jodie" was put through the ringer in her youth. Later, she made many bad choices, lost touch with all four of her kids, and was not the example she desired to be. Eventually, she was sentenced to prison. However, through this traumatic experience, she came to know Jesus. On a Freedom Ministry Chip Night, I asked her to give us an update on her life, otherwise known as her "testimony." She was able to say that she is a new creation in Christ, has a life that bears good fruit, and that restoration is possible. It was clearly demonstrated that what the enemy meant for bad the Lord used for good. That night, all four of her children, as well as many of her friends and extended family, were there to hear her speak. Currently, all of her children are now seeking Jesus, and one of them collected his one year "sobriety victory coin." Right before our eyes, we witnessed the healing and restoration power of Jesus. This was a powerful night of ministry with an amazing response time filled with repentance and deliverance. I am honored and blessed to share in these types of events on a regular basis.

CHAPTER 10

HOLDING TO THE VISION

Before anything good, such as a breakthrough, healing, or deliverance can happen, it must start in seed form as a word. The Lord can and does speak through dreams, visions, other people, sermons, and praise and worship, but, most often, He speaks in our hearts with His Word. Sadly, we regularly get distracted and do not make time to "be still and listen." Without this basic principle in play within our daily lives, we are just punching into the wind- attacking others, spinning our wheels, or never seeing who the real enemy is or what he is after. Apart from the devil, the biggest adversary you will ever face is in the mirror. The fast-paced systems of the world and false sense of obligation we feel are not designed to allow an individual any time to center. It is more profitable to the enemy if we digress as a people and never achieve our God-given dreams and potential. This is a fact. So for those of us who truthfully believe in Jesus: Listen up! People of God, ready yourself and receive this!

"I will stand at my watch and station myself on the ramparts; I will look to see what he will say to me, and what answer I am to give to this complaint.

Then the Lord replied: *Write down the revelation and make it plain on tablets so that a herald may run with it. For the revelation awaits an appointed time; it speaks of the end and will not prove false. Though it linger, wait for it; it will certainly come and will not delay."*
Habakkuk 2:2-3

If you have been struggling to overcome something, the power from the Holy Spirit is the answer, but in order to see this power alive and in action, you must first be willing to receive all that God has for you. Get to the end of yourself: surrender. Some of you will say, "Ok, I have done this, but I am still stuck." I understand. It happens to us all. Why is it that we get a Word from God and never see it come to pass? Why do we get a Word about relationships, restoration, healing, sobriety, finances (killing the debt), being a Godly man/woman, or our calling such as missions or local ministry and then things seem to just get harder and more difficult? Does this mean it's just destined to be a struggle and that we should all just quit and wait for the government or our "friends" online to bail us out? Surely, we can find someone to agree with us and tell us what we want to hear? Yes, you can always find someone to agree and sulk with you in your pity. In reality, we had better learn to seek out people to encourage our God-given potential. When the Lord speaks, He does so for a very specific, Kingdom advancing reason, and though it may linger, wait for it because it will certainly come. When it comes, do not think for a second that the enemy is going to stand idly by.

I know the struggle to be very real in my own life. I have testimony after testimony about God giving me a Word through various ways and then there is a war over that Word. First, I had to receive and acknowledge that the Word was for me. Then, I had to listen to the direction from God and walk it out. The Holy Spirit will give you faith, and trusting Him will help you obey and seek out the fulfillment of the Word given to you. The Lord will also put mentors and those determined to hold you accountable in your path. As with anything else in life, it is our choice to take action. Keep pressing forward with child-like faith and determination until your Word (dream/vision) becomes a reality that changes the lives of others. When you find the sweet spot of the bat (standing strong in Gods purpose), you will know that "this is what I was made for." Have you ever stayed up late at night or even for days wondering what life is really about? Have you thought to yourself, "There has got to be more to life than this?" There is more. The Lord has more than you can ask for or imagine. Everything I was ever seeking, I found through Jesus. "*Seek first the Kingdom of God, and everything else will be given to you*," says Matthew 6:33. This isn't just my story. This goes for all of us who believe!

Why does it get harder? Understand this: "Everything in the Kingdom of God is about seed time and harvest." Therefore, when you get your Word, immediately the enemy comes to steal it before it can take root in your life. The Bible says in John 10:10 that "*The thief comes only to steal and kill and destroy; I have come that they may have life, and have it to the fullest.*" This pertains to all aspects of doing anything for or receiving anything from the Kingdom. When God speaks life into something, the enemy will come with his tricks. For example, imagine that you heard God speak to you about eating healthier and changing your lifestyle. Don't be surprised if that same day you get invited to the all you can eat pizza buffet (someone's treat). That is a casual example, but it has happened to me in every single area that I seriously felt led to change, and I can promise it will happen to you also.

In most cases, Jesus spoke in parables, not clearly explaining what He meant thus giving us all something to ponder. Still, there are a few examples where He just "spelled it out" for His disciples. I believe He did so because it's just that important that they "get it". He did not leave anything to their feeble reasoning or simple understanding. Look at the words of Jesus in Mark 4:1-20:

1 Again Jesus began to teach by the lake. The crowd that gathered around him was so large that he got into a boat and sat in it out on the lake, while all the people were along the shore at the water's edge. 2 He taught them many things by parables, and in his teaching said: 3 "Listen! A farmer went out to sow his seed. 4 As he was scattering the seed, some fell along the path, and the birds came and ate it up. 5 Some fell on rocky places, where it did not have much soil. It sprang up quickly, because the soil was shallow. 6 But when the sun came up, the plants were scorched, and they withered because they had no root. 7 Other seed fell among thorns, which grew up and choked the plants, so that they did not bear grain. 8 Still other seed fell on good soil. It came up, grew and produced a crop, some multiplying thirty, some sixty, some a hundred times."

9 Then Jesus said, "Whoever has ears to hear, let them hear." 10 When he was alone, the Twelve and the others around him asked him about the parables. 11 He told them, "The secret of the kingdom of God has been given to you. But to those on the outside everything is said in parables 12 so that, "they may be ever seeing but never perceiving, and ever hearing but never understanding; otherwise they might turn and be forgiven!"

13 Then Jesus said to them, "Don't you understand this parable? How then will you understand any parable? 14 The farmer sows the word. 15 Some people are like seed along the path, where the word is sown. As soon as they hear it, Sa-tan comes and takes away the word that was sown in them. 16 Others, like seed sown on rocky places, hear the word and at once receive it with joy. 17 But since they have no root, they last only a short time. When trouble or persecution comes be-cause of the word, they quickly fall away. 18 Still others, like seed sown among thorns, hear the word; 19 but the worries of this life, the deceitfulness of wealth and the desires for other things come in and choke the word, making it unfruitful. 20 Others, like seed sown on good soil, hear the word, accept it, and produce a crop—some thirty, some sixty, some a hundred times what was sown."

Jesus went to great lengths in order to explain His meaning here, but do we really "get it?" I don't think so. A feel-good message or religious activity will not cut it. "Nice little church services" that appease the hometown feel will eventually lose sight of the big picture. When the Word goes forth sometimes toes get stepped on, tables get turned over, and people will gain revelation in Christ and who He designed them to be. We are talking about your God-given purpose. Do you understand your hopes and dreams, your position in the Kingdom, and the purpose for which you were created? There is a war for the Word every day. There is a very real foe who wants you to keep busy, prideful, defeated, discouraged, selfish, angry, lustful, distracted (watching television/playing games), indulgent, and destructive to yourself or others. This enemy knows every kink in our armor and knows exactly how to expose them. He will use anything and everything possible to keep you from seeking Him or holiness: past or current friendships, family members, co-workers, old relationships, church drama, forgiveness, loss, bitterness, pain, addiction, fear and insert anything and everything here!

The time between when you receive the "word" up to when you begin actually living it out will be a slugfest until the end. The enemy does not want to see you discover your calling or function in your anointing. Yes, you will eventually have your own personal anointing. However, there is much we need to be made aware. 1 Peter 5:7 says, "*Be alert and of sober mind. Your enemy the devil prowls around like a roaring lion looking for someone to devour.*" Who he is looking for to devour is not the lost or the "luke warm"- the posers. Who he really has an appetite for is the "called." You are of little danger to the kingdom of darkness until you truthfully "say yes" to Jesus. At that point, the fight will be on. The road is long and the battle can take its toll. Consider this statement. <u>Of those called with vision, few will make it into their purpose. Even less will sustain it when they get there.</u> It will be impossible to take a single step further into our purpose until we take the focus off our situation and shift it to Jesus. I write this not to discourage or condemn anyone. It is my heart to expose the enemy and equip His Church to "keep pushing." We must always be mindful of the battle raging in our mind. The devil and the world will fill our heads with fear and lies. When the lies come into our mind, we must learn discernment and resist:

"*Resist him, standing firm in the faith, because you know that the family of believers throughout the world is undergoing the same kind of sufferings. And the God of all grace, who called you to his eternal glory in Christ, after you have suffered a little while, will himself restore you and make you strong, firm and steadfast. To him be the power for ever and ever. Amen.*"
-1 Peter 5:9-11

Here is the good news. The enemy is already defeated. God opposes the proud and gives grace to the humble. Most of my life, and still if I am not careful, pride keeps me from learning and growing. Admitting that "my way" wasn't so hot was extremely difficult. In fact, it was painful. However, that was just some "pruning" or growing pains in my walk with Jesus. This happens to us all in different ways and is necessary for growth.

We are all in this together. When you get your Word: refuse to deny His command. Do not allow the enemy, yourself (flesh), or anyone else to rob you of your calling in Christ! Keep this promise in mind from Jeremiah 29:11-13, *"For I know the plans I have for you," declares the Lord, "plans to prosper you and not to harm you, plans to give you hope and a future. Then you will call on me and come and pray to me, and I will listen to you. You will seek me and find me when you seek me with all your heart."* It truthfully gets on my nerves when pastors do not share verses 12 and 13 along with 11. We all want to hear about prospering, but we tune out on the listening, seeking, and finding. There is much patience and diligence required. It all starts with receiving a Word by faith and allowing the Lord to guide you. It is as simple as listen, believe, surrender, receive, seek, grow, do, and go.

Jump back to and reread the verses in Habakkuk at the beginning of this chapter. When the Lord speaks or gives you a Word, write it down. When He shows you how your vision will come to pass, make a plan. I have already stated that the enemy has a plan: to take you out. How much more so should we have a plan? In *The Art of War,* Sun Tzu states "If you know your enemy and you know yourself, you need not fear the result of a hundred battles." Know your enemy, and, more importantly, know who you are in Christ. Jesus, Himself, took time to spend with His Father (see Luke 4:32, 5:16 and 6:12). He is our example, and if He had to make that time then so do we. The next part requires maturity: Holding to the vision. While you are seeking, you may not yet see the plan coming to fruition. However, you can still seek, serve, and prepare yourself daily. Continue to press onward because at the appointed time, you will be shifted into your vision (or word). This is affirmed in Galatians 6:9, "*Let us not become weary in doing good, for at the proper time we will reap a harvest if we do not give up.*" King David was a humble shepherd boy doing his "normal" routine when his opportunity arose, but, when he was called, he was already equipped, humble and prepared. It always seemed to me like he was "intently waiting" on something more while being faithful. Study the life of David and you will see that, though he may not have known it, he was clearly prepared for his moment. He was not qualified, but he was, in fact, equipped.

Thinking Point: God cannot promote you out of your current situation until you learn to be faithful where you are now.

In the name of Jesus, all things are possible (Philippians 4:13). Maybe you are stuck right now and just about ready to quit. Maybe you're burnt out from serving others and getting burned. I encourage you to keep pressing forward. Keep in mind Romans 8:1 "*There is no condemnation for those of us in Christ Jesus.*" You do not have to receive that your current difficult season is "just how life is." "Things will never improve" should not be your final answer. Do not build a house in the wilderness. Think about it like this: Maybe I am here right now, but I am only passing through.

His grace is enough. We serve a God of second, third, and one hundred chances. Unplug yourself from the matrix, and see the schemes of the enemy around you. Exit the cycle or system, and enter God's plan. When the veil is removed, you will experience the "love hurricane" that is Christ Jesus. He never wastes any of our life experiences, period. The Lord will use a willing vessel. He is faithful when we are faithless, and He loves us. His plan for us is good. Are you willing to hold onto your vision and seek your purpose? I promise you that it will be worth the cost. Keep fighting the good fight of faith! The battle is often fought and the difficult ground is gained in the trenches.

THE TRENCHES

There is a saying that "the key to success will be found in your daily routine."

The dogfight for our lives and destiny happens daily. This is why Jesus spells it out for us in Luke 9:23-24 when He says, *"whoever wants to be my disciple must deny themselves and take up their cross daily and follow me. For whoever wants to save his life will lose it, but whoever loses his life for me will save it."* Learning how to "die to self" or put our fleshly and natural desires at the foot of the cross is a process. It was an event for Jesus, but for us it is a revelatory process that we must walk out. God blesses us when we can trust Him through obedience. This is not the "feel good" message that itching ears want to hear. This is the reality: it cost something to follow Jesus. The blessing, reward, or natural (or supernatural) provision will always out-weigh the "cost." We are assured of this because Jesus says in Matthew 6:33 to, *"seek first the Kingdom of God and His righteousness and all these things will be given to you as well."* In most cases, it takes time to develop "faith muscles." Building them is a lifetime process of the Lord showing Himself, teaching, healing, and having fellowship with us. The Lord's mercy and grace abound through the Blood of Jesus, but we must be willing to do our part- even if that part is just allowing Him to do His work in us!

Arnold Schwarzenegger was a pioneer in professional body building. He was a seven-time Mr. Olympia Champion. Not only did he have natural genetics (and some admitted anabolic synthetics) working in his favor, but he invented new techniques of muscle growth in the sport such as the "Arnold Press." Arnold also had the best team helping him with his nutrition and supplementation. He possessed the raw determination and mentality to do his absolute best. Combine all these factors, and you have one of the most highly recognized and innovative body builders of all-time. Now, consider yourself here. You are, in fact, "fearfully and wonderfully made" by our Lord (Psalm 139). This means that every bit of your genetics, DNA, and giftedness comes for God. Though there may be some element of generational sin or propensity to sin that may need to be dealt with, the fact remains that we were made in the image of Christ.

If you are willing to accept Jesus Christ in His fullness, then you are on the road to healing and purpose. If you are willing to allow the Lord to guide you in what, how and when you should be reading, seeking, praising, and praying, He will guide you. You may be wondering, "where are my steroids in this?" Where is my boost? Where does all this determination come from? Here's the good part. The Holy Spirit is our steroid. There are no negative side effects from the Holy Spirit, only gifts and new levels of intimacy. The Holy Spirit will come, and you will receive power, tongues, prophecy, healing, anointed teaching, and evangelism; and it will naturally happen. You will also feel the love of God. Eventually, you will become more focused on pleasing God than on pleasing anyone else. God's power is so real that it amazes me. The wisdom and direction that comes from above will change your life. The Lord will provide a "support team" or church family and put special people in your life to equip you for service. The Bible says, "Ask Him" and "seek and you will find." In the heart of every believer lies the passion of a champion. Are you willing to pay the price? First, you must fully understand that the price has already been paid! All we have to do is receive the deeper things of God and "walk it out." The choice is yours.

CHAPTER 11

THE PAYOFF

*15 "Watch out for false prophets. They come to you in sheep's clothing, but inwardly they are ferocious wolves. 16 By their fruit you will recognize them. Do people pick grapes from thorn bushes, or figs from thistles? 17 Likewise, **every good tree bears good fruit**, but a bad tree bears bad fruit. 18 A good tree cannot bear bad fruit, and a bad tree cannot bear good fruit. 19 Every tree that does not bear good fruit is cut down and thrown into the fire. 20 **Thus, by their fruit you will recognize them.** "*-**Matthew 7:15-20** (red letters, the words of Jesus)

Several times throughout this book, I have mentioned that the blessings will outweigh the costs. Simply put, the blood, the sweat, and the tears will bring results. This is commonly referred to as the "fruit." Jesus provides us all that we need for victory. Allow me the pleasure to share a few real-life examples from my own life. All of my struggles and "issues" held me in bondage (chains) for years. There is only one word that I can use to describe why I am alive: grace. The Lord was able to turn a wasted, broken life and use it for His glory. He will do the same for you. Please understand this: God gets the glory in everything that I am about to share. I am still a work in progress. Without receiving Jesus Christ and the fullness of His love, nothing good would come from me. I cannot tie my shoes without Jesus.

BEING A BLESSING

Ten or fifteen years ago, I never would have believed anyone if they told me I would be a missionary, Bible teacher, or preacher. It is a good possibility that I would have laughed or cursed you out of the room. I was "voted most likely" to become a casualty of the street. However, God picks the foolish to teach and shame the wise (1 Corinthians 1:27), possibly so that He gets all of the credit and glory. The blessing for me was not only becoming sober and rejecting the street mentality, but it was discovering my purpose in Christ. He wastes nothing we have ever been through, period. Everything started to slowly come full circle. There were a number of milestones along the way (which are important), and it was a gradual progression and process for me.

Just the fact that I stopped using drugs and going out created a shock wave with my old crowd. Many people thought, "This is just a phase." Several others mocked me by saying "You don't need Jesus to change your life." and much worse than that. My redemption started at the bottom, and I had to trust in Jesus to work my way up. Every less than desirable job I held allowed others to watch God elevate me and make connections Jesus still uses to this day. Little by little, the desires of my heart and bad attitude began to change. I had no idea that I was building my witness (my testimony to His love). Many times, it seemed like I was just "hanging on" to the Cross for dear life. People were watching me like a hawk for failure. Some wanted me to fall off so that they would not have to continue feeling the prompting of the Holy Spirit to seek God or change. The enemy likes to produce disclaimers (I'm a Christian, but I still…) or set us up for less than desirable public moments. Sometimes he uses our "friends" to distract or act as wolves in sheep clothing. I learned that very real lesson many times in my early walk and in dealing with people in ministry.

After a few months of consistency, people began coming to me to ask what time church started or what class was I taking that helped me change my life. People that I had not seen in years would wonder what was going on in my life that produced such a radical change. A close friend of mine, who is still on the fence about Jesus, came to my Baptism. I asked him, "So, what did you think, bro"? He replied, "It was better than your funeral would have been." Even someone who does not believe exactly what I do could see what Jesus had done in my life. The before and after speak for themselves. It is possible to gain the respect of people who do not share your faith or, in some cases, do not even like you. The Apostle Paul writes that we should be all things to all people so that we might win **some** (1 Corinthians 9:22). Not everyone is going to understand it, but some will. He also urges us to live at peace with one another "whenever possible." When walking with Jesus, you will have plenty of opportunities to develop faith and eventually good fruit that will last.

One of the largest steps for me to take was attempting to teach or share what God was showing me in His Word. My first attempt at teaching a Bible Study was extremely awkward. I had two or three of my friends from my past attending it that knew exactly where I came from. They, in fact, had witnessed me at my worst. This was both good and bad. It was good in the sense that they knew there was something going on to produce such radical change in my life, but it was bad in the sense that the enemy tried to make me feel like a hypocrite. The enemy used to try and beat me down with fear and a horrible sense of inadequacy. Fortunately, the Lord turned my hardheaded nature into determination. I refused to quit. These studies grew larger and the faces of the people changed. Eventually, the Lord gave me the ability to lead a Word-based Bible Study. All of the Word that was in me began to come out. The Lord is still teaching me to be obedient and sensitive to His Holy Spirit. The small group time I get to lead in our Freedom/Celebrate Recovery meetings, known as the open share, is both humbling and mind-blowing. Taking and teaching classes like the "Disciples Cross," "Experiencing God," "Purpose Driven Life," "Life's Healing Choices," and "Necessity of an Enemy" have been a tremendous blessing to experience as well. However, the real blessing is living out what the Lord says and teaches you.

COLLEGE GRADUATION

My college graduation was one of the greatest "moments" that God has ever given me. I have already shared much of what I have been through; therefore, the fact that I had a 2.4 GPA when I dropped out of college, and life, in 1999 was a small miracle in itself. I spent the next few years drawn into darkness and depression. However, after I really met Christ and began taking in the things of God: Jesus changed my life. I was called to the mission field in Lithuania from 2006 to 2008. The last few weeks I was there, I began intensely seeking God's direction. It was strange for me because for years, I sought out this calling, and now it seemed as if the door was closing. This troubled a goal-oriented person like myself. I went to all my secret, soul-seeking places and found no answer. My answer came in seed form, strangely enough from an afternoon trip to the movies. I watched a movie that had many overlapping stories, and one, in particular, was of a college professor challenging a student to reach his maximum potential. I realized that I had missed the mark as far as my education was concerned.

I arrived home to a great blessing in late 2008, but 2009 was still a year of frustration and transition for me, but the Lord opened the door for my return to college through grants and encouragement from others. When my first day back to college came, I found myself frozen in my jeep, afraid to walk to my first class. It had been ten years. I had traveled the world and conquered addiction with Christ. Yet, the same familiar fear I had as a teen returned. I started praying, hoping that a dove would land on my jeep or that some other sign or wonder would convince me to move. In my desperation, the Holy Spirit gently spoke to my spirit and said "Go. I have provided you with everything you need for success." I sucked it up, and said, "Ok, Jesus. Here goes nothing."

I could write about several awesome testimonies of how God worked through me and showed Himself to me through my return to college experience, but, for the sake of time, I will just say that He held true to His Word. Temptation and trials in ministry both stretched me and refined me. Three part-time jobs, full-time ministry, and full-time college will take its toll on anyone. There are two verses in the Book of Hebrews that helped me through these trials, not to mention Spanish 101/102 and Statistics 231. I would like to share them before continuing with this story.

"Now may the God of peace, who through the blood of the eternal covenant brought back from the dead our Lord Jesus, that great Shepherd of the sheep, equip you with everything good for doing his will, and may he work in us what is pleas-

ing to him, through Jesus Christ, to whom be glory for ever and ever. Amen."- **Hebrews 13:20-21**

In God's time, everything came to pass. I was able to graduate college and raise my GPA from 2.43 to 3.0. Once, I even made the Dean's List. Those things are wonderful and attest to the fact that anything is possible through the Lord, but, for me, the next testimony was the greatest of all. The dark areas and seasons of my life really began during the same time I dropped out of college. Obviously, I put my mother through hell in many ways. In my own outlook and in the opinion of the world, it was not likely that I would ever return to college or do anything positive with my life. But, Jesus had the final say. Little did we know that twelve years later I would "walk." In an arena full of people (even with my bad eyes), I was able to look back and see my friends and family "in the house" to encourage me. God is so good. I really cannot see as well as I used too, but, miraculously, after all the names were read during the final walk away, I looked back and saw my mother clearly. In that split second, I looked into her eyes and raised my diploma case. The Lord called me back to college and after much perseverance; He gave us that moment together. Be encouraged because Jesus wants to make our dreams a reality-especially when God gets the glory!

WALKING "POPS" HOME

Life can be tough. Period. The enemy likes to set us up to fail whereas God likes to set us up to "shine" our light for Him. During the last few months of my father's life, some of his "old ways" began to surface. Other people close to me were also struggling. It seemed as if everything landed at once. Money was tight, and my plumbing was beginning to fail. Responsibilities of a Recovery Pastor never stop. There is always a need or a situation to address. Much planning, studying, praying, calling, texting, and meeting are involved in weekly ministry, including pouring into leadership and ministering to broken people. Stress was also a constant factor at my full-time day job. I was handling all these situations simultaneously. The enemy is relentless, and, if nothing else, he was succeeding in making me worn out and stealing a good amount of my joy. I have never claimed to be Superman, but I am guilty of attempting to be. Only by the grace of God and faithful prayers of others was I able to continue in ministry and concurrently handle such a workload under immense pressure. This much I know: God is good and God is always faithful.

The Lord had done a great work in my father and I's relationship. The last twelve years was a gradual healing process with a great deal of trials and tribulations. Looking back, there are a lot of things I could have done, said, and addressed sooner and much differently, but Jesus gave us many "moments" in communication for which I am forever thankful.

My father was an interesting character who cared about people. In many cases, Danny was a good listener. Most of his life, he was a better friend to others than he was to himself. A poem he wrote will be included in the back of this book. He was well read, liked to "debate," and, at times, was very hard to read. He had problems with high blood pressure, health issues, and other struggles. The last few months of his life, no one, including the doctors, could figure out exactly what was wrong. We all assumed that it was something to do with his blood pressure or other possible medications that he was taking. In 2005, when he survived a heart attack, the doctor told him to stop smoking. He never did. He was famous for saying, "A man can smoke in a certain way; a man can drink in a certain way." When a person's pedigree consists of a large part of Irish descent, that certain way was "all the way." His Chronic Obstructive Pulmonary Disease (COPD) had gotten worse at an alarming rate. Each year, his bronchial related illnesses got longer and longer. He was just so tough, hardheaded, and full-of-it that, at times, no one could "read him." A few trips to the ER and regular doctor appointments gave him no real improvement. Eventually, we formed a rotation of people routinely checking on him, and it is a good thing that we did.

One day, I was driving a friend to a Celebrate Recovery rehab/half-way house in West Monroe (Awaken 514), a town about four hours away. Earlier in the trip, I called Dad's doctor to schedule another appointment for him. The best that they could do was schedule him the following day. An hour and a half later, I received the call that he was rushed to the hospital. Even though I was only 200 miles away, it felt like I was a million miles away. There was already so much turmoil in my personal life, and my mind was racing as I began to process the news. Adding to the helplessness of the situation, there was a miscommunication that he had already passed away. I was frustrated and powerless. I thank God for the prayers of my church, family, friends, and Brother Larry Breaux, who was driving me home.

Thankfully, it was not yet his time. This would begin two of the most difficult weeks of my life. He was put on a breathing tube, and he was pumped full of fluids and nutrients that he was lacking. The doctor said that he had never seen anyone obtain CO_2 levels that high and live through it without some type of permanent brain damage. He was "stable" but sedated for two days. They finally removed the breathing tube and put him in a regular room. When he began to recover, he was ready to eat and talk and proceeded to tell everyone that he was just "dehydrated." The Lord appointed and sent a doctor who owned racehorses, which would be the only reason Danny believed anything he said. Late into the fourth or fifth day, he was moved into his own room and could eat "Baconators" (from Wendy's). It really seemed like the worst was over and that it was time to start handling the logistics of getting him home and properly monitored.

I am so thankful for those three days. I only wish that I would have spent more time with him. It was such an emotional ride. To say my heart and mind were utterly exhausted would have been a drastic understatement, but the talks that we did have were special. We were both optimistic and thankful. The first two nights that I spent with him, I prayed with him before I said good-bye. On our third night together, we talked about life and our generational struggles. The LPB network was trying to raise money so they had music artist guests playing live and encouraging others to join their cause. I can remember that John Cougar covered Bob Dylan's "Like a Rolling Stone." As our visit drew to a close, the television was turned off, and he said, "Let's say Psalm 23 together." I knew the contents of the Chapter, but not necessarily the correct order. This time, I just listened to him quote it in its entirety, verbatim.

Sunday morning came, and I received a call that they had to rush him back into ICU. They were evaluating and deciding what exactly to do with him. The last words he would actually be able to say to me without a mask or a tube went something like this: "How is that situation we prayed about going?" He was short on air and in a seemingly horrible situation, yet he took the time to check on me. Dad had really listened to and engaged in our conversation the night before. My dad had many struggles throughout his life. Sometimes, I thought he was frustrating my purpose in life. However, reflecting on that moment, I can see that in many ways, he was his own worst enemy, but he always was my biggest fan. He knew I was grounded in faith, and he wanted this other situation to work out for me. This was the real heart of my dad for everyone.

"Ole' Danny Boy" would remain on that breathing tube the last week of his life. My life revolved around ICU visits, work, full time ministry, and holding it together by the grace of God. Before each visit, I would pray for strength and that Dad would see no fear in my eyes. I prayed that he would only see the love of Jesus. Every hour of every day was a constant battle. I thank God for family, friends, visits, support, and prayer because pressure seemed to mount from all angles. There was so much happening that I could not understand. At this time, no one knew how it was going to turn out. All I knew to do was to pray and to trust in the Lord. I remember being on the phone with one of my mentors discussing Dad and other life situations. The conversation turned and I said, "I don't want him to be alone if he passes. I want to be there." We rallied the troops, got the oil and the Bible, and prayed with all our hearts in expectation that God would heal him (in Jesus name). He never had a bad report until his last day. Every time the hospital would call to give a casual update, my heart would drop.

In 2014, on Saint Patrick's Day, the call I dreaded came. I had already gone to visit him that morning and was at work trying to "be a man" and hold it together. The nurse, who was always a sweetheart, called and said that I had better get up there. I worked at a car lot, and I had just let a customer use my jeep to bring her child some medication at school while we waited on her car to be fixed. I had to either wait on her or my boss to show up just so that I could go to the hospital! I prayed, "God, if his time is now just grant me this one request of walking him home! I humbly serve you and do not ask for too much!" Eventually, I couldn't take it anymore. I jumped into a little sports car on the lot and zipped to the hospital. "Fire and Rain" by James Taylor was playing on the radio. That song pretty much summed up his life. The night before, I came to visit him and witnessed my mother holding his hand. He looked at her like she was an angel. They had been divorced for thirty-six years, and did not see eye-to-eye on many things. That was a precious real-life example of God's amazing grace.

I made it in time; God's perfect time. In his last moments, I held his hand and read Psalm 23 and some other scriptures aloud. I told him not to be afraid or ashamed; that he had run his race and that it was my honor to be there with him. My mother, myself, and someone special was there with him to walk him home. Many others were in the lobby. I closed his eyes as he passed, fell limp across his body, and told him a temporary good-bye. While in that position, I received a hug from the other person there, and I truly felt the love and comfort of Jesus like never before in my life. That hug sent a pulse of Holy Spirit love that helped recharge me enough to get through the rest of day sanely and handle other responsibilities. The surrounding days were extremely difficult. However, his memorial service was a blessing. People came out, family sent flowers, and others helped by giving time and effort with finances, cleaning, testimonies, and music. At times the service was like a "roast" with legitimate laughs promoted by those who shared. I would like to again say thank you to these people (you know who you are), especially Pastor Francis for rocking out the "Star Spangled Banner" on an electric guitar. Danny's life was honored, and more importantly, Jesus was magnified.

Why would I share a gut-wrenching story like this? Simply because it is real life. There is no way possible I could have made it through these events without Jesus. Before, I never dealt with pressure, powerful emotion, loss, and responsibility without some type of self-medication without moderation. Life is tough and filled with adverse moments and difficult choices. We are all just one phone call away from life changing news. Sometimes, the healing process does not come the way we wish it would. The way we wish life to be is, generally, not how it is or seems to be. However, God is on the throne. Jesus is real. Christ did show up in this situation through love and support from His people. He gave me the strength I did not have and continues to do so. That is the power of God. When you get into the place where you are powerless or at the end of yourself, He can shine the brightest. When the Holy Spirit opens your eyes, you can see. Life is not always pretty, but with Jesus it is always beautiful. God is not a respecter of persons. Which means this: Just as He turned my life around and gave me purpose, He can and will do the same for you (Romans 2:11)! There is no area of your life that Jesus cannot heal, touch, teach, or improve. You only have to make the choice to allow Him to do so. It is only by walking with Jesus that we can make every day count.

TESTIMONIES

These testimonies are from people that I personally know and hold close to my heart. It is my hope to reach and connect with as broad an audience as possible. Hopefully, if you could not identify with any part of my own story, you will be able to connect here. Therefore, these testimonies are from the young and the more experienced, alike. They address different topics (relationships, missions, deliverance, forgiveness, depression and grace) and are from brothers and sisters from my home church and from others who hold diverse doctrinal and denominational foundations. It is a beautiful thing how the Lord draws people from all backgrounds and walks of life into His service. The unity is found at the center of the cross. It is my heart to share these stories of others who have also "finished their milk."

"Mrs. Ellen-Child of God's Grace"

When I was 19 and newly married, I was certain I was pregnant, but it was not to be. Instead, it was the beginning of years of female problems. It was so rare that I was sent to a specialist in Houston. I saw the third top gynecologist in the world there. I was told by M. D. Anderson Hospital that I only had a 4% chance of ever conceiving. Three years later and without any fertility drugs, I gave birth to a healthy 9 lb. 9 oz. boy. After having been told I would probably never have children and then miraculously having this son, you would think that I would have been over the moon thrilled. I was not. I couldn't explain it, but I had a feeling I had never experienced before.

Fast forward 15 months. After many months of playing mental games, having horrible thoughts of harming my baby and shaking my baby, and my depression getting worse every day, I decided to leave my husband and son. I lived alone for 9 months and saw him every other day. <u>I had NO IDEA that I had a medical problem</u>. It seemed the time away helped me to enjoy the time I had with him. It was nearing Thanksgiving and my son's second birthday when I unexpectedly had an encounter with Jesus at a Christian concert. I dove into my newfound walk with Christ heart first, asked for my husband's forgiveness, and moved home two days before my son's second birthday.

At about this same time, I was watching Phil Donahue, a popular TV talk show host (pre-Oprah), and he was interviewing a woman who was describing exactly how I felt. There is so much shame and guilt when you don't have the "normal" feelings toward your baby. After hearing her story, I started researching and found there are "baby blues" or normal post-partum depression and then there is "Severe Post-Partum Depression." I had the latter. The most misconceived notion is depression only last a few weeks whereas mine, and many others (as per my doctor), can last up to two years.

I made an appointment, went to see an ob/gyn, and told him everything- all of the horrible thoughts and feelings I had toward my child, my miracle, my own flesh and blood. He said that based on my hormonal history (see above), I was a prime candidate for SPPD. He told me that if I would have come to him in the beginning, he could have given me anti-depressants and that it would have been "normal" in about two weeks. To think, I missed out on 9 months of my son's life.

I did get on medicine for a month and felt like my old self again. I did not have another bout of depression until 13 years later after the birth of my fourth child. Do you recall that the doctors only gave me a 4% chance of ever conceiving? They forgot to add God into their mathematical equation! I recognized the signs and sought help immediately and never had to be away from my children. But my story does not end there.

Grace pardons our sins and heals our hearts.

Eighteen years later, I was on a field trip with a childhood friend of mine. We were sharing about our walk with Christ, and our many victories, and she stopped me as I was talking about deserting my family 18 years earlier and said, "You are living in self-condemnation, girl! God has forgiven you, and now, you need to forgive yourself!" I was not living in freedom-in the fullness of God's grace. It was as though I was telling Christ, "I know you forgave me, but your dying on the cross was not enough for me to forgive myself. It was not enough!"

Now I could not and would not ask Jesus to get back on that cross of Calvary, but in essence, that's what I felt I was doing. Scales fell off my spiritual eyes that day and I was able to see the bondage I had been in for all of those years. Thank you Jesus that I am set free and, like Job in the Bible, God has blessed me many times over for the time I lost with my family.

Israel Houghton's song, "Movin' Forward" sums up the direction my life is going now:

"Oh, hey, what a moment You have brought me to.
Such a freedom I have found in You
You're the healer who makes all things new.
I'm not going back, I'm moving ahead
Here to declare to You my past is over in You
All things are made new, surrendered my life to Christ
I'm moving, moving forward!!!"

If the beach is your sin, then the waves that engulf it and wash them away is God's grace. Grace pardons our sins and heals our hearts.

Grace is so much more than just the forgiveness of God.

God's grace can be defined as God's undeserved, unearned favor, goodness, kindness and love toward us.

My name is Ellen, and I am the Poster Child of Grace!

Reflections on Mrs. Ellen

Mrs. Ellen is the "real deal" and serves with all of her heart. She organized the church coffee shop, serves on the worship team, and has been involved with a number of other young ladies' ministries. She and her husband, James, have raised children and pointed them like arrows for Jesus. James serves on the Security Team and, for years, drove the church's van to pick up kids for various activities. They deal with adversity with a smile, and I can personally testify that Jesus gets the glory in all that they do. The Lord speaks through Mrs. Ellen frequently. I traveled to Nicaragua with her and a church team and prayed over our flight, which she was nervous about. We shared many laughs, saw many children accept Jesus as their personal savior, and encouraged local pastors. On this trip, it was my joy to watch the ladies battle giant insects flying around at the hotel. I know her and James pray for me and love me no matter how imperfect I am. That is what it's all about!

"Mrs. Karen-Overcoming Offense"

Some of my friends laugh at me because they say I am "un-offendable." When something happens in my life, they say "Were you upset?", and I can honestly answer no. I say this not to boast in me, but to boast in the Lord. My friends and I were joking the other day, and I said that God has given me the superpower of being un-offendable. Like Wonder Woman's bracelets, I can just zing those offenses right off me. However, the truth is that I have not always been "un-offendable," and I can still be offended today if I choose to be- but for God's Grace.

If we are all honest with ourselves then we know that we have all judged people at some time by their outward appearances, actions, or behaviors. We look with our natural eyes and say things like "I can't believe he just said that", "I can't believe she is wearing that," "How dare she!" or "How dare he!" We get offended every which way we turn.

But GOD! He got a hold of my heart and gave me revelation of His Grace! From all outward appearances, I was a pretty nice person, but inside, I was quietly evaluating, judging, forming opinions about people. I can remember one particular time when someone had done something that I did not agree with. I did not like the way something was handled, and truly, it was none of my business. In fact, it did not affect my life, my family, my property-nothing, but I chose to take an offense. I was busy formulating opinions and judging the situation and condemning the person involved. I was judge, jury and executioner, when that still, small voice said, "Do you know her heart?" My initial response to the Father was "I am pretty sure she doesn't have one?" The Lord gently responded, "Do you know her heart? Do you know anything about her? Do you know what she has been through? Do you understand my Grace?"

Honestly, having grown up in church, I could give the standard answer to that question as "God's unmerited favor," but what did Grace really mean? Like boots to the ground... what did it look like in my life? How do I live it out as to reveal God's grace to people around me? I understood Grace was God's gift of salvation, and I had accepted Jesus' finish work on the cross; however, was that it for Grace- just that one act then it was done?

(John 1:16) And of his fullness have all we received, and grace for grace.

(John 1:17) For the law was given by Moses, but grace and truth came by Jesus Christ.

My friends know I love to look up the original Greek and Hebrew grammar of the words of the Bible because, most of the time, our English language just does not do it justice. The original Greek meaning of the word "grace" in this verse says, "especially the divine influence upon the heart and its reflection in the life."

Grace came into being through Jesus to divinely influence our hearts and lives. It is a continuous action, not a "one time" event. We can choose to live in grace- allowing Grace, God's presence, and God's power to influence our hearts and lives, or we can choose to walk in our own ways, understanding, and what seems right in our own minds.

If you know any Bible history, the word Pharisee immediately makes you think "bad guy," but, you know what, from the natural eye, they were not bad people. They kept the law. In fact, they made up more laws to keep. They were responsible, good citizens. They were not stealing, or killing. They did what they thought was right. From all outward appearances, they were good people, but what did Jesus say? (1Jn 3:15) Everyone who hates his brother is a murderer, and you know that no murderer has eternal life abiding in him.

Jesus is not looking at the outward appearances. He is concerned with the inward attitudes, perceptions, and intentions of our hearts!

When the priests would go into the temple to offer sacrifices to the Lord, they had to, first, wash in a bronze laver. This was basically a big bronze bowl, but the cool thing was that the bronze was highly polished. It was actually made from the women's mirrors of that day. It was highly reflective. Therefore, when they washed they would see their own reflection in the laver.

God is so faithful when we honestly seek Him and who He truly is, and when we seek Him, we will find Him. I have learned that in order to live in a manner that reveals God's grace to others, I must daily, hourly, and moment by moment check my own heart, my own attitudes, my own motives. Like the Pharisees, we often condemn others because we have lifted ourselves above them to a place of self-righteousness rather than planting ourselves firmly under the covering of grace.

Now, when an offense comes, I stop, breath, and ask God to show me my own heart rather than concentrating on their heart (because we wrestle not with flesh & blood). I ask myself "Why did this upset me? Am I trying to control a situation?" There are only two things in life that you can control-your choices and your reactions? I also ask myself, "Am I trying to make someone conform into the image of how I think they should look, behave, walk, talk, whatever instead of allowing the Holy Spirit to transform them as He has so graciously began His good work in me?

The Word of God was meant to be a mirror so that we can examine ourselves not a magnifying glass so that we can magnify other's weaknesses, faults and failures.

(2 Co 1:12) For this is what we boast about: Our conscience testifies that we have conducted ourselves in the world with pure motives and godly sincerity, without earthly wisdom but with God's grace—especially toward you.

Look at others through the eyes of Grace through Jesus and check yourself in the bronze laver. Conduct yourselves in this world with pure motives and godly sincerity, not earthly wisdom, but with God's grace, God's presence, and God's power! Sometimes, the only thing that needs to change is your perspective.

Reflections on Mrs Karen

Mrs. Karen is a loving, down-to-earth woman. She worked at the bank that our church uses. The Senior Pastor and others used that circumstance as an avenue to build a relationship with her. Eventually, she accepted the invitation to visit The Gathering. God has given her the ability to love certain people with a "Jesus love." However, she can give "tough love" when necessary. Through life's various trials and tribulations, Mrs. Karen has learned to trust Jesus. She has served in the office, in Celebrate Recovery, in the Women's Ministry, on the Altar Team, and by doing whatever that was needed. It is abundantly clear for all to see that she enjoys her new ministry as a grandmother above everything else. Recently, she has witnessed The Lord answer her prayers. Her daughter Brandi has a strong walk with Jesus and now serves faithfully in the Freedom Ministry. This word about offense was recently tested before the printing of this book. Karen has chosen kindness, compassion, and humility over offense. We are all learning that conflict can be a relationship building tool, instead of something to fear. Karen and her husband, Mike (security team), love the Lord. It has been a blessing to know them and serve with them for over ten years now.

"Allie and Patrick-Never Too Young To Be Used by God"

Allie's Testimony

When I was five years old, I lost my dad. When I was ten years old, I thought I was going to lose my mom to a very aggressive form of breast cancer, which, thankfully, she survived. These are just a couple of examples of some of the bat-

tles life has thrown at me. Fortunately for me, I knew God from a very young age. I didn't actually become a Christian until later in life, but I knew who God was. I knew He loved me, and I never blamed Him for my dad's death or my mom's sickness. I cried to Him when I missed my dad and begged Him not to take my mom, but I never blamed Him or turned from Him. Unfortunately, kids are smarter than teenagers.

When my teenage years began, I started down a sad road of an insecure girl who was flattered every time a boy showed interest in her. I thought I was fat. I thought my hair was too frizzy and that my legs weren't long and skinny enough for boys to want me. Therefore, when they did, I let them have things from me that were meant for my husband. I lost my virginity when I was thirteen years old even though I was a worship leader for my youth group. I was about as fake as a person could be. There were times when I had sex on Saturday and led worship on Sunday. Thankfully, when I was fifteen years old, I was doing so much stupid stuff that I got caught. Then, I got caught again. And then, I got caught again. It finally got to the point where I wondered how I became the person that I was because that was not, at all, the person that I wanted to be. This was the point in my life where I turned to Jesus and truly meant it. This was the point in my life where I was ten years old again. I loved God even though I was hurting, and I knew He loved me back even though I had hurt Him. It wasn't until the end of my junior year that I decided that God is what mattered most. Unfortunately, I had already wasted almost my whole high school life being stupid, so I really wanted my senior year to matter. No, I was not perfect, but I tried a heck of a lot harder to show God's love to everyone around me.

Half way through my senior year, a super cute guy started pursuing me, and I finally decided to say yes- not out of insecurity or flattery but because I thought it may have been what God wanted for me. Nine months later, when he was nineteen and I was seventeen, we got married, and I knew for sure it was what God wanted. We had both had sex with other people before we started dating, but we did not have sex with each other until we were married, and that was a beautiful thing. Regardless of all the judgments cast on us for getting married so young, we have loved God and loved each other because we know we serve a God who is bigger than our age. Now, two years later, we are loving and serving God together and fighting battles together. God recently blessed us with a beautiful little girl to join us on this journey and we could not possibly be happier. We will always have battles, but we will also always have God, and because of that I pray we will always have each other.

"Don't let anyone think less of you because you are young. Be an example to all believers in what you say, in the way you live, in your love, your faith, and your purity." 1 Timothy 4:12

Patrick's Testimony

I grew up in a broken home where my parents struggled with drugs and were in and out of jail. I smoked, drank, and partied like every other teenager raised without a purpose. I accepted Jesus when I was seventeen, and three days after my decision, I was back into an immoral life style- chasing after whatever I desired. Later that year, I woke up on a couch that I was living on completely changed and burdened about the blankness I was living for. I had a deep impression to change the world. At first, when I woke up with this "why do I feel so good" mood, I was not thinking about Jesus, but, soon after, I rededicated my life to Him after realizing that the only way I was going to change the world was if I changed myself, and I could not do that on my own. For some reason, I just knew that Jesus could. I started my journey that morning, but I fell off more times than I can remember mainly because of girls.

I realized somewhere down the road of faith in Jesus that I was not going to be able to do this without that "special lady." I would pray every night for God to send that one girl that would help me run this race of faith in Jesus. One night, after leaving a party and smoking something that I do not know, I was in my bathroom on my knees crying to God because I was tired of falling off, and I already knew the road where that led. I was sobbing and begging God to send the girl that would change this. The next day, my future wife texted me to come hangout with her and her family- we are still madly in love with one another and Jesus today. We are still in need of God's grace constantly, but she has been my most precious blessing.

Uncle Sean's back story on Allie and Patrick

Allie is my blood niece and to me the "Baby," although my sister kept having children who all love Jesus. I knew of some of her struggles, but I also knew God blessed her with favor and talent. She is and always will be precious to me. I knew she was seeing Patrick, he was a real follower of Jesus, and that they were honoring God. Their being so young and not that far removed from the world's fire, I was concerned. Never in fear, just a genuine concern because I know the enemy hates "love" and will stop at nothing to destroy it. I also was in "love" at a young age, and it did not work out for me. However, I had no positive support system and no one ever spoke life into any of my relationships. God showed me this as an opportunity to encourage him.

The Lord told me to bless Patrick. For days, I listened to the Holy Spirit on how to do that. I said, "I sure will," and then I will kindly tell him that if there was ever a serious problem there will be no police called, and that Uncle Sean would gladly go back to jail smiling if something ever happened to Allie, he broke her heart, or any of that type of stuff. That is the flesh- a street mentality that I still have to kill when it surfaces. The Lord clearly said, "No, that's not how to go about it." I saw the way they looked at each other. The fact that they both have Jesus and learned from their mistakes meant they were mature beyond their years. So, I met with Patrick in private, and the Holy Spirit used me to "speak life" and wisdom. I am thankful that I am learning to listen to the voice of the Lord. Later, he texted me and said how much he needed that. Down the road a few years, while we were together doing prison ministry, he commented that we have this "wild kingdom connection". There is no doubt about it. God is good.

Today, they are still married, serving the Lord, and now raising a family. Patrick is "best-friends" with my mother (Allie's Maw-Maw) and is a blessing to our family. He can be found reading the Word of God, T.D. Jakes, Francis Chan, Steven Furtick, Bill Johnson, or any other challenging author. Patrick has recently finished his first book and it will be published soon. He is always learning, seeking, serving, and growing. Allie and Patrick are very gifted and use all that the

Lord has given them to further the Kingdom of God, serving with youth, children, the Altar and Worship Teams as a unit and bearing fruit. They are awesome examples that Jesus desires to use young people to further His kingdom. Clearly this speaks to me and others that there is no reason to waste years in the world when God holds your true purpose. There is no limit to where God may bring them if they keep saying "yes" to Jesus.

"Mr. Curtis-Timid to Bold"

My name is Curtis Duplechain. I was born in 1949, and I am 68 years old. I received Jesus as my Savior in 1962. I joined The Gathering (previously known as Life Church) in the spring of 2005. The first time I attended, the lead pastor and a mission team were out of the country doing a crusade. They went on several mission trips that year, and to this date, it has not changed. Each year, the church will go on several trips. I remember back then, one of the men saying how bold of a witness the lead pastor was on the streets, and I remember saying to myself "I want to be like that." Today, I say "be careful what you ask for," because anything you ask The Father in Jesus' name for He will surely give it to you! (John 16:23)

In 2005, Hurricane Katrina flooded New Orleans and displaced most of the residents, and many of them came to Sulphur. Our church opened its doors and helped many evacuees. Most of the members, which were about 75 at that time, did all they could to help. For about four weeks, I was burning the candle at both ends, running my business, and serving the evacuees. Then, Hurricane Rita almost destroyed Sulphur with wind damage. The New Orleans evacuees left, and near-ly all of the Sulphur residents were evacuated for an extended length of time. We had two large trees that fell on our home. After about 3 months, most buildings were repaired in Sul-phur, but there were some residents that lacked the finances to repair their homes. We had teams from other states that would come on missions to help these folks. Our church teamed up with several of these mission teams. I worked with these teams, and once again, during these times I was burning the candle at both ends. It was overwhelming to think about it at the time, but I had this mindset that I would do <u>whatever it took</u> so I had to rely on The Lord to give me the strength. I can look back now and see that The Lord was preparing me. I have found that all successful missionaries have this exalted mind set when they are on a mission.

I always wanted to go on a short-term foreign mis-sion, but I could not find the time in my busy schedule to go. I owned a business, and I had little time. Leaving for one or two weeks seemed impossible.

Our pastor would often tell the congregation that Je-sus commanded us to go to all nations and make disciples. He would say "The Lord Jesus said go, so I am only saying what He said. Go!" Soon, I began getting convicted to GO. Short-ly after, that Pastor Soloman Trejo, the greatest missionary I have ever worked with, came to our church. He preached the Great Commission of Christ also. He said, "Do you have a passport? If not, how will you go if the Lord tells you to go on a foreign mission on the spur of the moment?"

The next week, I applied for a passport, and I received it shortly afterward. I will say that there is something power-ful about taking that "first step in faith." The Lord started *opening doors for me to go on foreign missions. I sold my business to my son in 2006, and then I had plenty of time to "Go."*

In 2007, I went on my first foreign mission to Brazil. I have been on eight Brazil mission trips as of 2014. I have been on six mission trips to Nicaragua and two to Mexico. I have been doing ministry work in the local prisons with our team, and we have led many prisoners to The Lord. The Lord used Pastor Soloman Trejo, Pastor James Carson, and a few others to train me. As of today, I have had the privilege to lead several thousand folks to the Lord, and the sixteen foreign mission teams I've worked with have led a total of over 100,000 people to The Lord. So, you can see that no matter how old you may be or what situation you are in, nothing is impossible with The Lord. If He can change an introvert like me into a bold street evangelist, imagine what He can change a well-adjusted person into.

In closing, I want to give thanks to my special partners in missions Shawn Dugas and Dan Young. One could not ask for better partners.

I give all the glory to Jesus, my Lord and Savior. The Kingdom is His. The power and the glory are His forever and ever, amen!

Reflections and Back story on Mr. Curtis

Some people say that the Holy Spirit, at times, speaks like a gentle whisper. It is possible that Mr. Curtis has ministered to those same people because he speaks softly. However, you know when the Lord is speaking through him. I have been to Nicaragua, done Prison Ministry, and shared in various other ministry activities with Mr. Curtis for years. He is soft spoken, but when the Holy Spirit rises up in him, you not only hear what he is saying, but you "feel it."

The Lord truly wastes nothing. Mr. Curtis owned an Air Conditioner business, which his son now currently operates. Years ago, he did several service calls for my mother's house. It was one of those seasons when I had returned home as a young man in attempt to finish college. My testimony and history has been shared in this book. Unfortunately for him, when he was working on her A/C, the breakers were located in my bedroom. I was passed out in a serious way from whatever I had been involved with the night before. I woke up to see a strange man walking into my room in a uniform. Still not yet awake, I asked him, "Are you a cop or with the police department?" He said, "No" and kept on working. That was good news to me, so I rolled over and went back to sleep.

I had long hair, bloodshot eyes, and a general rough disposition. Mr. Curtis saw me at church years later one Sunday and gave me a warm embrace. He was shocked to see me in church. Later, we would become close friends. Eventually, he confessed that he felt like he should have talked to me about the Lord, but he was afraid. I told him, "No worries. I most likely would not have received it well." Jesus wastes nothing and eventually uses everything for our good.

When Mr. Curtis saw me that Sunday, back in 2005, he knew God was working at our church. I can tell you now that he misses very few opportunities to share the love of

Christ. Not only does he participate in missions, he worked faithfully for years with Mr. Dan in our "Purpose Driven Life" class and Prison Ministry. They were the soft-spoken "dynamic duo" of the church for several years. These laid back, soft-spoken men have an anointing from the Holy Spirit. It has been my blessing to grow and serve with them. They inspire me to keep growing in the Lord.

"Chel-From Darkness to Light"

There are so many things that shape us, mold us into who we become. With every one of those things, we make a decision, choose a path. Brought up in a Baptist church, I heard a lot about Jesus but did not see the power we talked about. I felt if God made it; He could fix it.

It's not easy for me to give a testimony of myself. There are some dark things back there that should be left buried. I would not glorify the enemy at all. The truth is, most would not believe it anyway- astral projection, telepathy, the casting of spells all with "good intentions." Where the Church leaves a gap, the enemy is all too willing and able to fill it.

Even to this day, I see the enemy at work, and I am quite unable to stop it. When people refuse to believe the enemy is manipulating them, there is little you can do. It breaks my heart.

I've been attacked every time I've stepped into the gap- by the enemy and people who are deceived by him. The religious people "throw stones." Gossip, I believe, is one of the greatest tools the enemy has against the body of Christ. I personally define gossip as two Christian believers speaking death against someone. While the stones are being thrown, the enemy will often throw flaming darts/arrows or temptation to get the ball rolling. The enemy rarely faces us head on any more. It is too easy for him to twist the hearts of others to say evil against someone falsely. So, watch what is being said; it is either fruit being examined or judgment on yourself. My LORD knows my heart while few have ever sought it out.

In the late 80's, I had a series of visions, and at the end, I was given a promise that when the dust settles, you will still be standing. So that being said, I'll jump to a point in time in 1985. I was dating a girl and went to church with her. Not that I had not been in church before but what I felt in my heart God would do and what was presented to me were different. I picked up a pamphlet on the Baptism of the Holy Spirit. Having bought a KJV study bible, I started researching this; what seemed to be the power I was looking for six years or so earlier.
God is full of mercy and supplied me with the perfect answer for my need. This is "Charis" the perfect solution for your need. A short while later, I cried out to Him on the floor of my trailer, and I asked the Holy Spirit to come into me and fill me to over flowing. It was intense, and I spoke in the tongues of angels. It brought concern to me because I had done something like it before, and it was not good. That Thursday night in a youth meeting, the new youth minister stepped in front of where I stood, a few rows back from the front, and he said, "Someone is questioning about the Holy Spirit." This happened three times as I asked God if this word was for me. The third time, he came and stood directly in front of where I was

and said, "It is about a prayer language." Ok, confirmation. I went forward. He called two young ladies who were visiting to come pray with me; one of which had dated a friend of mine a few years before. She was all smiles, laid hands on me, and prayed then I spoke the words I had previously received that night in my trailer. She said "that's it" after I spoke in tongues for a few minutes.

At the same meeting and a few minutes later, a girl fell on the floor and started slithering. I knelt beside her and commanded it to leave like it is written in the Word, and after a short time, it left. This would be the first time that I operated in the true authority of the Lord Jesus (Luke 10:18-20).

For two weeks, I spoke the same two sentences over and over again, but I wanted more. The Word spoke of diverse tongues, and I wanted all there was so I asked and diligently sought. I was by myself at the corner of Opelousas St. and Hwy 14 in Lake Charles listening to a song by Carmen. The chorus was "In Jesus name, satan you've got to flee." The light turned red, and I stopped and sang louder and louder "In Jesus name you've got to flee." As I sang, it was like a band was wrapping around my head and getting tighter and tighter so I got louder and louder. When it broke, my language exploded. It changed from language to language as I hollered praises to God. I have been told I can be intense and get loud sometimes.

I picked up a series of four small books by Kenneth Hagin on the topics of Satan, demons and demonic possession. In one of these books, it described what had happened that day in my truck. The strongman in me was broken and had fled. There are far more things that happened in this time *that I cannot reveal here. This is the abridged version. The battles for freedom were won by Jesus- we just have to proclaim the Word and stand.*

I'll end with this. The devil and all his companions and followers are nothing to the power of the Holy Spirit of the living God, and getting free of them is as hard as you make it. Power (Matthew 28:18), going (Mark 16:17-18), authority (Luke 10: 17-22), and the best for last, "For though we walk in the flesh, we do not war after the flesh: "For the weapons of our warfare are not carnal, but mighty through God to the pulling down of strong holds; Casting down imaginations, and every high thing that exalts itself against the knowledge of God, and bringing into captivity every thought to the obedience of Christ; And having in a readiness to revenge all disobedience, when your obedience is fulfilled (2 Corinthians 10:4-6). These have helped me keep focused on whom the enemy is truly. James 4:7 says, "Submit yourselves to God resist the devil and he will flee away." I do believe we spend too much effort dealing with stuff that if we would just do as Jesus said, Love the LORD your God with all your heart, soul, mind, and strength, and love your neighbor as yourself, the enemy could not get a foot hold in us. Forgive because you are forgiven. Love because you were and are loved. Give because you have been given to. Persecution will come from people and the enemy. They will try to get you out of love and into judgment. The enemy is constantly seeking whom he may devour (has permission to). There are far too many scriptures to share on this, and this is supposed to be brief. Love you one and all! He has changed me, and I will never be the same. Do not be afraid of the darkness for the darkness fears the light. In His name, Brother Chel.

Reflections on Chel

Chel is a brother, friend, and a person from whom I seek occasional council. I first connected with him and his family though a church "family camp" that was open to everyone. When I saw a guy in his mid-forties sliding and going "all-out" playing dodge ball at camp, I figured he was someone I would "click" with. He has a heart for hurting people and a desire to see them set free. Chel reminds me, more than any other person, that "It is the love of God that brings people to repentance." He will also be real about the consequences of a person's choices when it comes to reaping and sowing. In my own life, Chel has offered a listening ear to help me process things when I needed one.

It is often said, "New level, new devil." Jesus was in the process of bringing me to the next level. I was so busy and concerned about others that I did not realize it. My hands were on the plow, going forward, because I expect the Lord to use a willing vessel. My life at the time was a spiritual battle-ground. I found myself under attack like never before. People I love were also struggling. The enemy knew how to "get at me." Let's just be real. Leadership positions can become lonely places. As a pastor, I will carry many people's secrets to the grave (so to speak); however, in my own life, I found it difficult to confide in my normal support networks. This season was intense because the Lord was working and speaking in spite of these attacks. What I know God showed me went against the fruit in which I was witnessing. I was at a cross-roads; it was a war in my mind. The enemy used this turmoil and other situations as open doors to attack me. I know the enemy's goal has been to make me a "wash-out," thus derailing me from my higher calling in Christ Jesus. Thankfully, Jesus turned my hardheadedness into determination, and, eventually, my pride into humility.

All I can say is this- Chel was there for me through the battles. He helped me deal with some things that allowed me to continue to move forward in Christ Jesus. After a lot of prayer, forgiveness and repentance (confessing, being real), I was set free. Eventually, I received a prayer language almost ten years after I received the Baptism of the Holy Spirit. Now, my eyes are open to new levels of spiritual warfare. What the enemy was using to "take me out," the Lord used for my good and edification. Throughout the next year, I would learn about the "Under Armor of God" (Colossians 3:12-14), which is mentioned in the chapter about prayer. Layers of pride and a cloud of darkness had to be removed in order for Jesus to give me more of Him. Now, I can put on my "Armor of God" (Ephesians 6:10-20) and fight in authority, humility, and love.

I know my testimony and experiences differ from others. Read your Bible and you will find that none of the people documented there lived "cookie cutter" lives or all had the same experiences. Let me remind you about the thief on the cross. All he did was "believe." We have to be willing to seek the truth and follow Jesus. We must all be humble enough to ask for help, wise council, or prayer. There is no man or woman walking who knows everything there is to know or experience about Jesus or even the exact procedures to perform ministry. The Lord gives wisdom, visions, and dreams. He still speaks to His people. We must become willing to return to our first love-Jesus! We can never become all things to all people so that we may win some, if we do not love each other. What am I implying? It is past time that Pentecostals, Baptists, and all denominations stop treating each other like the "Crips and Bloods." We need to be "snatching people out of the fire" (Jude 23), and not allow fiery darts from the enemy to cause us to throw stones at one-another (I Corinthians 12:25).

"Kevin Fontenot-Deliverance In a Hut"

Below is an exert from Kevin's journal entry during our 2014 Nicaragua mission trip…

Nicaragua Day 4: Today was simply amazing, exactly the kind of stuff I came here for. It was just last night that I almost let the devil steal my joy when I was informed that I was being moved to a different team. It was nothing against that team. In fact, the team leader is Sean, my Recovery Pastor and sponsor. It was just that I was really enjoying the team that I was on and the church we had been attending. I had told myself before I came that it was ok to have spiritual expectations just not logistical expectations.

The day started with breakfast bright and early. I am the driver for this team so today was my breaking in. I was a little anxious but not because of my ability to drive this van with a standard transmission. My truck back home is a standard so I'm fine with that. I was anxious because the traffic laws there are non-existent in this country. There are not only cars and a lot of motorcycles pulling out all over the place, but there are donkeys, cows, pigs, dogs, cats, kids, and lots of other fun obstacles to maneuver around very poor roads. It went off well though, praise Jesus. After one day, I'm totally confident to drive for the remainder of our time here.

We were scheduled to go to a recovery house, which should have been something right up my ally, but I wasn't really feeling it. We pulled up, and it was closed; therefore, we ate our "flexy cookies" and switched gears. What a blessing it was! God was in control the entire time. We ended up driving up a mountain to a small, very poor village-exactly like the kind of stuff I had envisioned while preparing for this trip-very, very poor and lots of disabled individuals lost and needing direction.

We broke off into two small groups- Guy and I with an interpreter. We went from house to house ministering, inviting everyone to a 2:00 p.m. service, and sharing the gospel. We had mixed results. Some were anxious and quick to receive The Lord. Some, on the other hand had a deep fear of the Lord. It was not a matter of believing. They would say things like," But I like to drink from time to time. I need to think about it. You don't mess around with Jesus." They completely lacked the concept of grace and mercy. With other individuals it was simply a matter of divide and conquer. We felt that several people were confident and ready- clearly the Lord was speaking to them. Some were not as ready. As we would minister to them, they would make eye contact with each other and we would lose them. One woman was even in tears. I turned my back to the other women and looked her right in her eyes and said, "The Lord is calling your name." He was! Unfortunately, she again made eye contact with the group of villagers and decided to wait until she was ready to make that decision. I pray she has enough time.

The service was amazing. The greatest part was that it was completely done by children. Ninety-nine percent of the church was made up of small children. The worship was led by children as young as three. The guitar player was probably seven, and the guitar that he was holding was about ten sizes too big for him. There was another young child on the keyboard and two young ladies leading the worship. They seemed to love the microphone. They did a very good job of engaging the younger kids to sing along. Children poured into the small building, and it was amazing. Before long, we gave up our seats. In a short amount of time, it was standing room only. I honestly thought that they were about to start lowering people through the ceiling. Guy said, "We were about to have a revival up in there," and boy, was he right. The best thing was that it was led by the children.

We all shared our testimonies, and I closed with a small magic act mixed with my own testimony and an invitation for salvation. I had them close their eyes as I spoke to them. I asked them who in the room wanted to receive the Lord as their Savior. Eighteen of them raised their hands. I asked them to come forward. They were hesitant at first so I started leading the ones with their hands up to come forward. Soon, they began coming, and we led them in a prayer of Salvation. These young children surrendered their lives to the Lord. Afterwards, we stood outside the door, ready to pass out candy to the kids as they left. It was orderly at first. It then turned into a sea of little hands reaching, desperately trying to get just one more piece. It was a touching moment.

When service was over, the pastor asked us to pray for a woman who was struggling with dreams of Satan. She was seeking to rededicate her life to the Lord. This was getting serious quick. We broke out the oil and laid hands on her. We performed a deliverance session on her and cast out the demon tormenting her. She confessed the Lord as her Savior. Afterwards, we took a deep breath. That was deep.

Next, we were led to another man who had a bad experience in a church and wanted to rededicate his life to the Lord. He also had poor hearing and pain in his chest. We prayed for healing and anointed him with oil. We led him in the prayer of salvation and felt led to have him confess that he forgave the pastor who hurt him.

I could have easily got in the van after all this and called it a successful day. However, the best was still to come. We were asked to go into a couple's home who invited us in to receive the Lord. It was a very small, one room house that was packed with about fifteen people. For some time, the pastor had been trying to get this man to receive the Lord several times with no success. He was horribly sick and, the pastor was concerned about how much time he had left. As we went in, he seemed ready to say the prayer of salvation. When I got to the part where he must repent of his sins, he stopped. We began praying for him in the Spirit. It was as if the Spirit kept turning the volume up and then back down. It would get very quiet, and then the room would instantly erupt in loud prayers of worship and tongues. Afterwards, it would become quiet. It was as if every person was completely in tune with the Holy Spirit at the same time. This went on for about an hour. It is very difficult, if not impossible, to put into words the atmosphere of that little shack. Finally, the spirit tormenting him had departed! The man stood up and said, "Gloria Jesus!" He had been set free. He said the entire Sinner's Prayer. When we had finished, we did the exact same thing with his wife. It was very exhausting. We were pouring with sweat. When we walked out of that room, I felt as if I had just run a marathon. It sucked every bit of energy out of my body. I do not know if I am spiritually equipped to handle anything more intense than that. I will never be the same again after what I experienced today.

Reflections on Kevin

Truthfully, there is not enough space left in this book to share what God has done in Kevin's life. Kevin is in the process of writing his own book. He was a proud atheist and struggled with hardcore addiction for eighteen years. Eventually, he was led to get a Bible. He hadn't decided to seek Jesus. He simply wanted to find things "off" or wrong with the Bible to empower him to crush believers. What inevitably happened was his complete surrender to the Lord Jesus Christ. Honestly, I have never encountered someone with so much desire to learn and be used by God. He listened to the council and teaching the Lord was giving him. This helped him to not only learn from his mistakes, but also to learn from mine and others. This, coupled with his obedience in what the Holy Spirit was telling him to do, have produced much "good fruit" in the Kingdom of God.

Life threw him a curve ball shortly after he achieved his first year of sobriety. His son was diagnosed with autism. He was really upset and frustrated. At this time, he was finally not only living clean but living "all-out" for Jesus. Kevin briefly digressed from the fellowship, but he never returned to drugs. The Lord grew him through this process. He told Kevin, "There is nothing wrong with your son; he is fearfully and wonderfully made by me." God trusted Kevin, and He had a master plan. Eventually, he returned to the fellowship even stronger than he was before. Soon after his return to the fellowship, a door was opened in his life. Kevin was chosen to become part of the Louisiana Board of Autism. He gets to pray and speak during the meetings at the state capital. The Lord is still on the throne and in the healing business. In the last three years, his son has made tremendous progress. Kevin is also working with five years of clean time. That experience and the intense spiritual warfare that happened in the hut, I will never forget the rest of my life. In all these events, Jesus gets the glory!

When Jesus told me that it was time to re-start the Celebrate Recovery Ministry at The Gathering, Kevin joined the team. God was using him, even before he completed the "step study." Now, he teaches the men's step study, lives an evangelistic life, preaches, leads small groups, faithfully helps with pastoral security, and, in the past, has mentored/sponsored other men. He is an inspiration to us all. One of my life-long friends, Kent, often says, "Just another awesome testimony by Kevin Fontenot." We all laugh, but Kevin will say, "God is not a respecter of persons. Jesus wants to use us all." He is right! I am blessed to have Kevin in my life and a faithful member of our church. Kevin is currently in a season of sowing into his family, marriage, and "making time" for relationships. This is something we should all consider doing.

"Jill and Fred-Redemption and Reconciliation"

I wanted to walk out on my marriage. At the time, Freddie and I had been married for twelve years. We met and fell in love as pre-teens. We were smitten and inseparable! We had practically grown up together. Friends and family often commented on how perfect we were for each other, and we both agreed. We had a beautiful baby girl, a home of our own, and life was great!

I was attending a local church on my own and bringing our daughter Celeste. The only thing missing was my husband who did not want to attend with me because it was not the denomination he was raised in. I didn't want to go to his church; therefore, I just continued going to my own, alone, for many years. I wished he would have come with me but I understood his reasoning. I was not mad at him, but I began to hold a grudge that I had to attend church alone. I wanted Freddie to attend church functions with me, pray with me, join the choir with me, and all of those things. He was not interested. I began to lose hope that he would ever attend church, so I started nagging. The nagging turned into arguments and. eventually, I built up a wall. I was unsatisfied. I blamed him for my emptiness. I felt that it was his responsibility to make me happy and that he was failing miserably. I had a list in my head of all the reasons he didn't measure up. I had these thoughts that I could do much better on my own.

Eventually, I stopped going to church. It just wasn't worth the hassle. Looking back, I guess I gave up on God changing my husband and my marriage. This decision was probably the worst decision I had ever made. I began to verbally attack my husband. I called him names like "lazy" and "boring" (Now I know he's a steady phlegmatic).   He would argue back that I would never be satisfied with anything he improved. Deep down inside, I knew he was right.

I daydreamed about a better life and happier marriage. I wanted the all-American dream- a bigger house, a newer car. I even fantasized about being a stay-at-home mom and baking pies! I realized this was highly unlikely in our marriage. Therefore, I had the idea that I could simply find someone else who could make all of this come true! Of course, this person would have to love me, be faithful, be funny, compliment me, and support me financially. My wish list went on and on. I told Freddie to move out one June. He moved in with our friend, Sean Barron, while I had my pitty-party, realizing that I couldn't have everything that I wanted in life. My family kept bugging me to talk about my marital problems, but I didn't want to. I stayed busy, yet miserable. I thought that I would be happier with him gone, but I wasn't. Freddie would come by every morning with a cup of coffee for me and a note promising me that he would change (I still have those notes). He was making it so hard for me to stay mad at him.

There was a turning point that God used by allowing my husband to speak directly into my spirit. I will never forget his words. He said, "Jill, no one will ever make you happy. Only God can!" Those words cut me to the core. I had no words to argue back. I didn't like what he said, but, for once, Freddie was right.

Three months later, I had enough of my emotional roller coaster! I was crying in the bathtub so that our daughter wouldn't see me, and I had a conversation with God. I said, "Things have got to change!" I had absolutely no peace whatsoever about a divorce. Even though I had told Freddie to move out, I still loved him. We were both miserable, but God had joined us together at such an early age that it didn't seem right to throw it all away. I remember telling God, "OK, I'm giving you one shot at speaking to me through your Word!" My plan was to get out of the tub, wrap the towel around me without properly drying off, and march straight to my Bible, wherever it may be!? I did just that. If you have ever done this, I pray your answer was as clear as mine. I do not suggest putting demands on God the Father nor giving him "one shot," but I was desperate. I needed to know what to do. I flipped open my Bible and read the first scripture that my eyes fell on. "If you are married, stay married."

I fell to my knees and sobbed in my towel. I tear up now reminiscing about this day. How could the scripture be so "spot on"? How could my eyes zone in on the most perfect scripture in the entire Bible for my situation? I picked up the phone and told him to come home. When he did, moments later, we embraced and cried together. How had we gotten here? Why did I feel like I could do better or that my husband was a project for me to fix? I know now that the enemy hates marriages and doesn't want anyone to stay married. Shortly thereafter, Freddie and I started attending The Gathering in Sulphur, Louisiana. We took a class called The Five Love Languages, and we soon found out that we both loved each other very much but were speaking it in different ways. That book helped reshape our marriage and the way we viewed each other. As we sat in the class with Rick and Sunny Duhon, I envisioned Freddie and I teaching a class together in the future to young couples about marriage. I knew then that God could use our story of perseverance and reconciliation. I know if we would have thrown in the towel this could never be pos-

sible.

We aren't teaching classes together yet, but I have taught some ladies Bible Studies, and Freddie has done some mentoring over the phone with two or three different young men whose marriages were in trouble. I'm so proud of him. I catch myself eavesdropping, and I hear Freddie sharing on the phone how our separation was the darkest time in his life. However, it was also the time of his life where he drew closer to God. Freddie was now in the Word every day. He was memorizing scripture; he was listening to K-love Christian music in the car and even singing along! The first time I heard him pray out loud, I almost fell on the floor! I am so thankful that I did not give up on our marriage. God answered my prayer even though it wasn't as quick as I would have liked it. What Satan meant for harm, God meant for good. A divorce would have been the end of our family and the end of any possibility of us mentoring young couples. Freddie would not have been pouring into the lives of those young men and perhaps their marriages would be over by now. We would not have raised our daughter in a Christian home. The best part is that we took in our daughter's best friend, Katelynn, who has made a wonderful addition to our family! None of this would've happened if we would have given up. I actually rejoice for that struggle that we went through because He has given us beauty for ashes.

You may be faced with similar circumstance. You can choose to walk away from your faith. You can make one poor choice after another, just like we did, and you still have the opportunity to come back home! God never left us. He never gave up on us. He will never give up on you either. It took some time and changes in our lives, home, and friendships to totally get back on track with our marriage and with The Lord. We took baby steps. We started to attend church about once a month at first. We then signed up for some classes. Over time, we attended a marriage conference. We went on a mission trip together to Mexico. We then joined a life group. All of this didn't happen overnight, but God had patience to work with us. He chiseled away the hurt, the lies we believed, the neglect we felt, and He replaced it all with his love! When I realized that I had put the expectations on my husband to be "my everything," I had to repent and apologize to him. How could I have been so arrogant as to expect my husband to be "my everything"? That's humanly impossible!

We pray that God will continue to use what we went through to help others. We can testify firsthand about God's faithfulness, grace, and forgiveness.

Reflections and Backstory on Fred and Jill

Fred and Jill have been together since sixth grade. I am happy and a bit proud to call them my friends. That is how long we have all known each other. Jill is driven, determined, and now a true servant of the Lord. She is a bit hardheaded, and that is one thing in which I can relate. However, she is obedient when she hears the voice of the Lord. She is willing to submit to whatever the Holy Spirit is telling her. She is now on staff at The Gathering and wears many hats. Jill helps me tremendously because I am a bi-vocational pastor. It is good for me to have someone to keep me in the loop, consistently help, and order resources for the Freedom Ministry needs. Because of Jesus, we are all close friends serving the King.

Fred has been one of my best friends since sixth grade. I encouraged him to live with me when we were in high school. Fred is easy going and an overall funny dude. It was during this time of high school that my life was going wildly off the tracks. Not very many people knew the real me or the true desires of my heart. I shared them with Fred. He had my back, regardless if I was at fault or not. Much like Ric Flair had Arn Anderson, I had Fred Humphrey. It went the other way too. I would have (and still would) give Fred my last five bucks if he needed it. If you have paid attention to my struggles, you can imagine it was not always easy to be my friend. Jill was not my biggest fan in our young adult years. I would go so far to say that at one point she dreaded us hanging out, in fear of me getting Fred into trouble. Looking back, I cannot say that I blame her.

At the time of Fred and Jill's struggles, Jesus had changed my life. I had recently returned home from the mission field. It was a frustrating season for me as I sought the next step in His plan. I was not yet on the church staff, and God had not provided a woman for me to serve with. Even when I was totally lost, I would help people the best I could. Needless to say, when Fred found himself in a bind, of course, I let him stay with me. I found this happening quite regularly with others, also. I had never seen my best friend so crushed in all our lives. Fred was there with me through my break ups with women and various low points. It was an honor to actually be a good friend and point him to Jesus instead of partying, going out, or encouraging him to find a new woman. Fred made the choice to stay in a safe environment when he had other options. The advice I was led to share with him stemmed from me NOT doing the right thing and losing everything I loved twice. I tried to encourage him to let God have the final say and to claim that! I could see him slowly taking steps toward Jesus. However, I was scheduled to go on a mission trip and was a little worried to leave him alone in that condition.

When we were growing up, Fred was not interested in school. He would not even let me do his homework for him. I never saw him read anything but comic books or fantasy football magazines.

What I saw when I returned home was a shock! I opened the door and saw Fred reading my Gary Smalley book, "DNA of Relationships." Seriously, I looked around for the hidden cameras. I asked him, "Are you alright, Bro?" He said, "Yes, I finally hit my knees and surrendered to Jesus in the back room." That was a touchdown! After that point, we started getting more Christian-based relationship books and discussing them. God used all of this learning to improve my understanding and to equip me to minister to several couples in the coming years. The growth that I saw in my friend was such an encouragement to me. When the miracle happened, they began to grow together in Christ. Their testimony is such a powerful one, and I pray that it is an encouragement to many.

Sometimes in life it is the little things people take for granted that eventually get them. When I have gone to visit the "Humps" in recent years, it touches my heart. I see their family just sharing life together through trials and tribulations. They look peaceful- chilling in their little nooks with their fat cat, Muffin. They are just on the couches, playing games, cooking, watching movies, and even knitting. To the untrained eye, these may seem like routine activities. However, for me, I see something beautiful only my Jesus could have accomplished.

"Pastor Sean D. Barron -Freedom Conference 2017 Sermon and Reflections"

I recently returned from a mission trip from Pachuca, Mexico. The goal and purpose of the ministry trip was to help with the 2017 "Freedom Conference," and to not only share a message of Freedom but to empower the people of Mexico to walk in this freedom as a way of life. My friends, the Carranza's, planted and have a thriving ministry called Life Church Pachuca. My first cousin and her family are resident missionaries there and teach English, build relationships, and launch Freedom Ministries with the blessing of Pastor Johnathan Carranza. The ministry has taken root and lives are being touched and radically transformed through the love and power of Jesus Christ. I have been in deep reflection of this trip, what the Lord is doing in my life, our local community, and around the world.

First, I'd like to say thank you to Pastor Casey Rader (Sr. Pastor of The Gathering) for encouraging me to make this trip. I was careful not to just "go" because I wanted to and because I had connections and relationships there. I wanted to make sure the Holy Spirit was leading me there, and I received several small confirmations and "God winks" to assure me that it was time to purchase the ticket. Though it was challenging to cover my "normal" duties here, I am thankful that the Lord has surrounded me with servants who share the calling, who are willing to step up, and who are willing to serve and seek the deeper things of God. The Lord is in the process of "raising up" a "whosoever will generation." This movement is clearly seen in my home church, my community, and several other parts of the world. I am blessed in so many ways. I can tell you that I was truly humbled by grace and honor, not only refining circumstance. All the refining has led to a new level with Jesus, depth of love and goodness in all relationships. The more depth of the refining: the deeper love, power, anointing and general presence of the Lord most experience through the process (*John 15:1-17*). I know that I most certainly can testify of this being real throughout my life.

Considering my past and where I came from (drugs, addiction, depression, hopelessness, etc.) to the testimony and purpose He has given me, it keeps me thankful and humble. The fact that there is no ceiling with God is mind blowing to me, i.e. there is always more. Several times, I have wanted to cap off His Work and say, "This is wonderful. This is the way it is done." I am tempted to be thankful for the result in that moment when He has yet to speak the final word. Certainly, we should all be thankful for His Providence; likewise, we must learn to not overreact when change, attacks from the enemy, and "trials of many kinds" (*James 1*) come. Often, these very impedances are the bridge to knowing Jesus on a deeper level. Most people will not cry out to Jesus until Jesus is the last option. The refining process cannot be avoided; it can only be stalled by our unwillingness to allow change and receive accountability or prophetic words of encouragement or instruction. At any given time, we can jump off of the potter's wheel, but it is up to us as to what ultimate vessel will be molded. I encourage you today, as long as you are breathing, that it is never too late. No single figure in the Bible was perfect, except Jesus. Every other person was just an ordinary *human being with the same extraordinary callings that are still being bestowed on God's people today. Miracles can come from humbling and less than desirable circumstances. Why? In order that He, alone, gets the glory and no one can deny His hand at work.*

Throughout the process, you should grow in your understanding of all things spiritual, including missions. I can honestly tell you that I most certainly have. Serving as a resident missionary, a person learns a deeper grasp of culture and a unique general pulse of daily life outside of his or her comfort zone. That person may even realize that the standard American philosophy about world missions is not always on point and that there are more parts to the Great Commission than simply sharing the Gospel.

***"15** He said to them, "Go into all the world and preach the gospel to all creation. **16** Whoever believes and is baptized will be saved, but whoever does not believe will be condemned. **17** And these signs will accompany those who believe: In my name they will drive out demons; they will speak in new tongues; **18** they will pick up snakes with their hands; and when they drink deadly poison, it will not hurt them at all; they will place their hands on sick people, and they will get well."*
Mark 16:15-18

*"16 Then the eleven disciples went to Galilee, to the mountain where Jesus had told them to go. 17 When they saw him, they worshiped him; but some doubted. 18 Then Jesus came to them and said, "All authority in heaven and on earth has been given to me. **19** Therefore go and make disciples of all nations, baptizing them in the name of the Father and of the Son*

*and of the Holy Spirit, **20** <u>and teaching</u> <u>them to obey every-</u><u>thing I have commanded you. And surely I am with you al-</u><u>ways, to the very end of the age."</u>*
Matthew 28:16-20

      *In the broadest sense, "The Son of Man came not to be served, but to serve, and to give His life for the ransom of many" **(Mark 10:45)**. When we begin to understand servitude, that missions cost something more than two weeks of time and spending money for essentials and a plane ticket, we will begin to understand what serving truly means. It encompasses the entire premise of "dying to self," and it embodies our entire life rather than time frame within that life. We do not honor The Great Commission when we get a passport, we honor it as a "way of life." Every day we pay a certain cost- the cost of living our lives with people, being transparent with them, and embodying real Christianity. We are not truly living if we do not love people and sow into them without regard for being hurt. I am not talking about our inner circle of friends; I am referring to a lost, hurting and confused world. There is no fear in God's Love, but there is wisdom. The love hurricane that is Jesus will not always make sense, but I encourage you to not become shell shocked because of a personal betrayal or another person's sin (or struggle). Jesus took our hurts and betrayals on the cross over two thousand years ago. We may get hurt from time to time, and that actually may mean that you may be doing something right and are, in fact, blessed:*

*"Blessed are those who are persecuted because of right-eousness, for theirs is the kingdom of heaven.**11** "Blessed are you when people insult you, persecute you and falsely say all kinds of evil against you because of me. **12** Rejoice and be*

275

glad, because great is your reward in heaven, for in the same way they persecuted the prophets who were before you."
Matthew 5:10-12

Please do not misinterpret my meaning. I am not minimizing the importance of evangelism. It is needed and we all, as the body of Christ, should play a part in the advancement of His Kingdom. The point I am trying to convey is that we may all play a different role in one individual's life. Jesus spoke these words:

"35 Don't you have a saying, 'It's still four months until harvest'? I tell you, open your eyes and look at the fields! They are ripe for harvest. 36 Even now the one who reaps draws a wage and harvests a crop for eternal life, so that the sower and the reaper may be glad together. 37 Thus the saying 'One sows and another reaps' is true. 38 I sent you to reap what you have not worked for. Others have done the hard work, and you have reaped the benefits of their labor."
John 4:35-38

*The challenge today is for us to go deeper, beyond the self-imposed restrictions we set. We must realize that though our gifting may be specific, Jesus does not limit us. We limit ourselves. We take spiritual gifting or personality tests and label ourselves this or that in favor of actually developing our character. The goal should not just be "good at the time" but to develop "fruit that will last." Our problem is that we resist the process. Therefore, we may be gifted, talented, or even anointed, but our lives are missing consistent Godly fruit **(Galatians 5:22-26)**. Laying your life down or your dreams or your passions or what makes you feel good at the moment in favor of the plan Jesus has for you will not usually be easy*

*(Philippians 3:7-14), and it cannot happen until you receive Him and His goodness. In this fullness, you will come to realize that everything you have naturally been seeking is found only in Him. Do you trust Him? If your life's desire is ministry then you should pay less attention to evangelists on TV and actually read the Word of God. Paul describes an aspect of this in **2 Corinthians 6:3-13.***

As we mature spiritually, there will be times in which we wish our reactions or responses would have been different. Throughout our lives, we each will face our own "rich young ruler moments."

*"**21** <u>Jesus looked at him and loved him.</u> "One thing you lack," he said. "Go, sell everything you have and give to the poor, and you will have treasure in heaven. Then come, follow me."**22** At this the man's face fell. He went away sad, because he had great wealth." **Mark 10:21-22***

*When these moments happen, the key is to remember that Jesus first looked at him and "loved him," and He also loves you. Repentance, is not a one-time deal, nor is self-evaluation (**Psalm 139:23-24**). Without consciously being aware of it, we often put our own twist on things, build walls of safety that trap us, hold viciously to our denomination's guidelines, or continue to apply the "old method" because it has worked before rather than listening to the Holy Spirit. I believe this statement to be true:*

*"People destroy with their character what they have built with their gift unless transformation has occurred." **Graham Cooke***

We must be willing to allow this change to occur both individually and corporately. I pray that the Holy Spirit will not leave us alone. We cannot sit comfortably in our own private fellowship halls while our cities burn to the ground, sing "Kumbaya," and wait on Jesus. Jesus is alive, and He is the God who turned over tables and shook things up throughout the Bible. The time is approaching when we will be held accountable "as God's people," not as Baptists, Catholics, Pentecostals, Non-Denominationals, California Hipsters, Millennials, or insert any other group, past or present, here. We let our opinions and fears direct us above the sovereignty of our Creator. Many preachers want to rain down fire and brimstone from the pulpit in some kind of pseudo scare tactic, while the Father lovingly waits for His people to realize they are under a new covenant of grace. A lost and broken world looks for hope and love in Christianity, and all they find are social media rants, "Christians" condemning those who need grace, spiritual gift disagreements, and arm-crossed curmudgeons critiquing the ministry. Ask yourself, have you seen one life changed through this behavior, or do you see a long line of people who are spiritually cramming through the exit door? The stench of hypocrisy looms in the minds of those already teetering on the edge of surrender and often blinds them to moments when the actual loving and accepting of people as Jesus did is around them. The country club mentality and good ole' boy way of doing things may have been fun while it lasted, but where is the lasting fruit? There are churches on every corner of the "Bible-Belt," but where is the love, unity, or actual revival? Why is the divorce rate inside the church just as high as it is outside of it? Don't we teach of love and kindness and forgiveness and repentance? Why would our general population of supposed believers even expect revival when few are even willing to pray before the service starts or place a legitimate prayer covering over their church leadership?

*The Lord is calling out His end time remnant. Things are changing, and others in this region are seeing the "big picture." Keep in mind, revival and change start in the mirror. In my little community of Sulphur, Louisiana change is, in fact, happening. The culture is shifting and people are willing to take a stand. They see and understand the fact that "It is the LOVE (or kindness) of God that brings people unto repentance" (**Romans 2:4**). The stand will not be taken with social media rants, protesters with posters, and disrespect. It will be taken in love. Hurting people do not need seminary theology in 2017; they need grace, mercy, and love. They need to experience the signs, wonders, and miracles without the legalism. People need to be able to visit a church and feel like they can be part of something bigger than themselves rather than experience a local "clicked out," factious church that resembles a country club or hipster coffee shop. A movement across America is coming, and it will happen when the Lord breaks your heart for what breaks His. When your life is no longer about you, you will embrace the nature of Jesus (**Philippians 2:1-11**).*

In our local Freedom Ministry (which evolved from Celebrate Recovery*), we have an event on the second Friday of each month called "Chip Night." We celebrate testimonies of lives changed, salvations, deliverance, and healing in all forms. A general move of the Holy Spirit is welcomed and occurs quite regularly. At our last Chip Night, we had over one hundred adults and over thirty children. The most beautiful aspect was that six different local churches were represented there, all in unity believing that Jesus is the answer to the storms of life and that He issues purpose and hope! There was an anointing permeating the atmosphere, and the leadership that was present that night can initiate real and lasting revival. When we had our yearly event called "Freedom Night" in March of 2017, there were more than ten different churches represented. More team work ministry is to be done in the future. It is my heart to help other churches start their own ministry, but the big picture is working and standing together in love. As I learn more about His nature and His ways, the more I realize that without unity and love, true revival will only be a localized flicker when it could be an all-consuming fire across this nation.

When we submit to the pruning process, it always produces good fruit and builds character or Godly virtues (**2 Peter 1:3-11**). In Pachuca, Mexico, everything came full circle for me. God allowed me to help lead a team that was comprised of not only of a handful of elders but also of some individuals much more experienced in things of the Spirit than I was. The fact that they all referred to me as "Pastor" was truly humbling. I did not know everyone that God had assembled on this "Freedom Team" on a personal level. I only knew that my cousin and my friend vouched for them and that I would have one night to travel and to connect with them before the beginning of the three day "Freedom Conference." While traveling to the airport, during the flight, and taking the bus to our ultimate destination, I was able to mingle with some of the team. It was clear from the outset that they were all about the Lord's business and had spent a great deal of time in prayer. They fully understood that we were there to serve the people, love them, and empower and equip the church leadership in Pachuca. No one was looking for a "free-day" or a ride to McDonalds. Everyone had a heart to *see God move, get to know the people, and experience the culture (and speed bumps). I was impressed and relieved by all of the preparation and promotion of the event prior to our arrival and of the organization that was already in place to help things flow as well as possible. A great evangelist friend of mine taught us years ago that we should be prepared to eat "flex-e-cookies" because things do not always go as planned. It is wise to have such a "cookie" and attitude each day in life as well as a glass of humility as a chaser. It proved to be a challenge getting my ducks in a row for the onset of this trip. I did not rest much before-hand, and I finished packing at 1 am the night before we departed. Because I had many messages on my heart and in my mind and recently preached a sermon on these same messages, being prepared should have been easy. However, the Lord only showed me certain verses of Scripture and gave me no direct subject matter (except for the Altar Ministry breakout session). Ready or not, I embarked on an adventure with my new friends from the Vineyard of Moss Bluff, Louisiana, Church of the King of Lake Charles, Louisiana, and First Baptist Church of Gillis, Louisiana. We were all to meet with Pastor Johnathan and his Leadership Team, worship, praise, and, finally, pray over the conference and the days ahead. It was an amazing time of worship, bonding, and intercession (spiritual warfare). The vision was laid out clearly to us and we were all in agreement. I could sense that the Lord was ready to do something life altering through this conference and trip. Everything came to together and was in place for Friday night, which would be the first night of the three-day conference. We all came together for prayer in an "upper room" of the event center.*

The Lord had not exactly given me the definitive message, but he did give me the peace that He was going to take care of it. During the worship, the Holy Spirit clearly spoke to me and said, "This conference is going to change the world." God must occasionally remind us and shake us up because our vision is too small for His divine plan. I shared this message and the message that Jesus had already laid on my heart. The gist of it was simple: "Freedom is not just a ministry; it is a way of life." The theme verse of the conference was:

"2 When you pass through the waters, I will be with you; and when you pass through the rivers,
they will not sweep over you. When you walk through the fire, you will not be burned;
the flames will not set you ablaze." **Isaiah 43:2**

Upon sharing that message, I will never forget the response of the people for as long as I live. Our team was divided into pairs of two, and each team was given a translator. Pastor Johnathan and I were in the center. Two solid hours of ministry was poured out and upon, released, and imparted over the people gathered in the event center. Every possible gift of the Holy Spirit was in action. Each individual team had their own amazing testimonies. Prophetic words, Baptism of the Holy Spirit, deliverance, healing in every aspect of life, tongues with interpretation, confessions of sin, and even a renewal of wedding vows occurred during the time of ministry. This was one of my most special moments of my Christian walk because that's just like Jesus to do the unexpected. People were in a posture of receiving and believing. Forgiveness was an ongoing theme the entire weekend, as well as restoration. The levee broke, and we got the pleasure of ministering and bonding with the people on that level of Holy Spirit love and God's Glory (extreme goodness). Praise the Lord, and all Glory to Him.

The Saturday breakout sessions held just as much weight as the night before. Each person was prepared for His move, and more outpouring than anyone expected happened in each class. There were thirty to forty people in all eight daytime breakout sessions. I observed two full classes and one half of another before retreating to pray before my own class started. How Jesus allowed me to teach a small booklet of information in a one-hour time slot, I may never fully comprehend. All I can truly say is that it was far more "intense" than I ever envisioned. We simply shared from our heart, God's word, and our own personal experiences in ministry and with the Holy Spirit. Every class, the Lord did something unique through prayer, wisdom, community, love, truth, and power.

On Saturday night, I only knew that I planned to share part of my testimony. I was given no clear and precise message from the Lord prior to preaching. I normally prefer a precise outline so when the Lord pulls me off my own path, I clearly recognize it. During the worship portion, on my knees, the Lord again spoke clearly. By this time, the conference crowd moved into a different area of the event center which overlooked the city. The message that was relayed to me in my spirit was one of giant pitchers of living water were going to be poured out over the people, and a flood was moving out into the city of Pachuca and the rest of the world. As I was on my knees in worship, I looked down and saw a big nail on the floor (that I previously did not see), and the Lord said, "Tell them this how much I love them and I that I am not mad at them." BOOM. This was His message, not mine. I shared part of my testimony about losing my dad a few years earlier and of how only Jesus gave me the strength to stand with my father and relate bible verses and communicate everything I needed to say. I remember thinking how strange it was that I shared that story because it was not planned. The response time was breath taking and went on until they flickered the overhead lights to encourage us to leave the event. As an aside, this happened every night though no one was in the mood for leaving. God's love was poured out, and, again, forgiveness was a major theme. My personal testimony, for me, was for a man and his family who recently lost his father two months prior. Words alone cannot express the time of ministry I had with that family. Jesus had once again made himself known, this time though grace and a warm healing touch. Again, each different prayer team had their own Holy Spirit encounters and experiences.

On Sunday, the last and final day of the conference, we experienced another powerful time of ministry. The worship, message, and ministry time was a special time of impartation. The mantle of Freedom in Christ was released and received by the people. The people were commissioned to bring this freedom to the city. Testimonies were shared from lives touched by the conference and the amazing work God performed using my cousin, April, and her husband Jason (Red) Pilkerton and their family. By being obedient to the Lord, they had successfully planted a Freedom Ministry in Life Church Pachuca. The fruit from this ministry opened the door for this conference to happen.

The message of Freedom and hope that the Lord gently spoke years ago to Mrs. Sue Ellen Richard, and the "Godfather" of our local Christian recovery, Brother Mike Richard *and their choice to follow His direction launched a small ministry called Celebrate Recovery. Little did they or any of us know that recovery would evolve into complete "Freedom" and victory, and that same freedom would spread across Louisiana into the heart of Mexico. My heart's desire is to be part of a lasting work and to support others in the quest for unity and freedom in Jesus Christ. That is Jesus, and He is currently changing the world in unity (**Psalm 133**) and, love is what "He does for a living." My name is Sean D. Barron, and thank you for letting me share.*

Special shout out to Pastor Johnathan Carranza, his family and Life Church, Pachuca.

A "grande" thanks to the team of translators and host homes.

Much love to the "Freedom Team" of world changers that the good Lord assembled.

POEMS

"When Are We Educated" by Grover "Danny" Barron, all other poems by the author, Sean D. Barron.

"When Are We Educated?"
When are we truly educated?
When we can gaze out upon the universe:
How lucid and lovely
How dark and dangerous
Yet with a sense of our own littleness; in the great scheme of things

When we know how to make friends and keep them
Even more-so when we can be a friend to ourselves

When we can look into the wayside puddle and see something besides mud

When we can look into the face of the most forlorn mortal and see:
The picture in view and see something beyond judgment and sin

When we keep in our minds the importance of children
In our hands the sword for oppression and injustice
But in our hearts and on our lips lies:
A bit of an uplifting song

"The Struggle"

Life unfolds in many seasons
Things change with no rhyme or reason
My heart
My love
Myself
Treason

I push and push
To this very day-
To deny myself the old way

This air I breathe
I take it in
Living water change me from within
My heart is dirty
My motive unsure

Light the path of feet
Make my hands and heart pure
Give me this day my daily bread
Don't let me chase wealth or self in vain
I am a scarred man
But by HIS wounds I am changed

Even in the struggle-
As I take this breath in
I give thanks for the Blood-
That washed away all my sin.

Dying land

The wisdom of the world
Has brought suffering
What is in my heart....
Condemns my soul
Greed, adultery, lust
It is idolatry; no self –control

The tears fall for nothing
As my soul withers away
Confusion, anger, bitterness
Please, Lord show me the way
I must return...To the cross

My redemption has been purchased
I don't need this world
My debt has been paid
Freedom to choose is mine
Though I desire to be...
Clay on the wheel
As I seek the Fathers hand sometimes I feel...
Like a flower in a dying land

There is so much pain and loss
Many things I will never understand
But I know....
You came to set the captive free
Please break these chains
Help me to see

As I cry out; on my knees
Now I understand you've been with me

Search my heart's intent
Renew a right spirit within me
Help me O'Lord
To love and forgive like you
Give me the strength to stand

Hear my prayer…
Have mercy,
Help save the lost and hurting…
-In this dying land

The Present

Never was good with love or loss
-Always paid the price
-Always paid the cost

A lonesome good-bye
A flower for a fallen friend
-hide in the shadows
-numb to feel again
-won't allow for the pain

Giving my love -I refrain
The gain, Not worth the risk

No hope
No joy
Only sadness

Yesterday is bittersweet
Like burning embers in the fire

The past rekindles emotion
-rekindles desire
-it burned to dust
-left in the abyss

Question posed-Is there more to life than this?

From the bottom,
-I cried out
Please take my hand.
Rebuild my house
It was on the sand

Now every day is a new
Forgiveness set me free
No longer gonna waste the day
-Cause it's all a blessing

Perseverance and grace
Through some of life's hard lessons
I am living today
Therefore I see it's a "Present"

Seasons

Happy are the pure at heart
Although there is long-suffering
Nowhere does a promise claim:
It will be easy

To admit the need for the cross
To surrender the fight
Is man's only hope
From darkness to light

You may not be rich
Full of financial blessing
You may become rich
In how you see things

When you can feel real love
When you see children play
When your desires change
When He makes a way

Give us what we need
Only for this day
As the pain and temptation,
Pull on our very souls

No one knows,
for whom the bell tolls
As the thunder rolls
Seasons change

Stop the madness
Call on His name
Every tear we cried
He holds in his hands

So be still and listen
Pick up your cross

Everything we gained
Now we must count it as loss

You can't take it with you
No need to worry about tomorrow
We must be clay in His hands
Crying out for wisdom
Because, I don't understand

The enemy accuses
The lies seem true
It never seems to workout
No matter what I do

The folly of my ways
As self-will guides me
Lord forgive my sin
Protect me and hide me

Just give me the strength
To abide in thee

My heart's desire is found in You

To be loved
To have purpose
To serve with everything I am
My pain and loss is not in vain

I can relate to the hurting
Suffering was my friend
You raised me up
Yet my heart breaks again

Through the pain of life
You hold me
Through the trials and tribulations
You mold me

Even in the darkness
I will never forget
What you told me
You heard my prayer

Your mercy was with me
Your grace abounds
You took my pain and turned it around
Then removed the veil
Opened my eyes

So as the storm rushes in
As confusion is all around
In the name of Jesus
I will not stay down

Your plan for me is good
Your will is profound
Again I extend my LIFE to you
As you pick me up off the ground

Your ways are not my ways
Your wisdom is higher
I don't understand this pain
But to please you is my desire

Holy Spirit come- ignite - inspire

Here in complete brokenness
I cry out to the Son
I may never understand this season
But let thy will be done!

"Them"

When I was at the tender age of fifteen-
Life did not seem such a dream
I saw the systems of this world
I bled for the loss of my kin

Nothing in life but pain certain, so I fell into sin
The taste was so sweet-for a season
Had drawn me "all in"
I saw the world and the people around me
Then swore, I would never be like…"Them"

Without joy and peace
Not one single person to confide in
I would not sell my soul
Just so I could fit in
Reflecting on my family:
So angry, selfish, torn
Making the same mistakes over and over again
Working so hard, but absent from LOVE
Without an honest grin
My parents seemed alone struggling
Mad because of what might have been.
Again I swore-I would rather be dead
Than to ever be like…"Them"

By grace, I was granted the time
Sometimes, I cannot comprehend
Because 12 years later, I looked in the mirror
And had become the worst of..."Them"

My joy was sorrow
My fighting spirit - vengeance
My love -absent
My peace was rage
My destiny soon to be death or a cage

The wind of the Spirit
Brought change all around, Peace within

As we rage against the machine, fight the powers that be
As the world can harden our souls, drag us under or in
May we find peace in something greater than ourselves-
Before we relive the sins of our fathers awake and realize
That we have become...
"Them"

Fast Lane

Why are you in the fast lane?
Seems like you want to drive real slow
Was it your parents fault?
Perhaps they also do not know

Why are you driving 50?
When the sign says 75
The Left lane is not for those,
Out on a Sunday drive

I could flash lights
I could honk
I could cuss
I could wave

Unfortunately, deep in my heart
I know it would be in vain
Some things others may never know
Such as the science and design of interstate flow

See, I don't like to rush
I like to plan ahead and cruise;
Listen to music, good preaching and even the news
I won't be in the left lane giving others the blues

Therefore, when I ride along you will not find,
Me obstructing traffic all the time
It is just common curtesy...
To go with the flow

See, driving slow is not a crime
But, why the left lane all of the time?
Do you need a hug?
Perhaps, you need some coffee to wake you and get loose?
Do have the sense the good Lord gave a goose?

So please don't be offended
When my gas pedal hits the floor and I snake around
(Humbly)
Just so I can continue on my way and
Give thanks my momma raised me right
And proclaim to you....
"Have a blessed day"

"Press on"

These hands can strike with vengeance
These hands can heal with a touch
These hands turn to fist
When the weight is too much

I don't need an A-K, Glock 9 or street sweeper
The 357 was my choice for a heater
I can't judge the liar, cheater or scoffer's mode
See for years I lived and died by a self-righteous code

These hands can build
These hands can destroy
Still driven by passion
Less man, more boy

These hands can catch a touch down
These hands can make a drug deal
In the fog I thought: "I was keepin' it real"
I used to believe only what these hands feel
When emotions burn deep
Seems only scars remain
Issues unresolved
Let's numb the pain

The world does not need more
Posers with tattoos of "the praying hands"
The world needs a few;
With the guts to be a man

See I can't judge you
For your a just a reflection of me

But Today I choose
Kindness, compassion and humility

I choose the armor
I pick up my cross
I will hold to the faith
When all hope seems lost

I never was short on words
I never was one to walk away
But this heart and these hands
Are no longer my own

So I'll turn my cheek
Guard my heart and **press on**

"It"

Some seek
Some run
Some build walls and refrain
Many never look back
Many refuse to let go
A few fortunate ones are never the same

Some know at first sight
Some are careful to be sure
Some become broken hurt like children
Many wander aimlessly
Many never know
Still, a few will persevere and grow

The road is filled with trials
They attempt to beat one's spirit into submission
You may find yourself;
Sitting alone thinking and listening:
To the faint echo of the screams of what might have been

Oh, but the warmth
The gleam in one's eye
That reflects in the moon
Seems to light the nights sky
Stillness of heart:
More than passion and peace of mind

I remain thankful for those times
Even more so for what will be
Balanced on the great scales it remains
More than worth all the
Lashes
Tears
Emptiness
Questioning
Pain
It can push you into brokenness
Or set you free from your fears

I shall not relent
Nor, regret the time spent
Now, I must stand
Without a hint of bitterness
In the distance I can see my deliverance

The conquest and pride
Does not define a man

Still, I will fight for what I desire
Die for what I believe
I confess
Many times, I have fallen
Many times, I have been deceived
At times, I have missed the point
Pushed several that loved me away

To learn to die to self; the thought for the day

Some lie and cheat
Some drink till they're done
Some land on their feet
Beat their chest, declaring: "I won!!"

The cycle of abuse
The pain that binds
Like rusty shackles and chains
Impairing the decisions of a weary mind
Still, through the ashes some will find…HOPE
Perhaps tap the source for the power to change
Yet, some will shrug it off and simply remain the same

Although, I am scarred
I will not refrain
This wall will come down
Brick by brick you see
Because life is:
Too short
Too precious
To me
To hide behind a wall
So no one can see

I have experienced several moments
Summers on the shoreline, surface in my dreams
I ran with the pack, I laid it on the line
I gave my heart away
Felt warmth I will cherish till my dying day

It can drive you insane or
Prompt you to sing a song
It is more than a notion
Kingdoms have fallen over this emotion

The "it" that I speak of is known as "love"
Though I could never truly give or receive "it"
Till I experienced "it" from above

"CYPRESS"

No words can describe
No dictionary can comprehend
The meaning
The definition of friend

For the many glasses raised
For the toast's and the "cheers"
But more for the ones present
For the hard times and the tears

For every ride that had no particular destination
For familiar places
For familiar faces
For "HOME SWEET HOME"

For every loss
For every win
For everyone who came to play
The games we remember
----To this very day

For the crawfish and rib-eyes
For the tree at Holbrook Park (and concrete table)
For the Outer Limits
But more for the light in the dark (the truth when it hurts)

For the shirt off your back
For a place to rest your head
"Just a Port in the Storm"
Someone once said

For the ones who would fight
The ones who really have your back
For the ones who help at all cost
When there was no turning back

For everything lost
For things only few know
For the ones you trust with your life
For the ones you'd rather not know

For the lies
For the cries
For the highs
For the lows

For the person you can ALWAYS call
For the person you can ALWAYS trust

For that love, that will not die
--When this world turns into dust

For a promise of forever
For a Summer that was a dream
For the memories that wake you
Still asking,
Was it at all what it seemed?

For the memories that burn
For the pain that makes us ask why
For the brothers (sisters, cousins, friends, family)
Much too young to die

For the ones that paid the cost
For the look in his mother's eye
For every broken heart
For the long walk to say (meantime) good-byes

When you reflect
Do not disrespect
And spend days pondering how or why
Cherish and remember the way they lived
Honor the ones that died

As I reflect on the people
who have FOREVER impacted this (thing we call) life
I try desperately

But still fail to express a fraction of what friendship means

It seems
Other than some folly of my youth

It's safe
Engrave "No Regrets"

Some things learned
From foolish and wise bets
-- One friend will always save you when you reach for his hand
--Follow your heart's convictions
--To learn from your mistakes
--To forgive
--To lend a hand or an ear
--To befriend one's self
--To grow
--To just be a better man

Before the we are called home (that day comes)
Before the final trumpet blows (It will)
Before this world comes to an end

Lord if you teach us (me)
--Nothing else
Teach us to be a -"FRIEND"

This poem is dedicated to everyone who has lost someone close, to every single person who has impacted my life past or present, and to the few who NEVER turned their back on me.

*"Perfume and incense bring joy to the heart,
And pleasantness of one's friend springs earnest counsel."*
Proverbs 27:9 (NIV)

"Greater love hath no man than this, that a man lay down his life for his friends."
John 15:13 (KJ)

"You have taken my companions and loved ones from me; the darkness is my closest friend."
Psalm 88:18 (NIV)

You have to understand the text to see that, in spite of it all, he is praying and communicating with God in Psalm 88.

Brief reflection on "Cypress"

When it comes to learning, growing, and chasing your dreams, one must be willing to step out of their comfort zone. Often, that means aligning yourself with those who are more experienced, skilled, gifted, successful and/or intelligent than you are. Always be willing to "expand your circle" without compromising your beliefs. This applies to the realms of business, ministry, relationships, and all avenues of life. This was the reason I chose to pop in at the McNeese State University Writer's Club. I was definitely impressed with the talent and the diversity that was present at every meeting. The first couple of visits, I did not share anything, but I was allowed to give feedback on a few things I heard. I could feel the Lord prompting me to share; therefore, eventually, I did.

This was the poem I shared, one of the few times I was led to share my works outside of this book. I was concerned (to an extent) of some of the possible responses I may have received. The curiosity eventually outweighed the cost. The Lord gave me this poem as I traveled across the Lithuanian countryside on a train. The subject of friendship, relation-ships, and all of my various life experiences whirled through my head. After the completion of this poem, it was shared two weeks later at close friend's funeral. This poem encom-passes much of my youth and young adult experiences. With that on the line, eventually I said, "I'll share." In a room of professors, published authors, aspiring writers, and future scholars, I laid my heart on the line.

The responses varied. One young man's reaction led me to believe I had achieved the level of depth which was tar-geted. The professor said, "That's good. A little heavy on the 'for' usage, but good none the less." Although he was correct, the Irish blood inside me smiled. One of the young, published guys said he enjoyed the references to the crawfish and rib-eyes. That was good because "that's how we roll" in Lou-isiana. A young lady smiled and said, "I like how you closed it with a prayer." That was sweet because I was not meaning to sprinkle salt, just perhaps stir the pot. The first guy who commented had tears in his eyes. He said something like this, "That makes me think of my ex and good times in high school." He then excused himself and left the table. This told me that he did, in fact, relate to the depth of this expressive piece. I am sure those who commented spoke the truth but took it easy on me. I always enjoyed hearing them share their efforts to understand works of prose, but to the young man who left the room, only the Lord knows the depth it meant.